A KISS WITHOUT ANY SHAME

IN EVERY PERSON'S SHATTERED HEART IS GOD'S MENDING LOVE

ANNABELLE SABELLA-REZA

A Kiss Without Any Shame
Copyright © 2019 Annabelle Sabella-Reza

All rights reserved. No part of this publication may be reproduced, stored in a retrieval system, or transmitted in any form or by any means, electronic, mechanical, photocopying, recording, scanning or otherwise, without the written prior permission of the author.

Unless otherwise indicated, all Scripture quotations marked NKJV are taken from the New King James Version®. Copyright © 1982 and 1995 by Thomas Nelson. Used by permission. All rights reserved. NKJV is a trademark of Thomas Nelson Inc. Scripture quotations marked (NIV) are taken from the Holy Bible, New International Version®, NIV®. Copyright © 1973, 1978, 1984, 2011 by Biblica, Inc.™ Used by permission of Zondervan. All rights reserved worldwide. www.zondervan.com The "NIV" and "New International Version" are trademarks registered in the United States Patent and Trademark Office by Biblica, Inc.™ Scripture quotations marked (ESV) are from the ESV® Bible (The Holy Bible, English Standard Version®), copyright © 2001 by Crossway, a publishing ministry of Good News Publishers. Used by permission. All rights reserved. Scripture quotations marked (ISV) are taken from the Holy Bible: International Standard Version® Release 2.0. Copyright © 1996-2013 by the ISV Foundation. Used by permission of Davidson Press, LLC. ALL RIGHTS RESERVED INTERNATIONALLY.

A Kiss Without Any Shame is a true story. In order to protect the privacy of the people involved, certain events, dialogue, characters and names have been changed, combined, or blended.

∼

Library of Congress Control Number: 2019901053

Edited by Joseph F. Reza
Cover design by Michael Lirag

ISBN: 987-1-7325308-0-5 (eBook)
ISBN: 978-1-7325308-2-9 (paperback)

Published by AZERiNK PRESS
Montebello, California 90640

∼

Printed in the United States of America

~ WITH LOVE ~

I lovingly dedicate this book to my husband, Joseph. I also dedicate this written account of my life to my beloved children—Paul, Sabella and Deanna —and to my daughters lifelong partners: David and Christian.

To include my precious grandchildren: Jonathan, Ezekiel, Zen, Marley, and Navi—I pray this book inspires you to trust the Lord, and have the hope and vision of your lifetime, and to remind you our God can do amazing things. Jesus loves you.

Finally, to my mother, Dolores Juaner Sabella, may the legacy of your selfless love lives on through the future generations to come.

This book is a chronicle of my life—a love story written on my heart for you.

I pray that my life story will give hope and move those who need to find the healing touches of God's mending love. May you be encouraged to trust our supreme God, regardless of what situations face you.

— ANNABELLE SABELLA-REZA

CONTENTS

1. Failed Attempt — 1
2. Voyage with the Great, I Am — 4
3. Kiss to a Child's Heart — 8
4. Perfect Life — 11
5. First Girl Member of the Boy's (Only) Group — 16
6. Oh No, Not the Lice! — 25
7. Eight Migrates — 32
8. All Eyes on Deck — 40
9. Typhoon's Darkness — 47
10. The Year of Losses — 59
11. A New Day — 69
12. Father Figure — 76
13. Salted Wound — 79
14. Inborn Quality — 87
15. Perfecting Lies — 98
16. The Good, The Bad, and The Ugly — 103
17. The Truth of Reality — 112
18. Fatal Touch — 135
19. Taking Control — 149
20. Guilt vs. Shame — 164
21. Meeting God's Grace, Face-to-Face — 172
22. See God's Image — 185
23. Priority Number One — 194
24. From Salesgirl with Love — 205
25. Kisses of Love — 220
26. The Truth and Why (I) Say, "Yes" — 227
27. Freedom — 232
28. Glory be to God — 253
    Words of Love: For You — 274
    Words of Love: For a broken fellowship with the Lord — 276
    Words of Love: Kisses for Our Heavenly Father — 278

Unmoved, Circa 1958	281
Acknowledgments	283
About the Author	287

1

FAILED ATTEMPT

*A*nother heavy rainstorm had left the Island of Luzon with a fitting humid feeling on this very warm day. Yet, a chill factor has occupied the room's atmosphere. A troublesome sensation I feel ill-at-ease.

The storm's most targeted place is the densely populated City of Manila, Philippines. A hub to many typhoons, the town and its locals come against the cyclones' pattern of leaving damaging and harmful effects. Quezon City, where I live is only six miles north. I feel out of place; far from home. There is a clear irritation in the flesh—a throbbing feeling is surfacing.

For the locals, any outside activity is a fearless feat during a storm's nuisances. The islanders are immune to the isle's environment; though, most often disastrous. Even with that, a wrestling feeling inside me takes center ring in this tempestuous day.

In casing, seeing the room's window showcasing what I'd call, *water life's* amusement park. In mindful viewing, *I can't wait to cross their paths.* The sight of tadpoles would once again inject cheerful water-world childhood memory.

I see right below its dew-covered glass window a narrow spring mattress, fitted on a metal frame. And it's hard to miss, looking up high above on the ceiling is a fresh damp patch over older stains—an obvious sign of leakage. A sign that is not surprising. Water damage caused by the unrelenting heavy rainstorm that just passed left reminiscent nuisances of past years.

Adjacent to the well ventilated dampened room is the entranceway. Several feet outside are people moving, showing urgency. And those others, are merely pacers. Lined-up on its well-trafficked linoleum covered floor are individuals—two appear engaged in most serious conversation. Sure as can be, I could guess the profession of both people whose stance could prove to be who they are. Both the man and the woman wearing identical attires are talking medical terms in the world-wide used foreign English language. I hear them speaking to a third person having a familiar sound, but was out of my sight. Guessing by the tone of his voice, he asked a question.

Followed with more. Though brief, their "Q, and A" dialogue echoes across the narrow hallway and wafts into the room. This ends their conversation and the man wearing a white coat responds as he steps inside the room.

"She is lucky, very lucky. *It* only required few stitches."

Distracted by the sensory unfolding, I stopped listening.

For now, inside this poorly lit room, I felt the ceiling fan's cooling air rotations—awakening my skin's senses. A tingly sensation. My forearms' standing hairs proved the thermostat's cold degree reading.

I sense something strange is coming. My body's pain receptors are at mid-way in queuing endangered form. Just then, an irrefutable pain signals trouble. Emerging from the inside passing each three protective layers of my skin, shoots cringing ache.

Why am I lying here? Please, what is going on? But no one answered.

Can anyone hear me? or, as *they* often claim… am I "Hallucinating —again?"

It occurs I have misplaced any memories of today's happenings.

Didn't I celebrate my sixteenth birthday? Oh, that was weeks ago. In my attempt to move around, I felt a long sharp pain coming from my left wrist. I now *see* wrapped tightly in thick bandages.

More probing. *Why is my wrist burning? And why is it bandaged up?*

Further movements brought sharper and stinging pain. Physical awareness help lift the haze over my confused mind. At last, the familiar voice reveals an identified presence—made way into the room —carries a dead-pan face. And in my sight. With the obvious accent, he spoke in low notes.

"I'll take you home now!"

Then silence—nothing else said. No other words were retractable for decades with anyone else since that day I failed to end my life.

2

VOYAGE WITH THE GREAT, I AM

I had unspoken words for many years following that dreadful day—I failed to end my life. In remembering the hours leading up to that moment... seeing the blade laying on the shelf as I looked for hard drugs. Any medicine hard enough to end all, relieve the pain, and forget everything in my life. I imagined the relief. To not feel. That attraction of cutting all the sensitivities inside of me, brought about the sharpness that would stop the pain entirely.

No reservations. With no one to think about. Nothing can hurt me anymore than *they* have. I picked up the metal and aimed at my left wrist. Right thumb in sync with the point finger pinched together, my eyes pulled in closer onto the area where the radial artery might be. Then, I angled the razor-sharp blade's tip on the targeted area... pushed in deep through my skin. And with no hesitation, I sliced my wrist from left to right.

I didn't feel a thing.

THE PAIN I buried propagated to deep anger, and I built resentment towards my loved ones. The lies—feeling bitter and defeated in life led me to entertain more lies.

For decades, I remained not living, just surviving. I hungered for the lost love. I carried weighted emptiness—thrusting me deep in the sand of hopelessness. Feeling no sense of security, I became a suspicious adult individual. Only trusting in myself. One might say, "paranoid!" I questioned people's intentions conforming only when it suits my life's plan.

A deceitful trait of God's enemy, the adversary, directed a fatal spear to his target. Leaving me in shame and guilt—my spirit shattered, I pursued a fabricated destiny—death to my soul.

~ TRAVEL WITH ME ~

PLEASE KNOW, there is love beyond telling. Love beyond human understanding. It is absolute. Love that is everlasting. Love that is available to everyone.

I believe love is a universal wish and want—a necessity, one may say. Humans are relational beings with a need for connection, and whether we find genuine affection, our hearts long for adoration. We strive for unconditional acts of devotion. Find congenial friendship with lifetime partnership and companionship. We are created to care and love another human being.

Yet in all of these, deep in our heart's blueprint is a space. A special place for absolute love where no human creation can fulfill completely.

You may shadow similar attempt to end your life; an aggravated assault to self, a fallacious relief. There is no feeling of guilt and, or shame that could keep you away from the true love that awaits. Please believe you are enough. Somebody fully understands. Somebody loves you—unconditionally.

Yes, the Almighty God Himself is the "Somebody," Who loves you and I. There is no requirement needed. He takes us as we are. In His divine ways, awaits at the door of our hearts.

My voyage throughout countless storms of brokenheartedness is not uncommon to this world. Perhaps, you or someone you know may have traveled in the same life journey, unable to thrive in life. Or you may know of a person on a destructive road. Likewise, presenting good intentions in helping a friend or a loved-one may provoke further distance and resign from help altogether.

Hiding in the dark is safer. Truth is harder to accept than a lie. Guilt and shame make a harder place to express truth. It is tough to face shame. Especially when one is convinced to feel guilty of *it*. Having a shattered heart, I believed the lies. With this lie, I stayed—buried in the bondage of darkness.

In my quest to finding the truth, reading came the least confrontational. Faces of goodwill individuals may present as militants and so I spent hundreds of hours in stillness. I read. I listened. In my desperate cry for help, asking, seeking, and knocking—the door to my heart opened wide. And I answered, *Yes,* to God's calling.

In newness, I consider the many great Christian authors and other good-willed self-help writers to be perfect third party validations in so many ways. Yet, the best endorsement I share with you is the Word of God—unceasingly adorns me with His everlasting love. His grace and mercy—sufficient. His true love pours in. I am no longer in bondage of sin. I am heaven's royalty, God's Princess—His child.

Every single day, I hop on the love boat and have my coffee time with the Author of the greatest love story ever written, God Himself. I delve into His mighty infallible word with eagerness. In complete attention. With patience. Seek His purpose—closeness of the moment.

Always present. His Spirit of love equips me with His joy and laughter. He strengthens me in a moment of weakness. He empowers me when I am helpless. He provides for all my heavenly needs, never thirsty nor hungry. He protects my mind from all lies by His present truth—ever so peaceful and comforting. My High Priest. God's corrections place me on a humbling and righteous path. For His purposeful instructions for my day, there is nothing for me to fear; because the Creator of the Universe, my Savior's Holy Spirit lives inside me.

"A Kiss Without Any Shame," was written for you. Inspired and guided by God's Spirit, I pushed through all the well-meaning stops with you as my aspiration to finish.

> THIS BOOK IS A CHRONICLE OF MY LIFE—A LOVE STORY WRITTEN ON MY HEART FOR YOU.

P.S. As you join me through the following pages, I pause at certain parts along the way to reflect on its central message. In hopes to shine some light on your lost for word moments of "Huh! What? Why?" with "Hmm," and other queries you may have.

I share **REFLECTIONS**, which are throw-back moments from when God intervened during the good and bad transitions in life. Of times, when I found and acknowledged the truth is in Him. In this parting, you will be there. Hopefully, to take part in one of the most exciting journeys of life. Excitement, in which God channeled His sanctifying moves in every situation for me, and for others around. Including the difficult people in my life.

God wants us to ponder. Reflect on. Be encouraged by His Word and loving presence. Our indifferences make us whole human beings. God's personal touch in each of His creations; man or woman makes one's spirit, authentic. May God lead your interpretation and understanding, blessing you—be it, partial or complete—Spiritually wholesome.

Encouragement: Our debt of sin vanished while nailed on those two crosspieces of wood and our Lord Jesus cried out.

John 19:30
"It is Finished!"
(NKJV)

IN JESUS' name, I pray:

Thank You, Lord Jesus for your cleansing blood as payment for our debt You didn't owe. For Your grace and mercy beyond human understanding and an amazing love that is pure and overflowing—never ever running out. Please mend our shattered life as you write Your story on our hearts.

3

KISS TO A CHILD'S HEART

I was born the fourth love child to a Filipino mother. An infant islander, and the first female offspring to Ricardo Sabella. My mother is from the Northern Island of Luzon, Philippines. I was too much of an infant to remember, but I can imagine those kisses given by my parents.

How do I describe those kisses?

With certainty, my mother, Dolores, bequeathed a series of absolute touches—linking eternal kisses as God introduces me into her world. I can sense her first sequence of loving smooches—ever so. Feeling Ma's Filipino *sniff-kisses* and sniffling inhales with its warm breaths' moisture against my face. Conceivably, Ma must have felt life's most grandeur moment in those first few seconds as she held her newborn girl lovingly secure! If only, imprinting facial mark to her baby's soft skin tissue was possible—so much like in Job's words: "... And the breath of God is in my nostrils" (Job 27:3). I also imagine as God created man and breathed into our human nostrils—His graceful and divine face *imprinted* on ours.

In similarity, etched permanently in my heart are sets of tender kisses devoted on my spaced-out forehead by my father. Love infused early on, I held on to a child's heart for many decades.

You may have been unaware of a kiss given by many others. Perhaps a kiss from your mother, father, grandparent, sibling, adoptive parent, friend, perchance a medical staff or an eager, nanny-to-be.

These greetings placed on your tiny hands, feet, belly, and foreheads—felt kisses of love. Acts of love completed by your responding gestures showed in your sweet cooing smiles.

We remember those periods as children discover their physical abilities and developing skills in the new world of playtime. The stumbling and falling. The scraping, and with puckered lips—display a bigger ache. An ache in their heart for the lack of preventive measures by their loved ones. A hard to understand situation for the hurting child. Health-giving, a kiss applied on wounded skin presents healing to a hurting heart.

Henceforth, for me, a kiss is a caring notion. Sharing a language of love. An act of deep loving feelings towards another—much like a soft touch of our lips grazing a baby's silky-soft facial skin, on miniature tummy, around tiny feet, and hands.

Encouragement:

Genesis 2:7
Then the LORD God formed man of dust from the ground and breathed into his nostrils the breath of life; and man became a living being.
(NIV)

IN JESUS' name, I pray:
Lord, we ask that you grant us the sweet sensation of Your Spirit's divine presence. May we experience heavenly belonging from Your throne above. And, may Your manifestation be ceaselessly transmuting in our life, and into eternity.

~ MY FATHER'S LITTLE MAIDEN ~

PAPA'S INSPIRATION to naming his newborn baby girl would unveil a love-mystery poem written in 1849 by the poet, Edgar Allan Poe, "Annabel Lee" (who) lived in a Kingdom by the sea.

The narrator, details his feelings in a fitting language of love:

> "It was many and many a year ago,
> In a Kingdom by the sea,
> That a maiden there lived whom you may know
> By the name of Annabel Lee; —
> And this maiden she lived with no other thought
> Than to love and be loved by me."

MUCH LIKE ITS poet's storytelling, Papa's fatherly love for his baby girl, "Annabelle," would prove a thespian tale unfolding, long after.

4

PERFECT LIFE

*R*EFLECTION: I remember my childhood filled with fun and exciting moments. The team work. Fun-playing on a spacious outdoors. With fourteen playmates, each one—up to sometime good and not—a good notion. Add to this, five adults, co-parents... later I would realize, childhood memories that have accounted for the healing step needed. In divergence from its sorrowful atmosphere, emitted into that clammy room.

The Creator of the Universe created and designed me in His own image; I say, idyllically so! He knows me deeply. Knows, my heart. And He knows its condition—all the time. His healing hands came to the rescue of my heart's brokenness—perfectly timed. In Sweet revelation lovingly tendered by God's healing hands; was, in remembering. Recalling good memories made restoration possible. I had buried my true feelings—all the emotions including those sweet fragrant times in life. Beautifully scented life, I remember and forever cherish.

MY FATHER, "PA," loves long sinuous hair, period. And he favors hair in longer strands on all females. The subject of shorter hairdos is nonexistent especially when the discussion is about mine.

Loyal to our father-daughter hair-combing, ritual at night before bedtime, I find myself seated cross-legged, on the reserved seating for Bibe. The King of Nicknames himself, my father, christened me after a baby duck, bibi! There were no explanations given. I went from Bibi to "Bibe!" Pa preferred the sound of the latter.

Blocked at evening times; hair-combing is exclusive and a tranquil moment cherished by the both of us. Pa is always on time ready for his task. Dr. Ricardo H. Sabella, an economist and university professor is a stickler for promptness. As an educator, the motto: "Be early, be on time"—is a rule practiced beyond his classrooms.

Pa's hair-combing motions attach love-beam smiles. Hairbrush in hand, he applies pressure so softly on my hair's lengthy strands. His loving patience would once more triumph on straightening out, most often matted hair. In concluding one more chunk of sweet moments, Pa would whisper into my ears: "You're done." Pa finishes by kissing my forehead and tells me, "Goodnight, Bibe." Other recipients of Pa's affection included my sister, younger siblings, and Ma.

In all honesty, he has shared loving moments with all his children, but kisses are rare. None seen in public viewing.

I WAS BORN in a culture where multigenerational household living is a common practice. Most often, one residence could house two or more generations. And in many cases, build two or more homes in one compound.

My parents strategically and carefully planned a perfect dwelling place with two of my mother's kinsfolks and their respective families. There are no lease contracts to agree upon. Simple! It's a cultural understanding, my father, the person financially able to help other family members; supports with no reservations. The professor and his wife bought an acre of land with two existing dwelling structures. They built the third and main building for the Sabella's, before moving in. Pa christened the new structure, "Villa Dolores," an insignia of love for his wife.

My family of eight lived in the Villa Dolores compound with three other adults: my mother's two younger sisters, a brother-in-law, and their children. Eight young *pinsan* (cousin) as co-inhabitants. Fourteen Juaner (Ma's maiden name) progenies oozing with combined energy dynamics. Allotted fun-time, doled out by our respective mothers—and for each, motivated an absolute guarded playtime. We custom built our own group of playmates with seven boys and seven girls! Well, six girls; except my sister, an enigma!

The compound offers a half of an acre playground covered in island green grass and tropical fruit trees, dressing the bungalow with various foliage. We have our own Disneyland and Neverland. Villa Dolores' dwellers enjoy life complete with kindness and love with each family member, helping one and the other!

Ate, pronounced, "Aa-teh," addresses an older female relative with respect. Ate Claudette ("Ate C") my half sister, Ma's eldest and first love child, is German-Filipino descents. There were no questions on who had the German blood, was it Ma or Pa? None! Both my parents are from the northern and central islands of Luzon and Visaya, respectively.

REFLECTION: Much later, I would find out that Ate C's father was a U.S. WWII Fighter Pilot and had met up with Ma for a short period of time! My Ma's short-lived love affair ended when the flyer left the Philippines after completion of his duty.

Leaving Ma with child… did he leave not knowing about his child, my sister to be? And if he didn't, God had other plans. In less than two years and at toddler age, Claudette, meets her Papa to be—the professor himself, Dr. "Doktor" Sabella.

Ate C's beauty stands out in our neighborhood's profile. Her skin's light tone, an uncommon sight from the neighboring residents. My sister's beauty reminds me so much of Amalia Fuentes, a legendary local actress who mirrors the Western world's, her Gorgeousness, Elizabeth Taylor's, inimitable attraction. Ate Claudette's shiny brunette locks complimented her hair's natural waves. Her usual short hairdo showcases her chiseled face with high cheekbones, narrow bridge nose, and designer-shaped lips. Should happiness grace her, she'll bless your day with a sweet smile, paired with beaming jawline. Smiles, though cagey; I desire to see more.

In overall appearance Ate C, was the most beautiful young girl in our neighborhood. While she displayed European heritage, the Negrito ancestry is clear on my olive hued skin. An added reasoning to my sister's much lighter skin color... she stays inside the house most days. Never left alone outside our bungalow. Even the early morning sun-ray's subtle attempts couldn't reach Ate C. Her early stationary life—devoted indoors.

Shielding of Ate C was obscure. I didn't understand the reason they held her away from us "rough and tumbles!" She received exclusive care by our parents—by the adults. Perhaps her extra-extra petite stature commands for tighter parental protection. In other respects, none of us other siblings thought of anything visual or mindful reasons to ask.

INTER-FAMILY SUBSISTENCE in the Philippines is as solid today as it was back on the islands' pre-discovery period.

Fourteen children in one compound make for a ready at all times, playmates. However, an association who could be in trouble and have been at many times; I admit never leaving out a good-time portion. The expansive half an acre of green grassed playground provided the young residents with an everlasting play station. Imagine fourteen assorted minds with mischievous and strong-willed personalities! For which, I share the stage with my abstruse sister and four gregarious brothers. Ate Claudette, "BB," Rolando, Rex, and Ramon; drum rolling sound of pride I am to claim, are my closest and forever playmates!

REFLECTION: Branded by family tradition, my parents reared each child to respect and practice complete obedience to the elderly—with no questions asked. The family's culture is loyalty, togetherness, "I have your back" and "It is us against the world." We practiced this mantra mannerism throughout our childhood and are like-minded in everything. Reading our minds is with ease because we aimed to please.

Encouragement:

Psalm 13:5-6
But I have trusted in Your mercy
my heart shall rejoice in Your salvation.
I will sing to the Lord because
He has dealt bountifully with me.

(NKJV)

IN JESUS' name, I pray:

We delight in Your presence, sweet Jesus. Because of You, we are free to stroll down memory lane; discovering a treasure chest filled with fond memories from our past—bring loving healing to our souls.

5

FIRST GIRL MEMBER OF THE BOY'S (ONLY) GROUP

*R*EFLECTION: I bask in God's glory when I think about how God molded and touched every fiber of my heart—leading up to a tipping moment in life. Love infused in His creation. While I was still in the womb; as each life forming matter, God finishes a perfect string enabling me to find my way back to Him. God knew exactly what was to happen, and He was faithful to design a back door. He equipped my DNA's mechanism to find my identity is in Him—giving me access to the sovereign God. The many loving memories were to be my treasure chest of healing.

Similarly, a valued stock of gems is in keeping your hidden treasure chest. Take heed, you may house many rare pieces with brilliance waiting to behold. Your chest may hold that sweet smile given by a passer-by leaving you with hope for another day—a dear friend who sat with you in peaceful silence—a medical staff giving curing attention, a sibling sharing many fun-filled days.

Allow yourself to indulge. As you travel back to a time: when you first met your spouse-to-be, held your newborn baby, received your acceptance letter for higher education, or became the first elite member of a pre-school age athletic group—bask in the beauty and brilliance of times past. You may get a glimpse of God's grace face to face!

I travel back to those moments of such time when...

. . .

FIRST GIRL MEMBER OF THE BOY'S (ONLY) GROUP | 17

FILIPINOS PROTECT and honor each member's birthrights within a family structure. The parents, in most cases, decide and direct every child's path in life. Everyone from the youngest to the oldest has a set of rules to abide by and each with particular tasks to do. More common is that greater responsibilities fall on the shoulders of older children.

With each member's responsibility moving hand-in-hand into the family's teamwork. Not individualized. It's a group effort.

Kuya, pronounced, "Koo-yah," is the male counterpart of Ate. With this; the oldest brother, sister, and/or cousin carry two differing positions—dominance and duty. As in, Kuya BB, my parents' firstborn, commands, not *may* but demands—respect. He is skillful in using birthrights! To his tomboy sister and middle child here (emphasis, me) I follow Kuya BB's decrees, respectably. But not without a "clause," stressing on my personal conditions. Though, I can be more flexible in his call for order when having fun!

All kinds of fun activities and playtime, with mine (in particular,) is non-negotiable. I would not miss out on fun and enjoyment. This includes my desire to be a member of the irrefutable fun group, "Boys (only) Group."

By the unanimous member's votes, they voted BB, leader of the reputable fun crowd. They confirm new membership through successful completion of challenges given by its leader. Fact is, they much prefer having the group's participation inducted by a male. The group has not thought of the female gender as a member. And topping the reason for a male preference; strength, followed by endurance next. So it goes, if partaking and completing in all the challenges and dares admit association into the group, *Allow me to try.*

Backing off from any challenge is not in my DNA. Allowing for great playtime with the boys ensuing excitement outdoors; I say,

Why not the girls? In particular, *Why not, me?*

First, I must pass both an agility and endurance test most of the girl cousins avoid. No problem. *That's easy, I can handle any test.* Simpering!

REFLECTION: Those were the days for me that rough activities were more fun than playing with dolls. Take in account, dolls were rare child-commodity and not accessible nor affordable in the 50s. Adding to its price tag—doll's delicate appearance made for an obvious in-door's only play.

Now, back to the daring challenge handed.

IN TOTAL DISAPPOINTMENT. The infamous boy's group handed me a test to climb a mature Aratilis tree. These small size trees bear fruits looking like mini apples with a taste mimicking cotton-candy's sweetness. Aratilis matures into small-framed trunk with slightly drooping branches. Whoever thought of such a precarious dare... made for an effortless tactic to join the club. Perilous it may appear to the group, but for Bibe, the aspiring candidate, whose size and age would be an issue. So they thought. Wishing instead, I embroil physically with any of them. "Prove myself, it is!" I took the test.

Kuya BB, the leader—aka, the Boss, was not aware of his little sister's *monkey-like* abilities. Why should he? It's he, calling to omit all girls through rough-playing—altogether discourage girls. I did not have an ounce of hesitation. A quick assessment of this amazing fruit tree, I kicked off my two rubber flip-flops to the ground. Barefooted, my ten toe members were in-sync, grabbing each bough with a cautionary step on each ascending branch. Deep breath in, then out. 1-2-3, I stepped up—with a few more to go. Breaking a few twigs here and a few more there. On my way up—twig-scratching accompanies slapping motions around my toned and obvious indigenous, ancestral dark legs. Ten toes' gripping motion kept my feet on magnet-like pulls and placements. On-and-off, positioning my footing carefully on each step up to the next stable sapling's growth. Not quite to the top... one hard push upwards.

Sigh! Finally, I settled atop the tree's crown. It was an intense feeling to think I passed the test. It didn't take long; I became distracted. Noticing, within easy reach are ready to pick delicious mini red apple-shaped fruits. I realized... I was hungry. From where I sat resting... seeing these yummy-looking clusters in delightful abundance; I picked and popped, not one or two but four or five, ripened fruits into my mouth. Yes, all at once!

Adding more enjoyment to my sweet success—in quick motion, I picked several of the over-ripe fruits dripping in its sweet juices. Pumped up with this added fun idea, I aimed the handful miniature sweet explosives toward the sweaty heads below. I tossed the berries hard on the boys. *Bam!* All fruited explosives hit the targets. In a flash, again, distracted. And this time, by the cotton candy-like taste drippings on my fingers. Reacting to its sweet-smelling aroma, I closed my eyes and slipped into a total heavenly realm. Having my eyelids shut, added sensation to both the sweet aroma enhancing my taste buds. I consumed the honey-tasting fruits within seconds. Overwhelmed with good feel hormones and satiety, my eyelids at half shut, half open—I say, a good call. In between savoring moments, I see from narrow openings between my fingers, a sighting identical to bullfrogs' bulging eyeballs fixed on… me. With my mouth open, smeared with honey sweets around, I couldn't concentrate on the happenings below. Still, those about-to-explode eyeballs are readying for something.

O, oh!

Surrounding the Aratilis tree trunk are three senior group members, bursting in uncontrollable rowdy laughter. Each of their lips puckered, and pointed. Then laughed more—mouths and fingers pointing upwards at my direction.

A unanimous vote tallied. And coronation swift. For Me, the only girl and youngest member of the boy's group. It's time to rename this crowd. Thrilled, my association… effective immediately.

Yay! I jumped up and down then ran out to play elsewhere. I have achieved my goal with the boys. *Now, where are those girls?*

Crushing the challenge handed to the elite group's initiation, unlocked the gates to fun-land for one six-year old girl. Bibe!

Soon, I became a regular participant in the boy's games. Play activities, household chores, and family time squeezed in weekend hours. We stayed at a fixed schedule on school days. Outdoors playtime was greater than any of the slotted time for any indoor activities. I would forgo eating if I had to choose. My energy level never seemed to have dipped nor dropped! Strange, no it is not. "Energy begets energy." The compound's young male residents share my sentiment—yet, the girls —well, most don't.

Except for Ate C's un-proclaimed desires. I sense her inner

yearning for more outdoor activities. Sensing more on a stronger desire for camaraderie with the rest.

Encouragement:

∼

1 Corinthians 13:11
"When I was a child, I spoke as a child, I understood as a child, I thought as a child. "

(NKJV)

∼

IN JESUS' name, I pray:
A child's memory—mine with my sister is a spirit-filled connection. I felt her heart's desires, and I acted for the both of us.

REFLECTION: Ate C's struggle with unspoken and unmet yearning, catapulted a notion I regretted not trying—to include my sister in all the children's fun times. Many instances as a youngster, I had envisioned pulling my sister by the hand, holding each other as we skip and jump to her heart's desires. But Ate C was under guard. I couldn't have survived the isolation. An isolation I understood later in life.
God knew Ate C's deep longing, and as a child, I didn't.

Encouragement:

∼

1 Corinthians 13:11
"... but when I became a man (woman,) I put away childish things.

(NKJV)

∼

FIRST GIRL MEMBER OF THE BOY'S (ONLY) GROUP | 21

MOST FUTURE OUTDOORS'S games drove more energy into my unquenchable thirst for more fun! While more tough testing of my abilities continued, none kept me back.

During the game, "Follow the Leader," another favored activity by the club members, the "Boss" used his newly established obstacles comprising the compound's roughest running routes. Only the leader knows the course. Kuya BB will take the lead and take us through a secret run. Though, the other members have taken similar rougher routes before, I have not. The object of the game is to run the course from beginning to the end. Finishing last, attaches a *pricey* moment of humiliation. Our leader braves dangerous zones, but there are no obstacles anywhere in the Sabella-Land intimidating enough for me. The possible difficult route dances around my head. Knowing all senior members are one to three years older, there may exist a challenge here. I'm not sure about the other partakers but a secret run, is my motivation. Not backing out, I'm in.

Each participant prepared zealously to start the mysteriously daring track. In my mind, my feet are already running. And the green light went off. I picture us looking like the diverse mixes of long-distance, track and field Olympic Runners. Except, our pathway is unpaved dirt, with mini meres, wet, and slippery ground. Steering and circling around small trees, shrubs, vegetable gardens, while avoiding the pecking defense of the many aroused free ranged chickens. Be careful with our future meals here! "Bwock, bwock, bwock, bwock, bwock," pecking and defending as each feathered runner scurry about. Maintaining my position in the pack's middle, the leader includes his secret obstacle. Fast muscle reflex was demanding for more oxygen and my heart was pumping vigorously, it could. Eyeing our leader, I see him focusing on the added obstacle ahead. The circling route I was pushing through, blocked the view of the supposing—extraordinary challenge.

Running just ahead of me are my brother Kuya Rolando, with an older cousin next to him. I saw their hands lift dull barb wires and ran through them. Me, well—I for one didn't have time to think, let alone strategize. Instead, I focused on the goal ahead.

Here I come! I am now filled with adrenaline rush, like the Olympic Gold medalist, Wilma Rudolph, I ran with all my strength. Merely a few seconds behind my older brother, I aimed towards the same dangerous fencing he effortlessly slid through. My left hand reached for the top wiring and my right hand targeted the lower one, avoiding the razor blade sharp knots. With applied hand pressures, I opened the top and bottom wires wider. Halfway through, I pushed my last body part in between hard and forward, across through.

Aray! (Ouch!) I felt an intense pinch around my lower right calf muscle.

Is it my rubber slipper breaking?

I continued to pull and tug. Not feeling. Not seeing. The barbwire's knotted sharp ends had caught the top part of my skin. I pulled more. Tugged more. *Why can't I free up my foot?* I looked back to inspect. Blind-sided by the adrenaline flowing, but now I see... the continued pulling-and-tugging movements are causing the razor sharp knot... slicing down deeper into the second layer of my protective skin. The sharp wire lodged on top of my Calcaneus bone. *Now what?* Spotting the end of our track within a few feet in front of me, I wiggled euphorically, allowing me to free my blunt-cut ankle.

Yay! Yes, I finished and relieved that I dodged the humiliation of completing last.

I bask in the glory of 2nd placement. A brief whoopee, followed silence from the boys. In scanning... the cheering squad seemed to have frozen. I stood and held my breath. At that moment, my attention was pulled over towards a strong presence. I see, Ma, appearing un-spirited and was *not* jumping for joy. There from the bungalow's entryway, she screamed out my name.

"Biibee!"

Ma was standing by the peekaboo opening where she held on to the knob-less screened front door. Again, she screamed!

"Bibe, come here right now!"

She looked upset and worried at the same time. Perplexed, I stepped towards Ma.

"What happened to you?" she asked.

Ma's directional squinting eyes revealed its focal point—she pulls the image closer and sees my right ankle covered in blood. I couldn't answer Ma. Over to the side, one glimpse at the boys filled with mixed reaction of remorse and gladness, touched my girly side. Each "Follow-the-Leader" partakers were having surprising mixed feelings—

bad and proud of me. They like me after all. Kuya BB, the Boss and the group's leader, escorted me towards Ma's direction.

Meanwhile, within range of vision... Ate C, stood by a mere two-inch distance behind the screened door. Inside those big, beautiful, and deep-set brown eyes, I sensed Ate C's longing. She has a deep yearning to cross those invisible yellow lines embedded—to experience the outdoors. Stepping into the house, she locks her sight to mine as I passed by—sparks connecting mysterious frequencies that would repeat many more times.

Inside our family room, Ma cleaned the coagulated blood drips off my wounded ankle. My mother practices functional medical attention. After cleaning my wound, Ma carefully placed healing herbs to prevent infection. I walked away with my ankle wrapped with clean gauze. *Now, where was I!*

The cut I paraded with pride, measured four inches long.

REFLECTION: Several who have heard this *play-by-play*, storytelling, have challenged me a show of proof for authentication. Yes—I paraded, err, have revealed the decades-year old scar. I say, *Here it is—see and feel the proof!*

A FUN SO GREAT, there was nothing to keep me from the re-named, "Fun Group's," favored game of "Follow-the-Leader."

Encouragement:

∽

Proverbs 10:7
The memory of the righteous is blessed.
(NKJV)

∽

IN JESUS' name, I pray:
To remember You, Oh Lord, is to feel love forevermore. In our low

moments of bewilderment, help us find the back door and return to those cherished instants; recalling memories of pleasantries. Empower us with the sweet sensation of the past—loving smiles, healing touches, child-like hugs, and fragrant smells in clear visions throughout our day.

6

OH NO, NOT THE LICE!

Sweltering tropical weather places hassle to my outdoors play time. Following the most recent placement as *First Girl* member of the prestigious boy's group, I struggled with an extreme itch on my scalp. I felt somewhat frantic. I freaked out!

This can't be—No!

I don't want to entertain the thought of LICE.

Yikes!

Lice are nasty Vampire-like bugs that thrive in human hair and feed of people's lifeblood. These hairs and scalp loving bugs are very contagious and hard to eradicate. Radically, they jump from head-to-head, contamination. For me, the bigger issue... these bloodsuckers would be an annoying disturbance into my very busy fun-time schedule.

So who would have them? Yes, that would be me, ugh! I say, *really! You lice are nothing. I'll beat you too!*

I believe it was my scalp's new tiny residents' conscious intention that sealed Ma's pending case—cut off my long hair. Pa was seriously not hearing any of my mother's case, let alone consider the solution to extinguish this lice infestation by cutting my hair. He had no inclination for any change to the tresses that took a long time to grow into his hair brush, stroke-able length.

BOTH BATHING and showering are uncommon in the Philippines. We have body cleansing with the use of three bare necessities; water, soap, and a container. *Tabo*, is a customary hygiene tool used to collect water for washing or rinsing body parts from head to toes. *Tabo*, resembles a small coffee canister big enough to hold about one quart of water.

Since there is no system of pipes from the water well, we all pitch in to replenish water source to our family's washing space using a traditional bucket. Filling the large barrel-like container with water from the well extracted through the water hand pump. And for easier reach in the barrel, a *tabo*, floats freely on the water top.

No plumbing also means, no hot running water. And rarely, we use high commodity cooking firewood to heat water for cleansing. The adults did not do so; heating of water was not a practical consideration. (Not in the 50s.)

Island weather is hot and humid. So for most, body washing at anytime is a welcome refreshing time-slot. Each one has an allocated, five-minute body and hair washing. Fast in; fast out!

Imagine that!

Blood sucking lice deep head-scratching sounds, even from several feet afar, caused further sleepless nights for Ma and I. During those late night hours, Ma, derived a scheme. Morning came, she heard the rooster's crowing... *cock-a-doodle-doo*, she jumped up... fully awake ready to lead the battle. I see her now equipped with an imaginary armor viking helmet and weaponry. My mother waited for the sun up then she scurried and gathered powerful elements. She transformed into the muscular Amazonian Mother Queen. *What is Ma in a rush for?*

"Bibe, follow me," she summons. (*And bring those blood-sucking head lice!*)

I stepped outside and walked in rapid motion behind Ma as she headed towards the family washing space. A specified area for wash and release, the western world calls, "bathroom." Sometimes, the country dwellers refer to this space as, "outhouse." There is a slight similarity with the least of its configuration; it is also detached from the main house. Not plushy, a privy construction with two, ten-feet wide rectangular walls attached to one, six-feet cemented wall. Entry to the compound's wash and release space is a partial opening opposite to the cemented wall. Galvanized roofing material naturally heats the bottom space on cooler days and keeps coolness during hot days.

INSIDE THIS SEMI-PRIVATE SPACE, I smell a strong sour scent... resembling marination. Despite of this, I was not the least bit curious with the familiar scent. All the same, I took double sniffs to confirm, then ignored. I proceeded and prepared to enjoy, presumed to be, my refreshing *tabo* cleansing slot. Ma instructed me to sit *labandera*, (washing lady) style.

Odd... she washes me often with my body in standing straight position. My short height makes it difficult for Ma to bend down further and reach for the water and soap.

I sat and squatted in the washroom. In ready position, I asked myself, *Are we washing clothes at the same time? But, this is my personal beautifying, ('Calgon, take me away') moment.* I looked around.

Where is the soap, the kuskus (clothes scrub,) and the dirty clothes, where are they?

And, for what again—to save water?

Be mindful... were only querying thoughts.

Instigated by a strong breeze coming in through cracked cement, wafted the familiar pong revealing its identity. The vinegar stunk because it didn't belong in the washroom and toilet space. *Marination* held in a round metal container and placed within inches of my feet. *This*—means one thing, the Queen, is going for her kill—blood sucking, LICE!

Filipino children don't question a parent (back in my generation, anyway) it's all done in visual expression. A *language* seldom used in other countries—a lowly look. Safest place to be... if you know what I mean!

Who has it, Ma, you?

This was not funny, not even for a fun gesture. One countered look back from her and I knew the target was my head. My facial expression—a perfect *meme* (humorous image) with eyes and mouth wide open, I was in fearful shock! Not in the lice. But, in confronting Ma's strong, Amazonian arm muscle strength.

• • •

28 | A KISS WITHOUT ANY SHAME

LUFFA COMES TO THE RESCUE. Saturated with vinegar cocktail, Mama's arm strength in scrubbing off these masked sesame seed sized vampires, wasn't letting up. Instead, my mother's biceps and triceps muscles gushing with battling strength intending to annihilate. In between, she dipped the luffa then attacked; dipped—scrubbed more. My head bobbed down, bobbed side, bent front, then back to its opposite side. More battle of the blood sucking mini vampires and the Mother Queen, shifted into wolf imagery. Until, like Regan, being exorcized, I felt barf regurgitate in my esophagus.

Wait for it—oh yeah! BARFINGGGGG! Breakfast splatters from the esophagus up to my throat; from mouth down to my chin, sliming down over knees covering my feet. Revealing dried fish aka *Tuyo*, (dried salted herring) *mixées*, egg, rice, and yellowish appearing gook! "GOOK," an original term I made up for such repulsive blend.

The stench from the combined meals and stomach's yellowish bile was unforgiving. Loading up for a sequence of aftershocks; I regurgitated multiple unwanted combos all over!

MA GAVE way to the much demand of keeping my hair length. The solution for its infestation is to find and destroy its nest. I soon found myself seated in a beauty parlor and at this point I pictured myself donning a Yul Brynner's, shiny, no-hair style!

The owner and parlor's new beautician, chattered with Ma while the young protégé touched and pointed at my neckline. Ma, in clear agreement to whatever was discussed, motioned to my new and Personal Beautician to carry on with her afresh appointed duties.

This tough, rough-and-tumble girl wasn't at all interested in the subject of their discussion. Hairstyling, ugh! Too girly for me. I was obeying whatever Ma says. There is no choice to rebuttal, whatever it may be.

"Chop, chop," and she continued to cut off several inches of tresses. No sooner, the future beautician, Scissor Hand, had reduced my hair to a bob cut. There was no reaction from me. Either way, I understood my mother's dilemma. She had left me earlier at the care of the owner to run errands.

Two hours later, I sat with anticipation of my mother's return.

Entering the salon, I see Ma's physical gestures. The *I'm not amused* stance. Ma's clenching facial shows definite frustration. Undesirable to deal with. No sooner than after, the sharp petals came off, shooting out—Ma's un-complimenting, *colorful* words striking the parlor's young protégé. After some deliberation, the wrong-doing judgment declared a "no-charge" service to the plaintiff, my mother.

That evening, I overheard Ma's voice rise. In comparison; rarely Pa's octave notes ascend higher in our household even in disciplining his children. As I witnessed Pa's physical composure is like all other times; always controlled in Ma's presence. Yet, a tensed night had surfaced.

My parents' uncomfortable and jarring discussion resulted from my new hairstyle. Ma's explanation did not go well with Pa. As it went; lacking in experience, the novice graduate applied ammonia to my hair not once.

The goal of having that new hair-flowing curls called "perm" did not transpire. Instead, during the perming process, the trainee conducted what she thought an educated step. Unrolling the tiny hair-rollers to check for curls on my straight hair. She analyzed the curls. Then concluded the result did not produce the desired curls. She applied a second ammonia treatment. And when that failed, she applied the third damaging finale'. Resulting in an original—the 50s *Afro*! It was an accidental fashion statement. Unveiled by none other than, me, Bibe—a small girl with Malay-Negrito heritage, may well have started this round shaped hair trend!

It was not about his precious princess sporting an *Afro* tribal look that disturbed my father. After all, I'm part Negrito! Pa felt, a demolition of our special father-daughter's emotional hair-brushing ritual and connecting moments.

There was a nagging question in my heart from this scene—the reversal of an angered feeling—how it went, from Pa's to Ma's?

REFLECTION: In all honesty, I don't recall ever going back to our hair-combing loving ritual time with my father. Reason? Perhaps, in seeing my parent's discussion and to avoid more of the same, I unconsciously forwent the ritual. For Pa, my hair combing time may have been holy ground—formed only for him and I.

Though far and few, witnessing my parents argue was saddening. To avoid being seen by any of the children, they always vacated our immediate sight. Taking their dispute a few yards away from our kitchen. Both would play out scenes staged in the dimmed room at my Auntie's home next to ours. Often—a one sided scene for me. Ma at her usual fervent stance, shakes her right point finger at Pa causing tears to run down his cheeks. Pa was not a weak man; I believe his love for Ma just made him most vulnerable at times like these.

Unwanted scene that replayed over and over in my mind, creating dulling feelings inside my heart. It was disheartening to see my father with his head drooped down. With both hands placed on his face serving as wind-shield wipers, wiping tears off his eyes and cheeks.

I kept a mental re-reeling of those times. Ma's feelings were obvious— seethed with anger, she was making my father very unhappy. It saddened my Pa, who could do no wrong. He was in tears by what my mother was verbalizing.

When life became catastrophic and insanity was circling around my world, barraging and demolishing scripts staged before would replay in my mind. Using my, "Ma-like" finger pointing as I needed to. It was so much easier to pitch blame at the closest direction—at my mother who was unaware of my dreadful situation.

Neither did I have any knowledge of Pa's deep personal secrets. Skeletons buried so deep—only Ma can reach into its depth. They revisited his secrets in private, and sharpened dialog delivered by Ma on that night of my new do, *Afro* reveal.

Later in my parenting life, I played my mother's role. The script written in a perilous part was similar; appearing fault fell on me. Similar scene would re-enact with the character of Ma played out by me; and my part, portrayed by my daughter.

Encouragement:

∼

Philippians 4:8
Finally, brethren, whatever things are true, whatever things are noble, whatever things are just, whatever things are pure, whatever things are lovely, whatever things are of good report, if there is any virtue and if there is anything praiseworthy—meditate on these things.

(NKJV)

IN JESUS' name, I pray:

Pain causes our eyes to be blind-folded. But the truth surfaces at its given time. Jesus, Your steadfast faithfulness is praiseworthy.

REFLECTION: From all whose blessings flow, I am grateful for the richness of a parent's virtue displayed at peak form by my mother. I have learned to meditate on Ma's nurturing touches; many, have surfaced to identify the preponderance source of my personality. In time, my hope and personal prayer is that truth speaks to my children's hearts, as me.

7

EIGHT MIGRATES

*V*OYAGE ON THE PACIFIC OCEAN. Summer, 1959—the American President Lines express offered two class travel services to and from the Orient. In the 1940s, the company constructed two luxurious passenger ships. Naming them after two most powerful nation's leaders': President Cleveland and President Wilson. The Last Ocean Liners describes both ships: "They were shining symbols of post-war American technology, design, and style. Their 1940s modern first-class public rooms and pool occupied the entire Promenade deck. While the economy had a lounge, veranda, and pool aft on the lower decks."

My parents have taken a big step to relocate our family to the United State of America. We have heard so much about the western world and all its modern lifestyle. Imagine when we, the Sabella progenies, found out what Pa chose for our travel mode! The excitement I am feeling in sailing on the Pacific Ocean via American President Lines, is indescribable.

First-class or economy travel? I'll take the lower deck, the hull, wherever human survival is possible. I said nothing more. In place, I counted for the day to come.

We were oblivious of our parent's undertaking. Confirming my parents' decision made easier in seeing our thrill. Travel and moving plans took months to complete. Still, on time to board the cruise ship.

On our travel day—dressed prim and suited up, my family's steps lead us through a smooth cemented road towards the end of ocean terminal. Nearing towards our ship's designated berth, my vision was like a wet sponge dripping in awesomeness. It was an understatement. Seeing the ship's massive dimensions within a few feet from where I stood, was mesmerizing. Each one of us, remained in stillness.

President Cleveland is a gigantic ship with a maximum capacity of 778 travelers. The towering board in front—ostensibly stood four stories high. Truly, this is a gigantic boat!

IN VIEWING THE LINER, flashing imageries of how enormous Noah's ark must have been! I am a seven-year-old child looking close and personal at this massive boat.

Many story tellers of this great flood have described Noah's Ark, but it lacked showing off its surrounding details. As a child would further picture and think this through; the children present at the site of the newly constructed Ark. Hearing the many passersby mock and bully Noah for his God-imparted project in building the Ark. Like mine, sets of young eyes fixed on the transforming yet unfathomable view.

God warned Noah. Floodwaters will cover earth and He instructed Noah to build the Ark. The Creator established a covenant with Noah —saving his entire family. With much added greatness to Noah's calling, he built plenty space for Ark-dwelling for animals of all species.

REFLECTION: Imagine the magnitude of Noah's God-given project! Sometimes, I forget God's sovereignty, especially when I find myself at the end of my rope. In frustration and helplessness, "trust and obey," for reals, there is no other way!

Noah is one perfect example of trust and obedience to God. Imagine, the years following the blueprint provided by God Himself to build the Ark. Noah too, may have experienced frustration with himself. He became tired with the thousands of labored hours at hand, dealing with his immediate family, friends, and the complexity of gathering the animals. Yet, Noah's laser-sharp focus on following God's will, he triumphed. And as a result, the Lord spared his family.

Encouragement:

~

Genesis 6:14-15

Make yourself an ark of gopherwood; make rooms in the ark... And, this is how you shall make it: The length of the ark shall be three hundred cubits, its width fifty cubits, and its height thirty cubits.

(NKJV)

~

IN JESUS' name, I pray:

Oh God, help my lack of faith in You. My conditional obedience needs divine understanding—having a portion of Noah's faithfulness and obedience is for the asking. Whether it is mundane or exotically grand as Noah's, help me be fully in trust and obedient to Your day's calling. May You equip me to accomplish Your will faithfully, cheerfully, and for Your glory.

STEPPING towards the ship's sturdy metal steps, I continued to indulge at the ship's majestic presence. This liner is a monstrous vessel and I cannot contain the visions flashing before my eyes—fun moments awaiting ME! The steps up the first stairway are spaces in between. I see excitement in boarding activities below. As the distance gains and elevation rises, I looked back from my previous steps and saw the story-height I had climbed. Displayed were various emotions drawn on family and friends' faces bidding farewell to the hundreds of voyagers. Facial expressions, blurring and shrinking in stature as we gained more distance away from the berth—"Bon voyage family!"

For a young girl (noting me), it was to be a voyage of no return—entreated more excitement packed with a hefty touch of mystery. Eight migrants embark on an ocean travel to a well-known foreign land, which we received with much eager fascination.

THE DESIGN of family cabin was perfect for multi-dweller travelers like us—we could fit in one room. Pa based his requested cabin set-up similar to the accommodations we have at home. Adding sleeping arrangements for each of his progeny in assigning each, an exclusive spot. With a choice between top or bottom bunk bed. I asked for the bottom. "Please."

So this is what the infamous western luxury feels like! Pa assigned sleeping arrangements for each one. And mine, the lower bunk frame with a 4-inch, made in the U.S.A. mattress. A dreamland for reals! This beats my 2-inch bed padding, made local in Manila. What's more? The feel of the covering, is silky soft. Just copying Ma here. Why? Because, I didn't know what silk was... much less, felt like. Topping such extravagance, the ship's manning crew set this indulgence in sleeping with my very own pillow.

Oh, there goes setting my brain to thinking mode; I've got it hot of the-press idea. Yes, there's that light bulb again!

Sleep mate is a common denominator in dwelling with multiple human bodies in one room. I might add, back home at "Villa Dolores," bungalow, the dimension of our family sleeping room is rather spacious. Ma organized two sets of bunk beds for my three brothers with two full-size beds arranged side-by-side. Assigning one bed to my parents and their toddler, Ramon. The other, to Ate C and myself. Although, these sleeping arrangements are never permanent!

Occasionally, one of the younger siblings, sleep walks to Ma's side; and if that spot is unavailable, slumbers by an older sibling for comfort.

Ate C, a light sleeper, is also my keeper. Often, my sister keeps silent on most things she witnesses. Specially, all of her siblings' hustling and bustling. Primarily, she reduces to complete silence in my *going about*, for anything fun. Sometimes, my sister shares her desires silently with few word phrases. Nothing lengthy. With those big, deep-set, brown eyes filled with muted feelings—a mystery novel in the making.

OUR FAMILY SEA voyage at hand is so farfetched. It's a living reality in a dream world. Breathtaking! So far, I could think of nothing that matches the adventure. Over two weeks of newness in everything— well, almost!

Starting with the grandness of our ship, American President Lines offer ocean travel service like no other. Papa, a former U.S. Navy Man used his expertise in the matter. Sailing across the heart of the Pacific Ocean, he recognized the thrill his children would experience. An exploration I was eager to go on board.

Over two weeks of non-stop playing—if there was a Genie, I would have wished for zero sleep hours! Sleeping arrangement with an eager lonesomeness to the max—no sleep mate—enabling me to move and stretch my limbs, freely. I love you my sister, but I'm here to lavish in these glorious weeks of royalty-like venue and services.

Phrasing, "Icing on the cake," is the lusciousness with each scheduled meal prepared. In abundance, six times a day! Passengers feast in a well-thought design; strategically encased in a wall-to-wall, massive window. Imagine, overlooking the sea surface. Ocean water's bluest hue. Where visual limitation is imbalanced.

Great and troubling, waves splashed against the ship's hull, powering in between the bow and its stern. Pacific Ocean's morning reception in its richness brings visual light to the Bible's Apostles' justifiable fretfulness over a storm.

Encouragement:

∽

Matthew 8:24
Suddenly a furious storm came up on the lake so that the waves swept over the boat. But Jesus was sleeping. The disciples went and woke him, saying, "Lord, save us! We're going to drown!"

(NIV)

∽

IN JESUS' name, I pray:
Lord, Your words have ministered to Your people in times of furious storms. Continue to help us, we need Your anchoring presence in weathering our daily challenges. May we recognize Your awareness at all times; and know, You will never leave us or forsake us.

• • •

REFLECTION: 2,000 plus years ago, I imagine Jesus slumbers in peace on the boat's water-soaked floor boards as its seawater rises where He lay. I also imagine His disciples with their much failed attempt to stop the flooding; feeling distress, wake Jesus.

Oh Lord, I too, feel the fear of perishing. Afraid of the unknown in life. In knowing Who You are in my life; steadfastly, gives me confidence and peace in times of uncertainty. Lord, please help remove the seduction of the world's security in its perishing standards—enticing me away from Your divine and sovereign ways.

TWO-THOUSAND PLUS YEARS LATER—I, too, am seated in the juddering ship's dining room facing a wall-to-wall window of this humongous ship. Unlike Jesus' boat, the American Liner's ship is not flooding! The ship is pushing through its rough sailing.

We felt the balancing movement of the ship, often rough. For now, eating tables are sliding forward, towards the window. As we watch ourselves, still seated and chairs moving along with the entire room's furnishings. Then, as if choreographed, all the furnishings, return to its starting point. Yet, we, the motionless diners haven't fallen off our chairs. Instinctively, we placed our hands, elbows, arms and upper torsos on the top eating table to keep the plates, still with half-eaten food from sliding. Silverware, and glassware filled with beverages, tumbled and spilled. Other table utensils and water pitcher fell onto the wooden floor without breaking! There was no time to check on others. For the Sabella family, this is a... fan... FUNTASTIC time! While other travelers were fearful, we were uncontainable in exhibiting our awesome joy.

My family, engulfed by the vast scene before us; we kept still, in the thrill. The great visual scene paired with physical encounters—an incomparable experience we all shared.

We didn't keep still for long. To ease surrounding uncertainties, Pa immediately composes a natural response—a "matter of fact," and moves his upper limbs. He puts his hand into his coat pocket, pulls out a paper and writing pen. Notwithstanding, Doktor, (Ma's nickname for our father) in a calming voice had no sign of worry during an unstable environment. Pa announced the many amenities along with fun events on the calendar. He was the complete opposite of how the disciples reacted—in fear. There was no need for lifesaving.

Pa and the boys continued chattering while Doktor, in its ship's rough sailing and with mind unmoved, writes the family activities offered to passengers. After reading aloud to us, he pocketed the itinerary for future use.

Board games were the favorite foreign freshness in the boy's fun activities. The newness of these games didn't keep the group of three small boys and a grown man to pursue more of physical activities. We're talking about three monkey-like males who live on the ground, trees, and puddles most of their days. The now shelved board games are for the slow days—the rainy ones. There was no rain in the forecast, however.

After the ocean water calmed down…. to the deck, *we* went.

THERE ARE 6,929 nautical miles between Manila, Philippines and the State of California. The US-made ocean liner we boarded will take nearly three weeks of sailing to reach the docking stations in San Francisco. It seemed a forever fun-fun-fun! We milked on all the amenities. From games to food—we basked in the new world's entertainment ways.

Though burgers are free from the ship's lunch and dinner menu. My family discussed trying the fifteen cents, *hamburger*... McDonald's burger once we docked in San Francisco. My older brother whispered, "I hear Mr. McDonald sells, cheeseburgers for nineteen cents each."

Oh, this must be a heaven-like eatery!

In sharing, Ma loves treating her little youngsters in the "spur of the moment" thing. Back at Villa Dolores' bungalow, she announces sweet treats such as—making home-made ice cream forthcoming. An extravagance we savor on special occasions. Sometimes, more a year. When serving this wonderful ice-cold sweetened cream, she considers the physical size of each child. She pulls the littlest ones to line-up— served first. A time, I savor in... serving the youngest to the eldest in line. She measures a portion according to the height and body mass— taking to account, energy level—weighted in by Ma's eyeing scale. No more, no less. Such a clever instinct!

During our voyage, Pa introduced us to buffets—an "All-You-Can-Eat," dining on board!

"What, is this 'all-you-can-eat?'" I asked and all my siblings, chimed in.

Incomprehensible! Indeed, a new and eye-bulging experience for my family. Seen only on television commercials, we embraced this new dining experience. Being timid is not an option in this new calling. All our lives, Ma served us portions. It's more like: *all-you-CARE-to-eat* in this case. Stomach-boggling! So many food selections to choose from: desserts, chocolate milk, sandwiches, soups, and salad dressings. Oh, that Thousand Island Dressing! I can eat this so called, *salad* all day long.

If this is the new world's dining custom, we are one hundred percent in!

8

ALL EYES ON DECK

There are roughly one hundred cruisers on the ship's deck, making yielding easy, towards my weakness for fun. Imagine the various ways to do so in an enclosed area, with a free-for-all viewing access to the sky. *Hmm, what's out here...* instead of looking for things to do, I stood still. Eyes are all over (stressing on mine) on moving bodies. There were walkers, loungers, and those few like me, who brave the ship's edge—taking in a mental picture—the calming view of ocean waters. So many happy smiles everywhere I looked.

The moment we embarked on this gigantic ship, we quickly spotted the passengers most favored past-time... *people watching!* What is this *human viewing* about? I soon learned how and when to take part. It won't be long, my sight... enthralled by the vessel's crew and their physical characteristics. Especially noticing people with lightened skin, narrow-bridged noses, multi-colored eyes, excessive height; with blonde tresses in some natural brown, and red color hairs. I am blown away! (Remember, I'm Filipino!) These human creations are graced with careful attention to details in lovely appearance... my intended sightings are to the deck's crew. I size each figure passing. From the frontal, peripheral, and sometimes, an accented voice would cause my head to jerk in sudden movements and with great interests, I see the full image does not disappoint.

Every cruising day, six Sabella progenies rise early with a readiness to dive into the ship's schedule of fun events. After each of the six meals, on-deck activities were plenty to keep us occupied and out of trouble. Corresponding to the cruise's lavish theme park on board is an all-day affair.

Do I have to sleep? It is obvious, the fun time in this floating transportation is unlimited. Somewhat incredulous. Nevertheless, I trust myself to having the best time ever. I must put all my waking time to good use. *Think, think, think, Bibe.*

Sitting in our cabin, I entertained a daring and fun idea... *hmm.* Squeezing and tapping on my chin, this is it. *The* "serving on a silver platter" occasion and laced with fun-packed freedom. It would be so much fun to venture off on my own! Discover whatever may be waiting for me outside the family cabin. A surprising adventure for sure. And slithering off my own bed is made easy, well I must be gracious and make this happen. A quick design and a concrete plan in place is on a standby for execution.

I woke up the next morning with a strong desire to carry out my intentions. And while everyone slept, I glided down from the silk-covered mattress with ease. I ventured off away to pacify my ever-curious mind.

Several steps outside our cabin door is an entry to a dark narrow hallway. *I don't remember seeing this pathway before.* Albeit, it's the only visible exit route to take. And the close proximity from the cabin makes a safe way.

In front is a dome-like entrance constructed with what appears to be metal dividers placed strategically in a row. I stepped forward slow and easy. I can feel my heart beating. *Lub dub, lub-dub.* Moving like a *suso'* (snail) on its belly, I hear nothing... a muted surrounding. Still and quiet. Seeing now in closer view are separators in-between each section. Moving ahead, the path extends further into a tunnel-looking passage revealing more section dividers.

I felt cold chills released into my body. More beatings of my heart. An unwelcome coldness. Still quiet, too quiet. I stood still.

TWO DAYS EARLIER... my youngest brother, Ramon, was practicing his newly acquired walking skills. He wobbled, dropped to the floor, and crawled around. While the rest of the family were busy on planning for our day, Ramon, crawled towards the cabin doorway. The little guy reached for the knob and pulled himself up. The door opened, and he stepped out of the family cabin with no one noticing.

A few minutes later, upon the discovery of a missing child, half of the family jumped in readiness to search. Led by some ship crew members, everyone swept all the "nooks and crannies" in and out the surrounding area. Each one eager to find our youngest sibling, we followed behind the ship's Search and Rescue Team. My parents knew the group members would face a great challenge in combing through tons of metal to check for any evidence. They scouted every inch around the cabins, stairwells, and the lower levels. Identifying baby scent on metal presents a great challenge.

I joined in on the hunt and concentrated within the immediate adjoining upper level. No one thought this possible! There was no way Ramon could have stepped up. Yet, smacked at the north end of the stairwell, Ramon sat crying like a baby should. Someone alerted the S&R Team and my parents were on their way up to reunite with their missing child.

Meanwhile, Kuya Rolando, quickly picked-up and placed Ramon's buttocks on his right arm. The big brother and hero continued to console, pat, and sway the little guy around... unaware of Ramon's very soggy underwear. At that moment, some kind of liquid form seeped through the sides of Ramon's elasticized plastic diaper cover, dampened the hero's forearm. And BAM, an awful and toxic odor explodes into the hero's nostrils. Unwary, Kuya Rolando, instinctively wrapped his other arm around Ramon's buttocks as if to contain the foul smelling liquid from dripping further. The hero's face turned white-washed. Within a split second, he hands our toddler brother dripping in smelly GOOK to Ma. Our family's hero sprinted like a bullet towards the side of the ship, regurgitated and barfed. Kuya Rolando would forgo eating his favorite western special cheese-burgers and fries for the remaining of our travel.

UNLIKE RAMON, I am not lost. I am on an adventure—an expected, fun escapade. I planned this whole thing. Who was I kidding? (Scrutiny at my age is most uncertain.) There is no time to probe with self. Only time to explore—my eyes slowly focus on what is ahead. In front is a tunnel that appeared deeper than I remembered days before. In slow, continued *suso'*-like pace, I stepped backwards with much added traction. Steady steps kept me with a consideration for another venturing time... when an earsplitting sound burst out filling the tunnel. My body went air bound, 1-2 feet; and in a moment's time—a superficial moment, I glimpsed mentally on (what I'd compare now to) *Indiana Jones*, running.

Up ahead, I see a metal wall divider from the top dropping. Heavy and eerie mechanical sound seems to make its way out of each next bar-like dropping dividers. Like *Indie*, yet stupefied for a mere second, I continued to watch multiple wall metals spew downward! I was turning around, then a full circle around. Back in full frontal view and synchronizing behind me are these massive metal walls dropping. I heard myself.

Girl, you are in... BIG trouble! What now? So this is how it feels to freeze in fright! Am I still air bound?

The next sound from the tunnel came in humming note, slightly softer and less noise. Followed by more of the same sound behind me. My body boxed in, I was trapped by two massive metal walls. *What was I to do?*

There was hope, the divider moved upwards in front of me. My eyes fixed on the door rising, I see initially, at the outset; exposed a pair of shiny leather shoes. Curiosity coupled with much anticipation, I stared at the bottom track where the glare-producing shoes, still unmoved. The divider continued lifting more, and a silhouette came into vision. The heavy sound of clicking and locking itself in place at the top, opens a full view of the other side. Revealing the silhouette as a massive figure.

There he stood... a giant figure. Tall, light-skinned, HANDSOME, and looking down at me are his sea blue-eyes. Hmm... heavenly creature!

What is this, err, who is this... who are you?

No words came out of me, so he didn't answer. With eyebrows placed high and eyes open; our eyes locked, his face tilted down towards me. He stood smiling.

The ship's Third Officer pushes forward with a big giant step. He stretches his long arms as if to pick me up.

OH PLEASE DO, expressed by my eyes. No resistance came from my small human presence. Instead, I sized up his full body appearance—a perfect creation—a work of art wearing a bright and crispy, perfectly-ironed white jacket. I have no desire to figure out who he is.

I remained speechless. Not by choice. I held my breath; my voice box froze. Now, I am in tow and sitting on one of his massive arms. My deliverance was but a quick brush of heaven. Both parents, in seeing me; breathed, a big sigh of relief. My father stretched his open hand to my deliverer's, and they shook hands. Though still emphasizing, I was never missing. I had that planned.

Several more times post rescue, my hero's presence graced us passengers with his heavenly persona on the deck. Upon the news of my rescue, some lucky "people watchers," welcomed a chat with the officer. Yet his masculine authority, somewhat kept me at a distance. Though, only seven years old, it was clear I recognize what an elite human design looks like.

REFLECTION: San Francisco reminds me of the many melodious days with my mother. Ma's radio-listening ushered me into hearing songs by the likes of both, local and their counter-partner's western vocalists. From the local's own "Golden Voice" the Legendary, Diomedes Maturan, who serenaded Ma, while doing many hours of domestic chores. And from the Americas, there were the Legendary: Bing Crosby, Perry Como, and Tony Bennett, brought in various baritone voices in sweet tunes. Daily radio-listening was Ma's favored break time from the heavy load of domestic chores. Voices from singers to scheduled, local Novellas, often played aloud in clear radio frequency.

I remember back home at the bungalow, Ma's radio listening doesn't take a back seat. Instead, she listens to instrumental and vocal sounds for certain tasks. Noting, she rolls up her sleeves with a small and fine, tight-teethed comb in her hand. Yes, a background orchestra blasting as Ma faces her never-ending battle with her daughter's lice-infested hair. Most likely, inspired to charge from her listening time of a deep heated novella-dialog. And yes, gross!

Melodies propagated in my artistic musical interest, which, in ultimate timing served an opportune guest singing presence with a Filipino singing legend.

In the most vulnerable time of hopelessness, God was working into my days. He placed me in the company of the late, Rodel Naval. Yes,

Rodel, who sang a triple platinum single was my Voice Coach, and dear friend. Coaching unleashing deep-scarred feelings jailed in my soul for many years. Touching its meaning of each word in the song. I sang, "You Needed Me," sung by Anne Murray. It is a song about unconditional and undeserved love written by Randy Goodrum. Although, my relationship with God, as I thought, was void—how suitable—words spoken by God Himself. In private times, I sang the appropriate "You's," with "I," and vice a versa.

> *"I needed You: Jesus, I needed You."*

PA GATHERED his family on the eve we docked into San Francisco Terminal. His footing stern. The obvious family leader's brand, an authoritative stance. Pa outlines the process in descending order.

The Senior Sabella, unfolds a lined paper revealing several scribbled words and he pulled out a pen then points on the top, "To Do," list. Pa's professor-like demeanor looks at each one of his children. Then he addressed each one. Kuya BB and Rolando, me, Rex, and Ate Claudette with Ramon toted around Ma's left waistline—each assignment given and noted.

My family has disembarked, each one touched with some sadness in leaving the American Liner's President Cleveland, our temporary home on the ocean waters. Yet a new excitement awaits the Sabella Family. As instructed, all seven of us now stand side-by-side on the terminal grounds. My father charges, with earnest confirmation.

"It is now time to kiss!"

We held on to the two-minutes basic training, conducted by Pa. Each member in proper stance. Every migrate stood and waited. My father placed himself next to the progressive line formed, at the end opposite Ma. With feet, bodies, faces, and minds in attention; Pa, our family's leader instructs us to bend down in unison. Our father commanded.

"One, two, three—and down!"

Pa focused ahead, bent his legs and dropped to the ground on his knees. His lips puckered and readied—then with confidence, waited.

That was our cue. We followed. And each one of the Sabella family member dropped to the ground. In sync, we kissed the damp concrete surface we knelt on. Yes! We kissed the crisp and cool ground pavement of San Francisco's berthing station. The cooled surface was smooth with an earthen taste all right.

Strange, but something about kissing the pavement was fun. Yet a question stirred in my curious mind—what was *this*, giving love to the dirt about? The caring face of our father kissing—seldom seen and given, but to a handful.

As for the ground, I shook my head. Plus, something distracted my attention. Without delay, I adhered to the diversion. Looking straight at what Pa was slipping into my hand; Dentyne gum, a first for me. I immediately unwrapped and popped this berry color sweet-something in my mouth. This is so tasty, a new sweet-spicy taste of cinnamon. Chew, taste, chew, and taste more.

YUMMY!

I looked at Pa's hands for the rest of the packet.

9

TYPHOON'S DARKNESS

Typhoons, the Filipinos commonly refer to as, *Bagyo*, are mature and violent cyclones; and, most occur in the Northwest Pacific Ocean. *Bagyo* has a natural inclination to inflict destruction to its targeted place, delivering its most biased and life-altering effects to Asian countries. One of its favored and targeted country, the Philippine Islands, battle these typhoons all year long. Most *Bagyo*, enter from the Northern Island of Luzon. The islanders cope in strengthened will against its storm's damages and most often, for a lifetime.

Still, my fellow islanders are resilient people who offer their gratitude—giving God the glory in their daily provisions. Food, water, and shelters with a loved one's survival, is at its best.

SEVERAL MONTHS before the turn of the new year in 1960, Pa, showed obvious changes in his overall mannerism including a noticeable change in his physical appearance. To mask the change, he maintained his *strict* professor stance but the use of a new walking apparatus is a sure giveaway. It appears that his health is failing. And for this obvious reason, my parents have decided to go back home to Villa Dolores bungalow. In less than a year, we have docked in San Francisco, took a train ride to live in Los Angeles... now heading back home.

Air travel from Los Angeles is approximately seven thousand miles long to our final destination in Manila. The flight from L.A. International Airport is approximately seventeen hours. Even so, I have no memory of our flight back home, and none of my siblings either could remember.

―

COMING BACK to our bungalow in Tatalon, was a welcoming warmth to my soul. The silencing uncertainties of Pa's health lingers but in no way disregarded.

Our recent travel to the new world temporarily halted Ma's livelihood. And in resuming her active life back with full support—brought relief to us, her family. Seeing my relatives have the stability of the familiar neighborhood; and my mother's longing to come back to Villa Dolores, reassuring.

It was a long-awaited joyful reunion for Ma and her siblings—an obvious soul-sisters. A heart-tingling moment evidenced by the joy each sister was experiencing. It was clear—their longing met—as love transmuted around, amongst the three (of six) sisters. The sweet vision of many kisses given and received by one and the other sister encased in love. Each one embedded their faces with every sniffling and inhaling motions as they released kisses around each other's necks—revealed their deep longing for missed loved ones. The Sisterhood's love proceeded with no expiration date.

REFLECTION: Acts of love are oozing from an overwhelming longing for one another. My Pa had accomplished the task—given us—the grandeur and beauty of ocean travel. If his plans included taking a permanent residency in the US, it was not to be. My Father's plans have changed because of his unexpected failing health. And fueled by the love he has for his wife to reunite with her sisters.

A portrayal that is to be a saving anchor in my life. Love never fails. My parents' show of acceptance, gifting others with encouragement are collective traits. A marriage of personalities—fibers of their hearts prevailed in their lifetime.

Encouragement:

∼

1ˢᵗ Corinthians 13:1-3
Though I speak with the tongues of men and of angels, but have not love, I have become sounding brass or a clanging cymbal. And though I have the gift of prophecy, and understand all mysteries and all knowledge, and though I have all faith, so that I can remove mountains, but have not love, I am nothing. And though I bestow all my goods to feed the poor, and though I give my body to be burned, but have not love, it profits me nothing.
(NKJV)

∼

IN JESUS' name, I pray:

Lord, as I work on peering our mother's sister-love towards my siblings; continue to help me mimic and extend Your love to others. Your Spirit of love and understanding is the brilliance others need. As You place others in front, please aid me to identify and shower unconditional love on them. Human knowledge with astute skills as with the abundance of material belongings—"none profits me if I, have not love."

WE FLEW BACK a few weeks early in time to register for the new school year. My parents designed a perfect plan as we settled in the pre-onset of typhoon season lasting several months. During the wet season, heavy monsoonal rains and intense thunderstorms occur. With certainty, storms happen and localize with unpredictable conditions. Adding to the "welcome home" mood are the predictable landslides and often, floods.

∼

WET SEASON DELIVERS heavy rain downpours with a long and continuous flow. And most often, causes severe flooding in Quezon City. With our home at Villa Dolores in the midst.

At its first stage, the bungalow's petrified wood casing, rapidly gulps its rainfall. Saturating every fiber of its foundation. And with a typhoon's natural inclination to dumping more rain, it could be a matter of hours before the encased home overfills—a rare occurrence. However, this time, rain doesn't cease and the overflowing of a large amount of water is now causing flooding.

I WAS HALF ASLEEP, dreaming of the "all you can eat" feasting food selections. Unaware the elders of the family have now camped around in our living room. Each one waiting for the rainwater to ease and prays that the flooding would stop.

Still, in bed—in dreamland. Where? I was back in our recent voyage to the new world. Our route through the Pacific Ocean was a thrilling adventure. Adventure could become fearful and there were fun and fearsome moments. However, my family made it exciting! It was a balancing act of emotions. The new world's travel introduction impressed on my family. Oodles of exciting on-board amenities and activities helped change the course of *this* unpleasant emotion rather quickly. Seeing, feeling, breathing, living in the gargantuan vessel, President Cleveland, and everything having to do with the vessel diverted our fear.

With the liner's offering of unlimited free entrance to its cinema room, the discovery of two swimming pools; and the food... literally, an experience that is out of my world. From the moment I embarked on this huge ship to carrying me through new discoveries—a plethora of fun adventures—daring and exciting. I am convinced, this western living is... sensationally, FUN!

STIRRED BY AN UNUSUAL SENSATION, I snapped back from this partial dream, Rapid Eye Movement-sleep.

Oh no, I didn't! Ah... did I wet the bed?

I double checked and the bed was wet. Thank God, though, the moisture didn't come from my body! But, from where? Rising up, I don't see my bedmate. Ate C, is nowhere around. Following an alerting call from my cerebrum, I moved my feet downward, towards the bedroom's wooden floor.

Yikes! An array of questions and thoughts rushed in and out of my brain. *Am I still in a dream? Am I in a bathtub? This bathwater doesn't feel warm. (In the new world, I learned to bathe in a tub. Bubble baths are fun!) Wake up, Annabelle! And please be that warm bubble bath!* Alas, it wasn't!

My talent in physical coordination kicked in as I tried standing up to find a reason for my wet bed! As quick as lightning, fright consumed my entire body—feeling water instead of my house slippers.

What is going on here?

I now stand barefooted on the bedroom floor; in the one-foot deep water rising. My balance wavered. My fear increased This is not the ship and no fun at all!

My fear is concrete—it's real. And for the first time in my life, this fear engulfed my whole body.

NEXT TO TATALON, is the City of Manila, which sits at sea level in most areas and below, in other parts. Thus, affecting several surrounding towns with flood waters and can stay stagnant for a very long time. Only when the ocean tides are low will the water drain away.

So, the rain pours and the uprising flooding continues!

Sadly, more scared; I haven't seen Pa, who seemed to have taken residency at a local hospital since we landed back from the US. I miss him, especially now. If he was here, his presence would comfort me. And would have made everything okay and safe.

I pleaded inside… *Pa, please, come home—we need you! I need you!*

Pa graduated with a Bachelor's Degree and took the advance "PhD," doctorate education from the western world's George Washington University. In my personal domain, he can solve everything. Do anything. And is, indestructible.

So find him! Somebody, please!

The adults carefully kept secret of our father's health updates from us, the children. Without seizing, I asked about my Pa. With the flood at hand, I wish only to be by his side. He can protect us; he can protect me. I hear the powerful pounding of rain force now.

Why, where, and what is wrong I cannot be with Pa? There is no one around to ask. Elder family members are in full force addressing the imminent danger of rainfall's out-pour.

Flooding is gaining momentum! Shortly after discovering the rising water in the house, I witnessed my aunts, older cousins, and siblings—rustle through, from room-to-room in robot-like movements. Arms swinging, body balancing, with head looking straight ahead, and rushing to exit. What were they doing? Are we at war with nature itself? The water level is now below my knee. My body is moving along with everyone's motion to survive out of this fast-rising water. I am distressing over drowning. I do not know how to swim.

To see the controlled, fast-moving bodies around is not uncommon around the Sabella household. Ma and her sisters embody examples of an effective team. In my life, I have seen each sister's focus and work together in harmony. In difficult times, together; with respect to their Sisterhood, always prevailed. So, they focused on a solution to survive this imminent flooding.

Ma is dealing with her own high priorities. She is at Pa's bedside, and no one knows her comings and goings. Pa had placed Ma, his partner, the leader in his absence. But Ma is missing too. Now what? Unbeknownst to my parents, their family is fast becoming part of the ocean's depths.

REFLECTION: In the era of pre-technology, there were no cellular lines down to worry about. Nor computers for any internet search or "You-tubing," results to follow. *How to Survive in Case of Any Flooding?* Nor, *Learn How to Swim in Five Minutes!*

Our reliance; our survival is now in the hands of our older relatives. We followed the examples set before by the elders to us, youngins. It is an obvious opportunity to apply teamwork. I followed through that one narrow exit, the front door!

. . .

REFLECTIONs: In the story of Noah, following the great flood, he opened a window and saw the top of the mountains. I imagine, standing beside the Ark's Sea Captain is his wife: "Has water subsided enough?" she asked. Curious, Noah, chose two feathered friends: a raven and a dove to check for habitat condition. And eventually, both found dry land and did not return to Noah.

But in this flooding moment, I see no dry land.

"Don't worry about anything... go outside now!" shouted my aunt.

I was back to my reality, our aunties took over; and as trained team players, we followed orders and tread carefully towards the front. Right when I heard our acting commander's directions to exit, I was engulfed with paralyzing terror. I felt my bearing freeze. My brain stem aided deep breaths in full rapid motion. I was hyperventilating. My pulse rapidly rose. My heart kept that momentum as I stomped around in-and-out of the living room's water-covered floor.

Right at the front door, I continued my thoughts about God's chosen Sea Captain, Noah. Our bungalow may not be on top of Mount Ararat like the Ark was on; but, like Noah, I can see.

I see the water outside the exit door rising in terrifying high-speed movement. I hear the blaring sounds of thunderstorms. And discern visually, how along with the heavy rainfall, the reverberating sounds are causing distress to our neighborhood. The rainwater blanketing the earth's ground looks to be ocean deep. Continuous massive hailing wind and rain slam its power on the surrounding bungalow and the rooftop. Standing by for more instructions, I can see my Pa's parked vehicle emerge in front of the exit door. *Save me! Save me, Pa!* The frightening, chilling sounds of thunder and lightning, reveal widespread rain clouds. A shrewd and stormy proclamation that more water is forthcoming.

"Bilisan ninyo, lumabas na kayo!" (Faster you, go out now, all of you!)

My aunties kept on repeating: "Dalian ninyo!" (Hurry you all!) Call for the emergency evacuation. Then I felt a surge of water push me out the exit door. I fell to my knees outside into the rising water.

Behind me, in this continued commotion, my uncle and an adult male neighbor took one child in each arm and paddled hard across the yard and as the water deepened, they swam. Yes, they "swam" across its compound's half-acre playground buried in deep rainwater. As far as my eyes can see, there was water but unlike the Pacific's bluest blue ocean water, it was murky.

Upon rising from my knees in the water, I wondered, *where shall I go now? And, what do I do?* I could feel the water's force moving about me. Just then, in a forceful instructional vocal expression not understood, a man shoves me inside Pa's vehicle. The sound of the storm was so loud; he yelled and instructed me further,

"Stay inside until help comes back."

He took his attention away from me, abruptly turned around and pulled one of my younger cousin's body who was flapping his arms and hands, against the flood water's strong gripping movements. The man placed my co-inhabitant's small frame on his back.

Who is this man? Why was he here? And where did he come from? Because of the unpredictable current of the flood water; my cousin wrestled, looking panic-stricken, to stay on this man's back. A scary scene to behold. Soon, they swam away.

Why didn't they stay with me?

Now frantic, every physical movement went with such urgency. I merely followed this man's directions and stayed put. I realized after... I was alone.

I COULDN'T THINK. I felt isolated. Still somehow knew, help would come. It was a very lonesome time; my father is nowhere. And it's not that my young mind mattered, it introduced me to calamitous and severe situations to tackle by myself. So much more though, I feared not seeing my Pa again.

Would I drown?

REFLECTION: I am an islander who couldn't swim. Never learned. My fear of water was first introduced when, Pa, hurriedly threw me into the three-feet deep seawater and nearly drowned. He thought he could teach me similar to all the others; taught this unorthodox way. Later, fear came back after I was hurriedly pushed into a pool. Yes, also, almost drowned.

THE FLOODWATER IS NOW MOVING upwards all around, rushing about, and eyeing both sides of the vehicle's doors. I felt my body shake uncontrollably in seeing water seeping through. There is no metal door, strong enough to keep its powerful natural energy away from me.

This panic response is reminiscent of a time our family was on vacation. Bataan, a province north of Quezon City—a place for perfect respite. Where *soul-steering* walks by the white sand beaches is a haven for anyone. Living in the city is great fun having access to a playground with ever-ready playmates at hand is at its perfection. And the lusciousness of the province's beaches surrounding this small town is breathtaking. Both the sand and beachfront give a tantalizing invitation to step up and feel the calming sound of ocean water.

An irresistible and exciting invitation my family fully accepted. We strolled on the beach upon our arrival. The sand felt cool. I looked straight towards the Ocean's water and saw the endless beauty of seawater. The earth's wavy clothing amasses underwater creations; inhabited by unique marine life including animals and plants unseen by humans. God reserved His amazing work for each living matter underneath; staged so deep and separate from dry ground. No human can trespass an exclusive area in the deep sea world and survive.

In the midst of our family's pleasant stroll, I see Pa looking at where I stopped a few yards off the sand line—I know *that* mischievous LOOK! He steps hurriedly towards me. Seeing his wide-eyed thrill... *oh no!* But before I could run away, Pa swooped my small frame and tossed me into the air. Spotting the water below.... *here I come!* Fearful emotions rose. My body bucked up, and I felt like one huge uncontrolled dead weight splashing into the warm seawater.

Surprise took me. Panic ensued. Unprepared and unable to swim, I tried to breathe like the fishes in the ocean. Why not? My lungs are bigger than most fish! Plus, God designed human lungs with widened space for air fill. I didn't know how to hold my breath.

I panicked and swallowed more sea salt-seasoned water. An obvious hysteric scene unfolds. Flapping arms and legs, accompanied with jerking body movements, I was sinking. Right away, Pa fished me out of the sea water and carried me back ashore.

Lucidity showed up sooner than I expected. In respectful rebutting with my father, I explained to the regretful professor how the result of his "good intent," could have turned out favorably. If Pa at the least, provided his student (me here still coughing up water—cough, cough) the basic swimming lesson. Yes, I would have been swimming with the fishes by now!

"And, what might that basic lesson be?" Pa asked in humorist ways.

"Lesson Number one, hold your breath before going underwater, especially while still in deep seawater. Right?" I asked.

"Yes, Pa?"

He nods.

"I thought so," and he smiled.

THIS REMINISCING MOMENT broke quickly by the reality of what was happening in Pa's automobile. Tears came flowing down my cheeks with eyes fixated on the flooding floorboard. *I have to do something. I do not want to drown. I do not want to die. Not ready to die!* I moved to the driver's seat placing my bare wet feet on its clutch and gas pedals. *Do I drive this car? How?* Human instinct for survival jumped started; thanks to my nervous system. I paused and believed somehow he, *that* neighbor will come back to help me.

With my head bowed down, I whimpered and prayed.

God, please help me!

My prayer was sincere. It was a genuine prayer so much like I had witnessed Ma prayed many times—on her knees.

Scouting my surroundings, I looked up behind over the headroom and focused on the automobile's back window. And through the oblong-shaped glass, I see images floating. *Are those swimmers in the water?*

Rescue me!

Not! They are only floating debris and branches. Shaking in fear, I wiped my tears to clear my focal view. The scene revealed more floating unidentifiable items. This reminded me of movie watching on a giant movie screen at a Drive-in, cinema in Los Angeles. Except, *this* is not a movie. The flood in what now appears to be covering the whole earth is real (not *Augmented Reality*). *This* is for real! Uncontrollably, my body continued to shake.

At that point of realism, I looked outside and see a ball-like figure floating and swirling. I blinked to clear my eyes again and focused on the round shape, bobbing about. I felt anxious. It's not a ball. It appears to be a human head. More heavy rain and wind continued to clobber the car wildly around and about. I kept seeing distorted images. Like windshield wipers set on high; I wiped and cleared the consistent flowing tears off my eyes. I continued to talk to God.

Wherever You are — please, help me!

With such intense neediness brimming, I wish the ball-like figure to be a human head. In particular, be the head of *that* helper. And while in mid-wishful thinking, my eyes opened wide seeing the automobile's door handle shifting downwards on its own. On the other side, its natural force of water continued to press against the metal door, making it harder to open wider. After, as if it's looking for something... a human arm and hand appeared through the narrow gap and moved around vigorously. *Looking for what?*

With great force, the car door opened wider. That bobbing round shape on the flood water—revealed a full-on human form with a familiar voice. He stood unsteady at the opening.

"Ready?" he asked.

Didn't need an answer, he pulled me out from the driver's seat. Like my cousin before; this "man-angel," saved me. In no time, I found myself clutched on my angel's back as he swam across the rainwater-covered ground.

God answered my prayers in sending my saving angel.

Encouragement:

∿

Hebrews 13:6
The Lord is my Helper; I will not fear.
What can man (and flood) do to me?

(NKJV)

∼

IN JESUS' name, I pray:
Frightening floods from life's vicious storms cannot break down my Abba, Father's divine protective walls surrounding me. God, You created me—You were there in times of need, and You are there always holding my fear close to You.

REUNITED WITH THE FAMILY, we felt safe together in our neighbor's 3 story home, which stood high above the waters. On that stormy day, heroes from a close-knit community received praises and given much gratitude by many residents for saving many of their family's lives. I wished to have thanked my angel in person, but he was nowhere around. Seeing everyone in my family safe is comforting. Yet, this new feeling of fear has my entire body tied-up, dreadfully. It was a warm-up feeling, surrounded by loving relatives and concerned neighbors. Teamwork at its best form!

Albeit a temporary safety nest gave way to an intense longing for my parents.

Where are they? Is my Ma safe? Has anyone told her... she almost lost a daughter?

10

THE YEAR OF LOSSES

*B*YE-BYE, BUNGALOW. Relief is a welcome feeling to have. It took two days for the flood to drain enough to reveal the compound's waterlogged ground. Expressing much gratitude to the many available neighbors who helped in the Villa Dolores post-flood cleanup. Helping hands moving damped heavy furniture, wet clothes, water-damaged mattresses, and valuable belongings outside of the bungalow to dry. It appears to be a gargantuan celebration of a new and dry day—at least for the moment.

Taking advantage of the sun-shining day, Ma came home and was scurrying alongside her sisters. The Sisterhood is at their best foot forward and together again in all they do. A wondrous moment and a good day for household chores.

Joining in the delightful day are many chirping birds. In-and-out, amidst the colorful backdrop gracefully fly and arrange melodious twitters. Affixed up in the sky is the multi-colored rainbow, a heavenly sign of a promised relief. Adding to a tranquil moment is the sun's brightness amid clear blue skies made an orchestrated finale. A theatrical moment; filling the clear and bright new day with blessings from above.

IT HAS BEEN two weeks since the flood, and major changes are channeling through. Ma seems to pop up toting great life alterations for her tribe.

Soon, we were reunited with our parents. After a few days' stay in Pa's hospital room... all eight migrates felt relieved to be with each other. There were nine of us in total including a relative helping with Pa's caregiving needs. Yes, we all slept together on the floor except for our ailing father. Our minds reassured—nestling together in the safety nest of our parent's loving presence. Each one relieved. We have reconciled with everyone, especially with Pa.

In the wake of a life-threatening and frightening natural calamity, what mattered most is our safety. Material damages brought on by the floods were insubstantial at this point. I didn't weigh in any of the storm's visible damages. My family survived and are now with each other. We celebrated the joyful moment.

THE BUNGALOW'S foundation and its wooden sub-structure suffered extreme water damage. It was beyond immediate repair. Our *FUN-land* is not available for fun anything; it's closed until further notice. With the extensive repairs requiring weeks to accomplish, Ma, made moving plans to an interim home at once. We will move to a familiar neighborhood, close to the school we attend. I have been attending, Rosa Sevilla Memorial School (RSMS), the former *Instituto de Mujeres*, since kindergarten.

RSMS, was the first educational institution created for the Philippine Lay Women. *Doctora* (Dra.) Rosa Sevilla de Alvero, founded the school in 1900. She was an educator, writer, and one of notable suffragists in Asia who fought for the Filipino women's, "Right to Vote."

Later, the founder's relative, Dra. Josefina Alvero would presume the role of Directress and principal owner. She was my father's professional colleague. Higher education was a unique connection for these two. Both the professor and principal held very high reverence for each other's accomplishments. Needless to say, their engagement at any level attracted attention from any crowd.

The school's curriculum offered a full day's schedule in both the city and provincial (state) educational system. In the 1950s, both the public and private schools provided six years of primary level, followed by four years of secondary level. Ten years... packed with programs to satisfy the credits required for a High School Certificate of Completion.

The country's national language, Filipino or Tagalog, along with the English and Spanish languages, were part of the mandatory Language class curriculum. Eventually, the Department of Education, voted to remove the Spanish subject in favor of the *more* world-wide used foreign, English language. Offering English I and II at the secondary level—high school years. To promote to the next higher grade, a student must complete five core subjects with passing grades in the first three years. Finishing the last year's six subjects with passing grades, awards a student a high school diploma.

Pa preferred for his children to practice using the English language at home. Tagalog is a given and Spanish... well, Pa speaks it and nobody else did. So, we engaged—English it was.

REFLECTION: We conformed to communicating in English at home. Albeit, Spanish would have given us "tri-language" abilities—useful to over one-third, bi-lingual Spanish speakers in the State of California. Not to mention the fifty-three plus millions, nationwide. The hindsight!

REX IS in his usual stance with Ma. His undying philosophy connected to the scarcity of monies during the upcoming school is at hand. The not-so-hidden agenda; Rex's—both school expenses and birthday land in mid-June. There are no cash funds left for a birthday anything! He defends his unrelenting position in a yearly inquiry of budget handling! "Will maneuvering monies around, be possible?" Year after year, the response is, "Not this year!" A further plea was re-scheduled for next year.

Meanwhile, for the rest of us who are not facing birthdays anytime soon... well, we celebrated upon receiving new shoes, clothes, school supplies, and brown wrapping papers for our books. This time, we received the extras; wooden rulers and manual sharpeners—useful and convenient commodities. Exciting conveniences. This feels like... "a celebration." Yes, grateful to receive comprehensive allocation, beyond our basic needs. Even so, Rex was also enjoying new learning tools and apparel, especially his shoes.

Joy funneling! Yet again Pa is missing.

IN RECENT DAYS, our mother has been staying overnight at the hospital; unseen at home. And all the aunties could say is that the doctors have extended our father's hospital stay for more testing.

What type of testing? For what?

I don't remember spending time with my father's sister; and so, her surprise appearance at our home has no substance.

Who is 'this' sister again?

Auntie Supe, Pa's older sister and only sibling is a domineering *Headmistress*. I can figure it out "HM," as the counterpart of her younger brother. Equitably so. Many see my father, the strict household economist, as awkward-appearing in nature. I saw the opposite.

Perhaps being the eldest of the other aunties, Auntie Supe, elected herself the commander in Ma's absence. There is no countering her decision. So it is, the Sabella youngsters are under her averse ways.

ENDLESS TELEPHONE RINGING disturbed my wholesome dreaming... *Pa in slow motion, combs my hair, few strands at a time.* "Ring-ring, ring-ring." Then quietness. Oh good! One of my Aunties may have answered the call. *Now, where was I?* I tried to pick up where my dream was interrupted. But, before nodding back to my dream, the HM rudely awakened me.

"Wake up. You Bibe, wake up!"

The name is Annabelle. Though, I did not insist on formal addressing. I can hear. I see—she's wrought up over something—magnifying her stony-hearted persona!

I got up and followed Auntie Supe to the living room. I see my oldest brother half asleep—rubbing his eyes—trying to wake up and hear what flusters the HM. She stops in front and centered... Kuya BB repositions to face Auntie Supe. He stood like a Roman soldier—protecting whoever may stand behind him. I stood to his left side. I reached up and held his hand.

I watched... I have been on the look-out for my father, since the last time we had a family sleep over in his hospital room after that horrifying storm. Though, brief—it was a blissful family togetherness. At the moment, subtle piercing of the heart is coming at a heavy clouding time in life. Something dark is developing amidst all the unanswered questions about our father.

The eldest in a Filipino family holds a great deal of responsibilities. Kuya BB has been dodging arrows from the HM! She had it out for us! Her clear vexation turned into days of hackling phrases aimed at innocent targets; to each of her younger brother's children. Auntie Supe, armed with weaponry so dark; her sharp cutting jargon made its way towards Kuya BB. Looks at BB's direction and she utters one lethal sentence.

"YOU CAUSED THIS... ALL OF YOU CAUSED YOUR PAPA'S DEATH!"

Bull's eye the audible arrowhead splits sending sharp cutting words to its targets.

HM continued to say hurtful words, I covered my left ear to hear nothing more. Though sounds of muffled words, "Blah-blah-blah" came through. My heart ached so much, but she didn't see. She did not care. All HM wanted was to point a finger. To blame us, Pa's family! She reached her goal; unequivocally, made our youthful and innocent minds, feel guilt.

REFLECTION: Painful brokenheartedness gave way to weaken spiritual foundation that had lasted a lifetime. Harsh language wafted "lingered poison" into our atmosphere. Unrelieved for a very long time. The burning cut made by damaging punitive words were unambiguously deeper on my brother. I saw its fiery effect on him. And I saw the Roman-like soldier's broken heart, drooped in misery. I believe Auntie Supe's hurtful words—kept untended—ultimately resulted in a spiritual struggle to cause a young soul carry a very harmful load in his future life.

It was an act replayed in my mind over the years. Particularly, in more vivid re-enactments came during my brother's challenging times.

So it happened, I was the one around Kuya BB still holding his hand, when Auntie Supe took her stormy exit far away from our home—from our lives. No one can refute, I removed her name from my vocabulary. My brother and I abandoned the scene never to be discussed.

OTHER RELATIVES SHOWED up later that morning including Auntie Peling. My older brother, Kuya Rolando, who couldn't wake up earlier is now dealing with the sad news. He joined Kuya BB; sat and stared at the wooden floor.

I have been pacing around the family room for some time now. Though, I have many times walked around; stepped downstairs, down the driveway, and back up the stairs to shake off the gripping news about Pa. My heart broke, shattered to pieces... OH, MY HEART ACHES SO MUCH!

Upon reaching the top stair, I see Auntie Peling overwhelmed with sadness, blinks to replenish tears into her puffed eyelids. She steps towards where my brothers sat. Sensing her immediate presence to give an update... she's here to say, your *Pa is well and alive!* I walked towards her back and held the exchanges of breaths in my lungs, I stood still behind and begged.

Say it, please!

She looks down and touches my brother, Kuya BB's shoulder.

"Doktor, passed from complications of Diabetes and heart disease."

At that moment of horrible news, I did not know what "complications" meant. *What is Diabetes? What is heart disease? How does one catch these? How do you get rid of it?* All I heard was that Papa, my love, has died!

I didn't cry. IT IS NOT TRUE! It's a lie made up by Auntie Supe.

Not disrespecting here; I believe none of these. It's absolute nonsense. I know he is somewhere; where is he? I stayed up to wait for Ma to come home. Other relatives around tried to console us. But I avoided their hugs, comforting smiles, and ignored their cries. I didn't even look for any kisses. I only wanted my Papa.

Oh Pa, come back to me... **PLEASE!**

REFLECTION: I have lost detailed memory of the days following my father's death. How does an eight-year-old child process loss of a loved one? How did I process the loss? I didn't. And I couldn't.

All I remembered was the numbness. I deeply longed for my Pa. My heart failed—a child's heart sorrowfully attacked by the loss of a parent. An incomprehensible process I should NOT have to face. As a child, my father was my everything. My world revolved around him. And comparable, I saw my father's spun about mine. Pa's presence secured my existence; I knew of God's unconditional love through him. And Pa's love, too, is not dependent on anything I do. He loves me, period.

I felt blindsided by an unidentified force. I felt a major artery of my heart; the Left Anterior Descending artery (LAD) blocked. My heart skipped a beat that would follow sporadic charting for many years that came. Soon my heart's myocardium (muscle) enlarged. The wall of my heart thickened with its senses clouding each passing day.

The pain of losing, my Pa, to death was so unbearable that nothing mattered. All the outdoors' activities became unimportant. Everything I looked for on any day, meant nothing. I was blanking out. His hugs, kisses on my forehead, loving touches placed on my shoulders. Those body-guarding steps that followed me around all the days of my life.

Yet God knew. He was by my side—penciling memories that would be the key towards healing—to give me a future and a hope in life. God has the only Password that could unlock the module needed to unveil the brilliance that awaits me. Jesus is the source linking humanity—my mortality, to God. His Spirit of wisdom, power, strength, comfort, and healing—God's grace and mercy sufficient! Transformation to my Lord's likeness is, and only through, His cleansing blood. Repent and surrender—liberation in God, infused sanity forever into my life.

MY ENTIRE FAMILY is fast transforming into Zombie-like creatures. Nothing like the make-up or fitting costumes for a Halloween Party but in real life. Everyone was in deep sorrow with Pa's death. Ma has dark sunken eyes caused by lack of sleep; she dealt with endless tears in solitude. In her family's presence, Ma resolved to be strong. My sister and brothers are going through a harrowing time! Our heads were looking southward. Limp bodies in slow motion everywhere around.

Still, teamwork is at a high gear in prepping for my Pa's funeral.

I flat out refuse to take part. Even in a call for help, I dragged doing my part. Although I went with the motion, there was a protective seal wrapped around my heart. Pa is somewhere and without a doubt, he'll show up. Just watch! That dead body in the coffin is not him. I didn't want to look.

I proclaimed out loud:

"That dead body isn't Pa!"

I gave a spirited declaration with an intentional unyielding look. Everyone in the room heard me. Though they met my statement with great sympathy evidenced by their expected reaction, I denied them any satisfaction in seeing me with emotional *anything*. There was no caving in my deep plea to see my father alive.

FOR THE PAST FEW DAYS, visitors from far and near arrived to be with my family. Each one paid their respects, stopped by Pa's encasement. Some cried, others prayed ending with a soft touch as if avoiding to hurt *that*, dead body further.

Hundreds of consoling visitors came and left. Everyone in dark apparel was pale-faced, an expression of sadness. I saw many strangers; too many strangers. I wondered, *who they were and what they were doing here?* From a close distance, I also noticed several young adults who stood closer together. They appear to be teenagers. From what I can see, unusually sorrowful. I couldn't place where, nor remember when I might have seen them before; yet, familiar looking. The atmosphere quickly took me back to a blank stare towards the bottom of the coffin.

The dreadful burial day came. I didn't sleep much the night before... thinking of my Pa. I woke up with heart thumping! Still waiting for him to wake up from a deep sleep. So, I went along with this charade. I stayed quiet riding in the family automobile driven by a family friend. When looking out through the clammy car window, I see many funereal activities. Few are smiling. Somber-looking clothing too. Again, *Who are these people?*

A sad scene fitting the days' mood. From a short distance, mid-way between the damp stony burial ground and cloudy sky, umbrellas mushroomed protective coverings over the many funeral attendees.

The call for a rainy day didn't keep the mourners from their last opportunities to bid farewell, even to travel on foot. Many vehicles, both chartered jeeps, and automobiles, lined up in a procession headed to Pa's final resting place. One-by-one, each mourner stepped out from their reserved transportation and walked passed a small traffic jam.

A team of funeral organizers placed the coffin in front of my mother and siblings then stood behind, unmoved. The compound residents, many families, and relatives, along with dear friends surrounded us. After the priest ended a prayer, one-by-one, each said their final farewell to Pa. Then, I see several men advancing toward the empty marble tomb.

To the side of the tomb is a block of marbled stone. I am no mannequin. I can figure things out. I see ready mixed cement in a large container next to the stone. I stood on the front steps of the architectural artistry designed mausoleum.

My heart hasn't stopped thumping! It's pounding faster!

Lifeless body, indescribable in all aspect. I stand firm, un-accepting of the happenings—in deep silent moaning—desiring; Pa would move back into my life. I am in dire need to move backwards, into the arms of my love. Thenceforward, I saw the men who have been standing motionless around, move and prepare to lift Pa's coffin. I rushed in screaming and crying.

"Stop! please STOP!"

I aimed—then threw my upper body and face on top of the coffin's glass top. Seeing my Pa's face for the first time since news of his passing—I tried to touch his face but could not break through its glass covering. Seeing him now up close... his lip's top layers are dry and appear to be peeling, and his eyes are shut tight. I knew right away what was wrong. I yelled!

"Water, he needs water! Please, anybody, give him water!"

He wasn't moving—incapable of hearing me. My elbows hung on the casing's sides, waiting for any flicker of movement as I continued to focus on Pa's eyes. With sweaty hands and fingers on the glass, I tap to awaken Pa. I cried with deep moaning. Tap, tap, tap...

"Pa, oh Pa, wake up!" and I whispered,

"It's me... Bibe."

"Open your eyes, I'm right in front of you. Just open them, **please!**"

My kisses imprinted and tears smudged all over the glass cover. Two or three others wrapped themselves around me, and literally pried me apart from this poignant grip.

They dragged me—my body along with my broken heart, away and forever from *Papa, my love*!

Encouragement:

Psalm 147:3
He heals the brokenhearted and binds up their wounds.
(NKJV)

IN JESUS' name, I pray:
You collected our tears when we were in fear—during the floods of pain in life—in heart-wrenching losses and from desperate loneliness. Your healing hands have closed the wounds of long ago, replaced by Your bountiful love. We call out to You, Abba, Father, "Oh Lord, our Deliverer."

Psalm 136:23
Who remembers us in our lowly state; For His mercy endures forever.
(NKJV)

11

A NEW DAY

Limbo days are dragging and having fun was the last thing on my mind. I wanted my Pa. His death impacted each compound resident. We were all experiencing empty-headedness; which, lasted for weeks in the bungalow. My shattered life has frozen still—not knowing how to pick up the pieces. Not that it freezes in the Philippines. On a typical June day, when the sun is out, the temperature predictably gets to above 90-degrees Fahrenheit. The island's normal atmospheric extreme state of heat and humidity have conditioned us to adapt to the climate. Unbearable. But no, it is not the moisture in the air—it was Pa's death that made the climate unbearable. We are missing his presence in the bungalow. More so by me.

Though the hot and moist feeling is part of our habitat's environment; it is not necessarily an unwelcome condition for the youngins. If the clouds are not shooting thunders below, the children are out playing. Still, I couldn't get out of the mid-stream of sad and sadder. I didn't understand Pa's death.

I have too many questions. Topping the list is, *Why?*

There was no immediate answer to a question I could not ask! I would not ask! And frankly, I didn't want to hear the answer. I wanted my father back. I miss his loving strokes and touches on my hair. Oh, those loving kisses! How can I survive this tremendous emptiness, *this*, now a hole inside my heart—inside my entire being?

Each school day helps divert my attention. The daily fun class activity—Physical Education (PE) is my all-time favorite group school ground activity. We play with very few restrictions. Open options for PE activities and to its fun gadgets. Students have many ball selections in differing sizes. More favored by the girls are hand-clapping and jumping rope. Often, the boys choose games involving the use of playing balls. And sometimes, a traditional game and one of my favorite pastime, SIPA.

Sipa, means kick. This game uses core strength and balance with quick muscle movements. The object used to play the game—referred to *sipa* made with a washer, wrapped in colorful threads with a plastic or paper straw attached to it. *Sipa* is then tossed upwards for a player to hit or strike using only the leg, largely from the lateral or medial sides of the foot to above the knee. Participant must not allow the object to touch the ground by striking as many times while in the air, into mid-air without stopping. These striking moves continue until the object falls to the ground, which ends the player's turn. Skilled players can make several kicks without stepping down for a break. If the player touches the object with hands, their turn is over. Out loud, players must count the number of times they kick the object. The surrounding opponents calculate the running total. The participant with the most kicks wins the game. I have to admit, the boys mostly beat me—though, not by many. I would say likely by three or four kicks!

My siblings and I take part in most of the games together at school. *Sipa*, touch ball, hopscotch, and the simple rolling of marbles on dirt into a small hole; games we enjoy playing as a group. Being together brings security and hope for our day.

It's too soon to know my heart. All I know is it's another day without our Papa. Often, I wish the school day would not end.

REFLECTION: Moments of family togetherness give me so much joy, knowing God's presence is wherever I go. He held my hands on that dreary day, the news of Pa's passing exploded into my ears. God stroked my hair every day as One Divine Father. All along, never letting go of His little child's hand.

Having God in my life now, I can recognize that losing a loved one to death, abandonment, separation, divorce or personal reasons for leaving, is heartbreaking.

All the more—loved ones—some are torn apart by the ever-shaky family structure at home. Children losing security based on parents' undemonstrated affectionate love for one another. And devoid of communication with each other.

The effect of witnessing my parents in heavy verbal discussions was heartbreaking. Catching sight of Ma's finger pointing appeared, accusatory. Pa's head bowed with tears rolling down his face are like wringing pinches tearing through my little heart. Love leaking through a tiny tear would soon burst out and sustain damage so deep.

In time, repaired wholly by Jehovah Rapha—The Lord, our Healer.

Do you relate to any of these situations? Please know God is right beside you—wiping your tears dry with His omnipotent strokes! No wounds too deep, too wide for His healing power. Remedy the pain with His love.

Encouragement:

∼

Isaiah 41:10
Fear not, for I am with you;
Be not dismayed, for I am your God.
I will strengthen you.

(NKJV)

∼

In Jesus' name, I pray:

You call me by my name. Lord, only You, know the condition of my heart, securely cradling and satiating my appetite for love. Every move I make, every hope I feel, every breath I take—You are here with me. Strengthen me, O Lord.

∼

NIGHTS HOLD ALTOGETHER a contrast to its day's newness with each passing morning. The continued deep longing to see my Pa intensified, that I started, "naturally," hallucinating—if there is such an experience. Maybe closer to fantasizing, right? *Hmm.*

Our sleeping set-up is a duplicate of the old bungalow's family bedroom. We all sleep in one enclosed area.

One wistful night, I ended up on the top bunk bed. Sleeping on the fun spot was likely a prize I collected from a game of *Sipa*. In lying down on my side, gravity pulled my focus downward. On the wooden floor are reflections—square in appearance. Looking up and to the side along the north-side, high in the darkened sky is the moon shining down brightly through the wide French glass window. Pausing, I envision, my Papa, in heaven. Smiling and looking down at me. I deeply wish for his presence—see him even for just a moment. Shifting my vision straight ahead is Pa's armoire, positioned twenty feet from the bunk bed. Flushed against the bedroom's dividing wall, stood a solid wood cabinet, an artisan's pride—displaying its nature's etches. There are no visible traces of manual-buffing made, not to a pair of sleepy eyes. Not easily detectable in the darkened area.

The loving memories of Pa soothes my mind, setting off and are transmitting melodious lullaby notes rocking me asleep. Remembering the brush strokes he applied to my hair... wishing for the imaginary loving touch to continue. I fought to keep my flickering eyelids open.

From afar, Pa's spectral figure appeared. He came through the door next to the valued wooden piece. Re-adjusting to keep my retina zoned in, his footing headed towards the dresser, afloat from the floor. Pa's living-like image moves and brushes through the moon's beaming light. Now, becoming fully awake, I comprehend the scene unfolding. Pa is present. In front, moving his focus towards my direction.

Pa connects with me looking with a conversant smile. He moves forward ahead still with eye beams connecting to mine. He pulls two sets of his favorite custom-made suits out from the dresser; turns around, cuts off the connective rays. He then exits the room—fading away! I wanted him to come back.

Not a story to share with anyone at this time of deep loss. *What would Ma think?* As for the younger compound residents, I will be the center of jokes!

One more vision followed days later. Pa appeared through the same door and walked towards me... more steps came my way and as I was seeing through... *is this for real*? Now, I converse with self!

"Do I want this to be physically real?"

"Yes, I do!"

This time around, Pa's image comes within inches of my face. I noticed his lips—no longer dry and peeling. Looking supple and curved at both ends. He's smiling. I closed my eyes, hoping to feel his kisses on my forehead. Nothing. I stayed in my pause yearning for Pa's kiss. Still, nothing. Opened my eyes, and again, he disappeared.

HAVING everyone gathered together at mealtimes gives assurance and a visual reminder, each one is close by. Together, we will heal and cope with all the uncertainties. The relatives who have placed so much effort in helping my family move back to a routine, have tapered in numbers. Though limited on weekends, my two aunties who still live in the family compound are sure encouragements.

Whispers and strange looks between Ma and her sisters have developed to be the customary environment. In recent days, their body language show, something critical has levitated. Adults do not involve children in grown-up matters, but these whispers and looks are sending off a strange message.

Engaging in serious conversations with adults is off-limits for younger family members, but this one special time; by chance, I was around. Ma's facial language appears unrecognizable—rather mysterious. In my viewing assessment, perhaps she is rummaging nerves to talk. Now this is not like my mother. She never needs to build her nerves to say anything—words naturally flow out of her lips. Instead of the usual seating pose with both legs crossed over, Ma placed both feet flat on the wooden floor. Heeding to her full on body language, Ma has our full attention. She looks uneasy—I sense gravity unloading.

(Ma begins: "I have something to tell you about Doktor," she pauses. "Your Pa has another family!" My eyes, wide open, look intently at Ma's face — dropping my attention to her lips. As she contemplates, I looked at my three older siblings and Auntie Minga's faces for any reaction. Rather, they all kept quiet. Ma continued to talk, "And Your Pa has five other children!" Her voice echoed out. I wondered off asking myself, "Did any of my siblings know about this? Whatever, this 'mumbo jumbo is?'" I don't know what Ma is talking about!)

I asked no questions. It's simple; mine was a wishful clarification for all the scenes played out by the Sisterhood's guises in viewable public setting. Hearing the women's low volume grunts, heightened whispers, and seeing un-favored facial expressions with subtle questionable innuendoes—all these, now make sense.

It was a matter of fact atmosphere. A twist of fate, rounded-up at the family dining table. Ma gave appreciation to each surrounding ally in the family setting at hand.

REMEMBERING SEVERAL FAMILIAR-LOOKING GUESTS... those young adults (teenagers, maybe), who stood far away from Pa's casket. In reserved stances, stayed in the crowd. A great loss was clear on their sunken, somber, and paled faces. Were they the other family—other children—my half-siblings? In chopped up time slots, revealing the truth—Ma's demeanor with sure confidence—relief finally came together. In the times of sporadic sharing, the last missing information links into complete disclosure. Four daughters and one son by a different Mother—born staggered within six months to two-and-a-half years apart, paralleled my Ma's birthing days. I came in at number seven followed by three more siblings, in which two are from Ma.

Ma would face a legal decision within a short time. She followed the obvious and right direction—discloses the truth about my Pa having five more Sabella progenies; Doktor's children, my half-siblings.

REFLECTION: Bizarre! Hearing the news about "Pa having another family," with "more children," was unconventional and shocking. Oh, it crashes! Nonsensical. No doubt, painful. A deepened hurtful time for Ma. I identify her attributes of graciousness and courage in keeping the many hurtful secrets of her heart private, and now, public. She disclosed her secrets for the benefit of others! Ma's secrecy was selfless. The love she had for her husband was pure and respectful. Ma never used pejorative words on her husband. Contrary, she showered him much adoration and passion. Unconditionally loved on him. Ma stayed in love, beyond "til death, do us part!"

The perfect timing of a complete disclosure revealed—Ma moved to do the right thing. Responsible actions I would later come to admire. In signing legal documents certifying her husband, my Pa, fathered five other progenies—magnifying Ma's *modus operandi* to help.

They told few stories of the other mother. Who is she? It would be years of filling in the missing pieces in Pa's life. The very isolated and personal chunk of time and in his full awareness was hurting Ma. For certain, was hurting my half-siblings' mother. My respect for Ma went over the rooftop, into the billions of stars—bouncing its brilliance back into my heart. Ma is keen on keeping the good memories of Pa alive and lovely. And with Ma's extensive collection of colorful words; she never, ever roasted him off.

12

FATHER FIGURE

𝓑OY TAKES FATHER ROLE. Kuya BB has been out of sight for most of the days following our residential move to Matimyas Road. The school's activities have kept us busy. Rex comes about unusually still. He has said little. Unlike years past when June brings Opposing Counsel, Rex, before Judge Ma. Appearing wearied. Rex just turned seven years young and yet his vigor zapped by our loss... has forgone his usual appeal to having a birthday anything!

Kuya BB, displays visible changes too. He and I have not visited *that* forgettable scene with Auntie Supe. I am guessing he has tossed it aside. Teamwork is at hand. As the eldest male sibling of the family, Kuya BB, understood the best he could... the underlying responsibility of our culture. How will he deal with the latest news shared about Pa having another family? Is he wondering as I? How will his siblings process *this* hefty indelible news announcement? His sudden gain of parenting responsibility is staring him in the face. No dodging. No disappearing act. There will be no hide and seek. Other than being a big brother with zero parental experience; this is now his life's reality. Our life.

A FATHER's role is a huge responsibility and to take our Pa's—more so —intimidating and frightening. With a sound basis, Kuya BB, is just a young teenager, but he courageously takes on the father role with no reservations. He has a concentrated effort to follow the parental lead displayed by our parents. He is a natural in leadership. Strategizing to grow big and fast are now in play. He snacks on fruits and eats all his meats and vegetables. Focusing on his studies and sleeps well. All centered on filling *that* pair of empty shoes.

Kuya BB, born with remarkable intelligence and resilience, and in due time with an undying commitment, fills the hard leathered shoes left behind. At fourteen, reflecting from the mirror—a young man in the making.

My brother received his basic training in life. He endured and outlived much of Pa's sternest disciplinary actions; which, often accompanied with enforcing measures. I admire my brother in so many ways. His creative keenness in life and tactical approach to helping—genuine eagerness. The light is shining through and hope is on the horizon for our family.

REFLECTION: In a perilous time of our life, Kuya BB's courage led to actions necessary to provide, us, his siblings the much-needed security. His valor, beyond admirable. The call for military duty forced him to leave us behind. I am forever grateful for the many sacrifices, Kuya BB, has made in providing us emotional and financial support. For all whom he continued to shoulder.

I hold precious the heartfelt gratitude, my parents, sister, and brother in serving others. Enabling me to reciprocate at God's appointed time. Several opportunities have jumped in on the "pay-it-forward" wagon allowing me to do for others. God extends our kind generosity beyond family members—towards those He places around us.

"Charity begins at home," displayed very early in my childhood. I also took in as charity begins from the heart. My immediate family had everything we needed. My parents nurtured us with loving kindness—an attribute passed on. Their generosity in helping our relatives, neighbors, friends, and others in need is a gracious quality embedded by the Creator. A mix of Pa's frugality and Ma's generosity—equals me.

No one had to tell Kuya BB to help us. He acted with no reservations. He provided financial aid, emanated amid much self-sacrifice. Blessed with suitable DNA strings, he budgeted efficiently. Generosity went beyond sharing of money—bounteousness of the heart. BB's obedience in his cultural calling shared many valued resources with us, his family.

∼

REFLECTIVE THOUGHT: Are you beaming with gratitude for an individual—your special person? Cogitate on that person—find time to visit him—talk and listen. Enjoy a favorite meal with her. Read out loud to them. Watch their favorite television program or movie with them. Take pleasure in penning a letter of gratitude, snail mail—a tangible multifaceted treasure. And dig deep unearthing some precious time to express gratitude to Christ Jesus, Who funded our penalty with His life. Because of our Savior's obedience to the cross, we can come to Father God's presence—a privilege we have any day of the week.

Encouragement:

∼

> Colossians 3:20
> Children, obey your parents in all things,
> for this is well pleasing to the Lord.
> (NKJV)

∼

IN JESUS' name, I pray:

God sets His promise to His people. We receive redemption by faith in Jesus Christ's ultimate sacrifice; death on the cross for our sins. May You continue to bless those sacrificing others, affording unrelenting financial, unwavering emotional, and physical support to the many in need. May our obedience be a testament to our trust and reliance on You, Lord—an act of commitment—of our deep love and faith in you.

13

SALTED WOUND

*T*he saddest day of my life has moved and taken unyielding back-seat. Weeks of adjusting to the death of my father is a temporal mindset in each given day. Even more so with Ma, she is wrestling with intense (spiritual) warfare inside. The obvious loneliness, emptiness, and painful loss—intensifying in her whole being mostly in the night—at bedtime. Not only is she dealing with the loss of her love, adding to the enormous burden of filling in extra parental role is overwhelming. Yet, I had not witnessed quizzical notion from Ma. She delves into the day's process—gives way into her newfound and unexpected role. At forty-three years old... Ma is now a widow, single-parent, and provider.

THERE ARE busy noises coming from many activities off Matimyas street. A mix of tricycles, jeeps, and automobiles; passing and stopping. Picking up varied passengers from the corner streets bordering a school. School children alongside holding hands with their parents; sometimes, a *Lola*, (grandmother) or a *Lolo*, (grandfather) pronounced: "Lo-laa," and "Lo-lo," respectively. Each one talking, connecting, and engaging with the other. They walk on the farthest side, away from moving traffic. There are no sidewalks like the ones in the City of Los Angeles.

I remember the convenience of the residential sidewalks in California—are designed for pedestrians. These designated pathways exclusive for people are astonishing. Enlightening. Safe crossings on streets are... welcome newness. Not surprising, we were in a new world. Every new thing in America was a welcome change to us. My interest on its paved and smoother sidewalks in our old neighborhood —peculiar—yet, not far-fetched. For me, it's all about having fun.

REFLECTION: The small town of Tatalon's passageways accessible to and from our home are rough—gravel road made from a mixture of crushed stones, sand, and other granular materials. Motorized transportation and animal powered wagons; alongside, God's two and four-footed creations use these pathways. Walk down to a nearby *Sari-Sari* (Variety) Store and most often you'll find neighbors and furry companions pacing right behind or by your side. Likely, the soft footing of a dog, a duck's audible quacking, a rooster, or chicken's pecking are on rough walkways. Though rare, hearing of a cat purring is exclusive and fewer than seeing a Carabao.

Carabao is the Philippines' National Animal. They are most referred to as "*Kalabaw*; " which are swamp-type water buffalo and are notorious for their hardworking nature. This tamed huge four-footed domestic help are a welcome citing around the perimeters of Villa Dolores bungalow. *Kalabaw* is often the power used for pulling heavy loads such as a wagon-filled with varieties of produce, various domestic supplies, heavy items, and sometimes transports *people*. And if need be, these horned laborers can pull a small "stilt" house (a humble home made with mostly plants and bamboo).

Most neighbors and the compound children see *Kalabaw* alongside Filipino's four-legged *best friend*, equal to Westerners' dogs and cats.

IN REMEMBERING... living in Los Angeles, after school, I could always identify the "clicky-ti-tack" sound of Pa's walking cane following behind on our route towards home. I would turn around in gleaming gesture, exhibiting a loving awareness of his presence. Though, it wasn't always a welcome sound.

In a walk through the new neighborhood, it was fascinating to see the easy access to the neighbors' open front yards. There were no barbed wire fencing around! I thought of the many fun games shared back at the bungalow with our co-inhabitants on its vast Sabella-Land playground. Often, I walk far behind my siblings. Perhaps the rareness of being by myself, and even though it was only two blocks behind my siblings, infrequency was the enticement to do so.

RECALLING... several days leading up to the end of October, our neighbors' excitement captivated us by their much-anticipated celebration. Watching our neighbors placing decorations around their residences, street corners—front yards—in trees; was spellbinding. Causing unexpected silence in between my family—we had no clue for the "spooky" hoopla.

Strategically placed are scary decors spread around homes, trees, shrubs, electrical poles, and road signs. The celebrants even *ghosted* the fire hydrants! Various paper decorations such as Jack-O'-Lanterns, skulls, skeletons, positioned around make-believe graveyards, doorways, and windows. Then there were those, *wasted* yummy pumpkins —carved in scary images—guarding each home's entry-way. Light illuminating from inside the pumpkins often reveal broken teeth! Last and not the least were the "Trick-or-Treaters." There were no tip-off of who they were and why the getup? What's boggling—scary costumes with masks, these Trick-or-Treaters were wearing. Children mostly— beyond thrilled for the year-long awaited, event's arrival.

"Is this comparable to the 'All Souls' Day' we celebrate back in the Philippines?"

Unlike the old neighborhood in Los Angeles, parading around in those costumes in groups, we celebrate around DEAD PEOPLE! No dress-up, just *visit* with the buried dead people in the cemetery. Families and friends gather around our departed loved one's gravesite to celebrate. We eat dinner and share stories about dead family members and friends for two whole days—barely sleeping. Can't! Not me. I dare not close my eyes and chance falling asleep amid thousands of tombs. If there is any time for anyone to beat me in a challenge, the "All Souls' Day" would be *the* day! Clear visibility, a mere few feet from lit candles. Land filled with skulls and skeletons, other tombs house fresh lifeless bodies—a real sense of darkness.

• • •

ONCE MORE AFTER SCHOOL, on *this* Trick-or-Treat day, my footsteps lagged my siblings. A systematic sound coming from behind got my attention, yet I didn't look back. Curious at first, then fear followed. Strange sounds continued and moved closer, "clicky-ti-tacks!" I stepped faster. Imagining it's a monkey in stilettos about to jump on my back. Well, monkeys walk on fours sometimes. Right? Come on now... a monkey on the sidewalks of L.A.! Maybe on the dirt road in Tatalon! Really, Bibe? Focus!

I got scared. Repeated safety instructions by my parents replayed as I conjured a better plan. I would sprint my way home and never look back.

But, this is me—the curious one.

So, I vaulted ahead about one hundred feet forward and quickly turned around. And there was Pa, walking... wearing a big smile. He walked slower towards me although I thought nothing more of it. As with a personal routine, he kissed my forehead, and we walked home together. Pa, with bearing ears, listened while I chattered with never ending, "Blah-blah-blahs; " sharing the scoop of my day at school. There would be many more similar theatrical scenes played out after.

Pa may have followed behind to see if his children could walk home safely; and, an assurance to him—we will be okay—should his health deteriorated.

That was just a few months ago. Oh, how I missed those multi metal-footed "clicky-ti-tack," sounds.

OUR LIFE WAS NORMALIZING from its harrowing life cycle's changes. Ma has enlisted many of her relatives to come alongside for help in a somewhat frenzied future.

Auntie Minga continued to show genuine help since Pa's hospitalization. Ma and her first cousin are our home operations *Pinsan* Duo and hold a unique connection. No different from Ma's siblings is Minga's courageous heart. Her physical appearance gives off a strong Spanish lineage. Light in complexion, hazel eyes, narrow and pointy nose with chiseled facial structure. Beautiful, yet humble. The *I get you,* exclusivity is startling. It went beyond what I've seen in the other Aunties. It's transcendent; one in the other.

Auntie Minga accepted my mother's offer as her live-in all-around help at home; and in Ma's absence, mother duties. Minga's servitude heart complimented Ma's generosity. Together, the *Pinsan* Duo operated systematically and managed our family's very busy household efficiently. Life's premature and cold serving of death changed its course and gave Ma the perfect help.

Minga is strict, still approachable; quiet, yet intellectual; reserved, but loving; and best of all, a modern-type individual with a heart of gold. There is a glimmer of hope coming into my family's seemingly inconsolable life!

Minga's help with the heavy household chores freed up valuable time for Ma, enabling her to concentrate on other matters. Legal and real estate business affairs are new to Ma; best she could, tackled them in confidence and boldness. Adding to, Ma now has to meet with the school principal and teachers regarding our educational matters. Duties in which Pa, handled solely. Ma, had tackled all the things left unattended since Pa's passing.

Having help at home has aided and eased many of our future concerns. My two Aunties and their families are still in Tatalon dealing with the extensive house repairs from flood damages. On occasions, both came to visit my Ma. Again, the Sisterhood comes together—never leaving one behind—alone.

WE HAVE A NEW STAFF MEMBER—FAMILY car driver. He is a little older than the former. Mang, pronounced: "Maang" (Mister) Fonso is quiet, smiles with lips pressed shut, shortcut dark-brown colored hair with a faint but graying strands on both sides around the temple. He moves with consideration for others around and quick to respond when summoned. He appears calm and sometimes entertaining. Mang Fonso likes to be alone and stays out of my Auntie Minga's way.

Each time Fonso finishes his driving chores for the day, he cleans the family automobile—then parks it back in the garage. Though our new driver smiles in all manner, to all appearance—he is a loner.

He kept me curious and thus observed him more—witnessing the same routine. Every day he and I spoke a little more. He had a look about him that reminds me of my Pa. Maybe his aloofness. My heart was opening to another older male. It has been many weeks since I spoke with an adult man. In fact, since we landed back from our travels to the USA. I've only encountered the helping hand of an angel during the flood and an uncle who is now too busy helping in maintenance and house repairs.

As the days turned into weeks have come and gone, Mang Fonso and I, talked more. And always, set about in our small talks is laughter and I look forward to hearing more, especially from Fonso. A new feeling inside me is stirring. Most days I make myself available to see the new staff member. Besides talking, we played guessing numbers, "high-low" card games. If short of time, a quick game of "hide and seek," though sometimes brief... satiates *my* longing.

My deep yearning for Pa was slowly diverting with the help of our new driver. It seems the days were expiring faster and happy stages are resurfacing in my life. I look forward more to our family time, and I am seeing my empty cup filling up with joyful fun.

Rainy season is my favorite time of the year. The wet season brought many happy times in our old bungalow. Days seem to have moved faster back at Villa Dolores. After a long day at the university, I remember... most days, Pa came home and was present for *most* nights. Rain or shine, the special times we have spent together, were exclusive and moments cherished forever.

This rainy day felt special, the family's usual busy day brought an extra time to visit Mang Fonso. He seemed happy to see me, though I wasn't sure—he appeared unlike his normal self. *Is he feeling obligated to respond to my playtime needs, or what?* Maybe rainy days are not his favored weather. *We can still have fun—make up a new game, or something.*

Mang Fonso summons me to come into the garage. Though feeling somewhat baffled, I stepped just a child step inside. As I entered the narrow entry door, he moved closer and touched my shoulder.

"Today is special," he said!

"There is a 'new game' for us to play."

I was so thrilled to hear he was up to playing. Omitting the manner of how the game rules, instead, Mang Fonso picked me up. Quick. It was frightening. Still not a word from him. I felt his hands grab my legs and thighs, separated and wrap them tightly around his lower back. Our hips almost touching. My face to his chest level. He makes frustrating sounds; grunts.

He pulled my small frame upwards, positioning my lower extremities higher on his middle back. Afraid of falling, I instinctively tightened the wrapping of my legs around his. I grabbed tightly on his neck as he firmly placed his right hand underneath my skirt and with force, slipped his fingers under. I tensed up feeling his uninvited petrifying touches—immobilized. In fear of crashing to the ground, I hung on. From deep inside, I knew something horrific was happening. I wanted him to put me down, to drop me! But I felt tormented and unable to say a word. All I could do, was to hang on, consciously choking his neck with my small bare hands. His hands continued to explore; I felt more unwanted touches. He skipped up, down, and moved around like an untamed animal releasing grunting sounds, strange to my ears.

Perhaps disgusted from my lack of "participation," my perpetrator, abruptly placed me down. And he walked away, leaving me alone standing on the cold wet driveway. I welled up in tears—stepping away—touching my chest, my hands moved downwards my skirt. I straightened my skirt, shook my head, and walked away. Coarse salt grains liberally poured over, scorching my already wounded heart.

Though, he did not pick me up again, more coercion and frightening tactics continued in the proceeding days. Those distant, all the same "suggestive" looks; his hands "accidentally" brushing against my clothing, smiles... smirks; over and over assaulting my presence. The evildoer continued his scornful mockery of my mind. Killing my soul.

The father-figure I so wished for and wanted, has poisoned my mind for months. My body violated—mind afflicted—and spirit tormented. I suffered a deepened loss inside—further mortifying my existence.

My perpetrator had me believe the shameful act was a fault of mine—in needing of his attention. Salting the open wound of loss. To boot, he exonerated himself—no one will accept the truth of such grim account. Certainly, not from one who hallucinates and visualizes dead people. No one has the time to listen. The biggest lie led by fear... no one cares.

One day, Fonso, the masked perpetrator, disappeared. While others wondered *why*, I did not! I had no one to talk to. The shameful act made—tormented my soul daily.

I believed the wrongdoing was my fault.

Encouragement:

1ˢᵗ John 1:9
If we confess our sins, He is faithful and just to forgive us of our sins and to cleanse us from all unrighteousness

(NKJV)

IN JESUS' name, I pray:

Thank You, Lord, for Your cleansing blood ridding us of our own wrongdoings; and, for clearing and healing all the damaging acts committed against us. The destructive layer of our being has cracked and fallen—creating a new and pure soul.

14

INBORN QUALITY

*B*ACK TO REALITY. Continued financial struggle finds Ma sitting amid unpleasant reality. She has exhausted all possible financial avenues to keep us merely surviving. Unable to pay rent, we moved back to our semi-repaired but fully paid bungalow home—a great hiding place for my aching heart and soul. I am finally home. Remembering many varied games played on the expansive and well-established foliage playground was comforting. Playing outdoors is back on our agenda. There were too many heartaches in our former house on Matimyas Street. Compound living in Tatalon is a haven entrenched with sweet memories of my Pa and family.

MY FAMILY IS MINDFULLY RESETTLING in our bungalow home. The Sisterhood and the compound children are back to familiar activities. A sweet "welcome home" to the strong-knitted team players.

Ate Claudette and Ate Violy, though first cousins, are more like twin sisters. Born just five months apart, both have similar personalities. They match their likes and dislikes. I find it interesting that each one's knowledge of the other's attributes works to compliment the other. And as their number one fan, I define them lovely to the eyes.

Being the eldest of fourteen children, our mothers permit their firstborns with more liberty—freedom to give commands to their younger progenies. Our mothers, hand over to their eldest children selected authorities. Allowing for the Sisterhood to go about other duties in their respective homes. Similar to Kuya BB, they carry a birthright. Dissimilar, the two Ate are higher ranking than the rest of us, youngins. One can think to challenge the "parent-given" privilege; but, no one dares to.

An inherent business sense is one strong trait that stands out in our family. Our environment in the family mix offers home-school's economic topics. Accounting, with marketing and sales strategies bundled in one. Each family member is an integral part of a brilliant learning system.

MOST FAMILIES in the Philippines teach their children the art of *financial handling*; the need for bartering skills in product purchasing. And though rare, exchange of purchased goods. Besides assigned household chores, we often accompany our mothers with daily errands. Ma would take every opportunity to have me alongside, shopping in the "*palengke*" (wet market). I am always more than glad to accompany my mother. Shopping in a *palengke* is where you find fresh everything.

In looking for something of interest, quick scanning seems to help my mother, though she always heads towards the front vendors lined at the entrance. We stand over the entry line, preparing. We are setting to pace through; assess, inquire, haggle, and buy. Ma stands still. She looks into the stretch of vendors lined up inside and it's clear, avoids eye contact with shopkeepers. Instead, she looks from left to right... slowing as the center scene unfolds. Squints for emphasis. Then moves her sight unto the extreme right side.

A gifted bargain hunter, Ma would scout around adjacent retailers before she settles on the (in her estimation) best product. From produce, vegetables, seafood, and various meats—Ma commands freshness. Ma doesn't get involved in a lot of chatting. Putting her money into anything is a serious business, she aims towards her goal.

Abiding by Ma's own established and efficient purchasing system, she looks at the item of interest. Satisfying its fresh appearance. Then careful touches, and smell of freshness follow. My mother aims to catch naturally live scent—she sniffs and sniffs again. At last, she graces the shopkeeper acknowledging look. With a mere nod, Ma concedes the item of interest's freshness. She then places the family's impending main and side dishes carefully back in its respective baskets. Still staging, Ma turns around and endows test questions directed to me, and loud enough for the seller to hear. During Ma's strategic "silent bartering" method—facial looks alone questions whether both fish and *arosep*, (grape seaweed) are fresh.

"Bibe, what do you see?" My eyes focus.

"How about the 'feel and smell?'" My fingers and nose twitch. Sniff-sniff!

"And, 'What about the cost?'" I pause thinking about the task at hand. Funny, Ma never waited for my answer. Finally, a deciding factor.

"Do both items warrant the asking prices?" Applying some of my earlier days' training, I responded,

"Yes."

"How so?" Ma asked.

"I see bright colors inside and around the *arosep*. Colors of perfect ripeness in deep sea green."

"And?" she continued.

I added,

"Because the items feel plump and smell fresh; plus, the asking price is fair."

She smiles—proud of her daughter's improved purchasing skill.

The final step. The expert buyer gives a firm and lower bid for a *yummy* combo meal. Adding adept haggling to her body language—ultimately results in discounted prices for the best items. Shopkeepers have accepted a well-established purchasing system applied by their "*Suki*," (loyal customer) who negotiates firmly or she walks away. *Suki* to many, Ma closes her purchases involving me, her protégé. I help with the counting and all money exchanges of *pesos* and *centavos*. For today's meal, a much-savored meal combo—fishes and seaweed!

Home-schooling per se, hands-on applications made with "one-on-one" child, are practiced in group settings. Practiced within the mixture of neighboring children gave us compound youngins the edge in most classroom settings.

Unbeknownst, a dealing expertise learned for use in the near future. My near future.

THE LOCAL AGENCY approved a new housing development for our small town of Tatalon. And a local building contractor started construction on a multi-unit dwelling structure. A sure sign of hope for the under-developed town.

We have many neighbors; who, with their families, without exaggeration—are living in corrugated metal sheet box-like spaces! Our bungalow is nestled deep into this quaint residential area with unpaved streets, and where construction is now developing fast.

Rain or shine, hot or hotter, carpenters and construction workers labor in long and rigid hours, regardless of its rising temperature and high humidity.

We are in the hot and humid season, yet a welcome post-school months are in play. The two cousins, Ate's Claudette and Violy, grabbed its opportunity of the year's school break. In mindful steps, they drew a ventured business plan offering product sales. Selling *mid-day* snacks to nearby neighbors with special attention to the newly developing enticement... hungry laborers nearby.

"Ate's Kitchen," owners are aware of our humble neighborhood's need for a market, let alone a restaurant, to buy food. The closest *Sari-Sari* Store (Variety Store) has little food in stock. And, that's if you consider local candies as food!

Ingenious! With a little contemplation, the two partners' idea produced and placed a business plan in motion. No sooner the announcement via neighbors—*Word of Mouth Ad*, soon spread.

∼

"PALITAW MERIENDA"
(SWEET RICE SNACK)

"Merienda! Merienda!
'Ate's Kitchen' is open for business.
Daily fresh nutritious snacks scheduled for hand-delivery.
Pacify your stomach's craving calls.
Attention to Construction Workers:
Look for our Salesgirl at your construction steps between
2:00 and 2:30 in the afternoon."

~

THEIR PLAN OF ACTION—COMPLETED. Ate's Kitchen, scheduled its soft-opening date offering a family favorite snack—targeted at potential customers... the *hard at work* construction workers nearby.

Ate's Kitchen's Proprietors will sell a popular snack on opening day. "*Palitaw*" is a semi-sweet cake made with grounded sweet rice, water, and cane sugar. These ingredients are mixed into a dough; then hand-molded to size 3" by 2" in oblong shapes and cooked in boiling water. *Palitaw* rise to the top when cooked, scooped out, and prepped for mouth-watering toppings. Sprinkled on each is a *special* mixture of sesame seeds, white cane sugar, and freshly grated coconut. Topping compliments an already delightful snack and oh—the best "*merienda!*"

With a personal agenda in mind, I hovered around two cooks scurrying around the kitchen. Though, neither obliged me any interaction; both have something else in mind! I hung around like a fly, buzzing but for a morsel.

Amid all the excitement, both partners seemed to have overlooked a key factor in this business venture. Or, did they? The need for a salesperson. Who would *that* LUCKY soul be?

One glance at their stances and facial expressions—directed at me —the answer is clear! There is no experience required. No need for an interview. Zero salary negotiations. And no job offers made. By the authority vested at birth *to* the two oldest offsprings; they appointed me, the business kitchen's *salesgirl*.

IF IT WAS TO BE, it had to be me. I complied. I was more than happy to help with sales and for sure, with pay! *Palitaw* is not just our family's favored snack; it is a popular choice by most Filipinos. (An *easy-peasy* sell.)

Lined with fresh banana leaves, the "*Bilao*," (large platter) cradles thirty mouth-watering pieces of *palitaw*. The *Bilao* presentation is organically enticing. I cannot wait to see the looks of hungry workers when they see what is in stored for them.

Rain has just passed, and the sky shows signs of a beautiful day.

Looking up, I see the clear sky's cotton-shaped white clouds ever graceful, dancing about—reforming. I imagine its main attraction moving gracefully behind and up, towards the center shooting sunbeams—lunchtime is approaching.

Relieved—I figured—*now* is the perfect time to cross over. Just a few hundred feet past the compound is the new development's construction site. I assured my first employers not to fret about their investment. The thirty pieces of gold, err, I meant *palitaw* are in my good hands. There is no rain in the forecast. The walk would take me a short ten minutes to reach the targeted construction site. Ate Claudette slipped several centavo coins in my short's pocket for money exchange. Then she handed the *Bilao*-filled sweet cakes in my hands. With her hands tightly on mine, she fiddled the platter upwards and placed her sweet investment securely onto my body. Feeling confident that my grip is tight and secure, she gives me the "OK" to go signal.

"Now sell. Go make some money! And, remember to..."

"Bring back the *empty* platter and take care of the cash," she called out.

With the snack-filled *Bilao* in tote and secured, I slipped into my super comfortable, but somewhat tattered pair of *tsinelas* (flip-flops.) In eagerness, I stepped out of Ma's open-aired kitchen and within two minutes I reached the opening of the compound's barb-wire fencing. Walking by this prickly fencing brought wonderful memories. I glanced at my ankle scar, I slowed my steps. I could balance. Remembering, "Follow-the-Leader" was one of the best games I had with the boys. Feeling comfortable at last, I am at home and ecstatic for a new challenge at hand. I hear rustling from a short distance behind, Kuya Rolando and my older cousin, Kuya Pugao, bellow out.

"Bibe, hurry now... 'go make some money,'" they hollered.

Sounds of imaginary bell-chiming; a new endeavor with added excitement in being outdoors.

I couldn't help but inaudibly name a few of my favorite water life organisms—swimming along collected raindrops in holed grounding. Once more, I am enamored in catching sight of hundreds of watermelon seed-like tadpoles, fry (young) fish, and other squirms. Passing my small slimy friends; all, appear to wave, mini water splashing, *good luck, Bibe*!

I see several feet ahead are strategically placed patterned stepping stones—a sign of deep waterway is ahead. Together with the help of our neighbors, my family secured walkway placements of big rocks, stones and sometimes, wood planks for walking across puddles and mud banks.

Wanting to add more support in my already tight hand grip, I swayed to the right and placed Ate's *Bilao* on my hip. Looking ahead, I am closing in on an immediate crossing—over a well-flourished waterway. They made this path of *spotted* rocks and stones. But wait! Those are not naturally formed spots. Gaging, I examined further. My eyes scouted the surrounding area looking for ways to go around, but the muddy terrain encircled the path. The obvious algae spot that have formed on the rocks and stones are for sure slippery. And would be perilous! This passage would be like stepping on beach balls!

"Oh, now this is a challenge!"

"*Go make some money, Bibe,*" echoed in my head.

I had a sure plan in mind. Grip tighter Annabelle. One foot and one step at a time. Tighten your core. Keep the hip, and *Bilao* glued together.

Seeing the waterway has collected its water height at a full-point—two feet deep, I stopped and steadied my footing. Looking down towards my feet, each one on a stone, I noticed my right *tsinelas* rubber strap between the big and index toe has thinned. No qualm. Albeit, the flimsy strap appears ready to snap loose. Feeling unstable, all of my five toes instinctively felt for each other. "Team Toes," at their best grabbed the rubber's flat sole against the slimy top rock. Hold it. "O-oh!" With the right *tsinelas* snapping apart, gravity pulled my body—swaying to the left. In a nanosecond and led by my right arm, assuredly a reflex... I accidentally tossed all of Ate's priced *palitaw* up into the air. In slow motion, I saw sweetened grated coconut with sesame seeds rain on my head. Some, by tiny ones—landing safely onto the waterways. Then I saw the snacks floating around its flourishing "*kangkungan*" (water spinach) waterways.

"*Hay, naku... (OMG)* now what?"

I felt human hands pulling me out of the cold mess. However, there was no one in sight... just coconut flakes snowing down on my dampened head.

Are those small fish and tadpoles now laughing and smiling—eyeballing at some new snacks—swimming toward the *palitaw*?

"Those are not fish food! Go away!" Fanning hands, shooing.

In agitation and frantic motion, I gathered all the *snacks* minus two (the fish can keep those). I see each snack appearing bare and moist. Small unknown green and brown fragments have replaced most of the yummy toppings. In a hurried pace, I picked and cleaned the foreign fragments off the *palitaw*. Two missing pieces would mean lost of profit! What to do? I can't go back to the owners—to two *Ates*. The news of a loss investment! To admit and surrender, would be suicidal!

"*Go make some money, Bibe*," keeps echoing in my head.

Without a doubt, the *Ates* would order me to hand wash *their* loads of dirty clothes. For sure, I will succumb to being their personal *labandera* instead.

Oblivious of my surrounding; I gathered myself together. Then, I wiped any sign of misfortune off my light colored water soaked shorts.

"I sure hope it dries out soon." Confident with a tactical plan, I lugged through and reached the construction site.

About a hundred feet away, I see faces of hungry—expectant labor workers. Accompanied by sounds of dropping hammers and construction supplies tossed hurriedly on the wooden flooring. And seeing smiles and body language with hands going upwards, waving and yelling.

"ATE'S KITCHEN, WE'RE COMING DOWN!"

"Please God, make them be in the mood; appreciate fishy tasting snacks!" praying as I approach these hungry workers.

All six men are like transformed little boys-moving around in monkey-like swings and paces. Excited, the hungry construction team sprints over unfinished stairs then jump onto the ground. Amazing display of fitness, one would assume; Tarzan must have been the group's leader of these six hungry men—now, are hovering around me.

Eyes gleaming, twelve eyeballs focused on the hand-carried *Bilao*—each famished expression changed to squints and silent wonders. Hunger overpowered any reasoning; multiple hands scurried to handing me paper monies. Each buyer quickly grabs purchased items—no one took bites, in whole pieces straight to their mouths. Two sets of eyes see only small amounts of the "special" ingredients as advertised. For all that while four customers too hungry to comment; busy chewing, all the same, appear to be pondering with eyes viewing upwards. More sniffs and chews followed. The obvious watery taste in their palates did not affect satisfying moment.

Next thing I see large calloused fingers move to clear a few tiny foreign speckles off the next pieces they're readying to eat. I continued to watch labored-hands move. "O-Oh, here it comes!" In chorus-like still half-chewing, now half-speaking, in sync.

"These taste somewhat... fishy!" (Does this mean, they like the taste of fish?)

In utter calmness, I stood and straightened up immediately. I hand-ironed my now, dried and wrinkled light shaded shorts. No one noticed its subtle stain across. Phew! In front at face level... I sternly eyeballed at my first six new customers, with their heads bowed over. I placed the monies in my pocket; systematically, I gathered my belongings along few leftovers on its serving platter. Seeing the chewing slowed down, unfazed, I firmly asked.

"Let me be clear, are you saying my *Ates'* cooking is not good?" hands on my hips. Swayed to the opposite side. I did not wait for an answer, (thanks, Ma) instead...

"And, that it's yucky?"

For a moment, their chewing stopped. Then *pronto*, all eyes fixed on me. I sizzled for a breath and continued with my defense.

"Hah, if that is how you 'all' feel, I will not be back to bring you any more snacks. Or worse, you will... 'not might,' miss eating popular food selections included in the '*new*' menu!"

In fear of future hunger unsatisfied; like a chorale, all chimed in.

"You can keep the change, just please come back! And, bring the '*new*' menu with you next time... please."

In appreciation, a smile of gratitude—all stood up. Took the leftovers and continued to eat as we parted ways.

"Salamat po (thank you, Sirs.) I'll see you next time then," I responded with a loud voice, "Yes" as I watch the six heads, nod up and down.

More "Yeses" in yelling voices as they walked uphill toward the massive construction site. All six body languages proved satisfied. Or, was it relief? Assured that Ate's Kitchen would be back. A big sigh of relief for me too. What I calculated that might have been a total loss, was not. I will present the owners an even higher profit margin instead!

All along this fiasco scene; was it just a happenstance? Or was it planned? Two members of the Fun Group, were around when coconut flakes dropped from nowhere; and their saving hands, pulled me out of the cold mess! Both ran off while I dealt collecting prized snack items. Away from sight, Kuya Rolando and Kuya Pugao wore proud smiles, stood several yards behind. Later shared; watching my selling technique was, "The most lucrative sales play, ever."

Assisted by their first hired salesgirl, Ate's Kitchen's soft-opening day was a profitable day. The bonus, I received all the extra monies made. Sharing "lucrative" earned commission with my two cohorts; whom to my surprise, guarded my path. One peso and some change divided by three!

REFLECTION: *In-born* trait—I have grown to appreciate my family's variable dynamics. As God created humans, He designed each one with a unique genetic coding, DNA. Seated deeply in our DNA's self-replicating matter are fundamental and distinctive qualities that have proven enduring—are those visible traits in our children and their children's children! I have witnessed several characteristics that have passed through both my parents' "one-of-a-kind" genetic makeup. In my family dynamics, evidence of these unique traits within all siblings, and me. Pa's frugalness and business sense, coupled with Ma's generous and servitude heart weaved and passed on to us.

Our parents are two different people; not aware, find connection in their future generations. Relationship calls for fundamental yearning; to love and be loved. True love shines from deep within two individuals; my mother gave her whole heart to Pa. And he gave his best back.

~V~
UNDERSTANDING UNCONDITIONAL LOVE
CAME FULL CIRCLE WHEN I MET MY CREATOR.

~

Encouragement:

~

Psalm 90:14
Satisfy us with your steadfast love,
that we may rejoice and be glad all our days.

(ESV)

~

IN JESUS' name, I pray:
Lord, help me understand Your loving ways. My humanity melts in Your presence. Feeling Your Spirit alive inside my soul is indescribable; love complete, all that I need is in You.

IN THE CENTER of our heart's emptiness is a reserved seat waiting for occupancy by One Person in Jesus Christ. His amazing love alone satisfies; love unconditional—with divine commitment; sacrificial offering—patient, forgiving, and love complete.

15

PERFECTING LIES

*R*EFLECTION: The distorted journey is clear—dark secrets from my childhood have bred through into my body changes; now in my adolescence years. Learning the art of deception is fast and on track—refined by many opportunities—never available in my girlhood. The masked devious arrangement by the prince of darkness presented attractive temptations; served on many delightful appearances. As sure as any chef's offering, the "delicious" appearing—luring—is to entice my hunger for more. These lying choices kept me further away from the truth.

THE TRUTH IS HARDER to face; I am now a teenager. Every day passing without truth is a no day of dealing with my buried hurts.

Losing our bungalow amidst a political brawl-out, positioned the "icing on the cake," atop layered of hurts deep down in my heart. I felt the structure flooring under my feet; not wet—but had rotted.

IT DIDN'T TAKE LONG, my mother found a modern apartment housing on Scout Santiago, at the outskirts of Quezon City. Ma had registered me to attend the University of Santo Tomas (UST) a Catholic University Private School established in 1611. UST Elementary School offered primary education for children, K to 10th grade. Ma budgeted her finances tighter, allowing me to attend this elite private school.

Kuya BB, now, a full-blown father-figure takes the lead in helping Ma with the rest of us. From providing transportation to and from school to school-related tasks. He is at our disposal. On top of this newly developed responsibility, he completes assigned house chores and assignments timely. Daily, he never wavered in his position as Ma's parenting counterpart.

Meanwhile, Ate Claudette, complimented our mother's role in all the domestic affairs. She took a heavy undertaking, not unforeseen to the rest of the family. Although Ate C appears to be physically helpless, she never seizes to amaze me with her abilities. She performs the task at hand with a profound desire and steadfast action. My sister's help in all domestic functions filled in the gap between Ma and BB's tasks. They are: Ma, Home Administrator; Ate Claudette, Assistant Administrator; and Kuya BB as Chief of Operations!

Kuya BB is four years my senior; displays control, intelligence, and wit. At just sixteen years old, my brother has transformed into someone respected by the rest of his siblings. An exclusion to this regarded position is my Ate C. She is the eldest and remained inclusive of Ma's maternal position.

Though my big brother was not aware of the deep infamy I struggle with, rooting from shameful acts inflicted on me—he is refreshing in an inherited surplus. Embracing a father role was customary—offering only a one-way act.

And so-it-was, Kuya BB would sign-off on our homework assignments. As his schedule became increasingly busy, he loosened the tightrope in checking every page of all his siblings' assigned work from school. Every day, he would sign the signature page *Reviewed by*. BB felt relieved and at peace; he could trust on all four younger Sabella siblings to do homework!

TWO MONTHS PASSED SO FAST in our new apartment home. Unbeknownst, my activities have been under the radar by the COO. One afternoon after school, Kuya BB summoned me alone in his presence.

"Give me all your assignment notebooks... Now!" he demanded.

I froze and quickly turned about face. I dawdled towards where my school bag laid. Although Kuya BB was just a couple feet behind me, I sensed his seething presence emitting. Turning around, I see his body language; a sure-fire, that I am reprimanded. Yes, he may do so —even spank me. He is skilled in doing so.

Without further ado, I handed my notes for homework onto the palm of Kuya BB's stiffened, somewhat shaky and spread out fingers. He turned the notebook pages. The first, a blank page. Then turns fast, revealing more blank pages. His face began to rosy up. Not the pretty blushing kind but the steamed-up enraged blood, *aching to burst out* kind. And he did!

"All these days, I hustled to wake up in time to drive you to school. Reminding you of your assignments, books, and food while making sure... I am not late in picking you up."

I stood still—not hearing his words. If only he can see—inside my shamed spirit is a hunger—to be heard. Kuya, will you hear me? Be understood and accepted, be loved again. And I longed for a kiss on my forehead once more—without any shame.

Kuya BB demanded an explanation.

My response...

"Kuya, two months ago, I have been arriving at school late. One day, after you dropped me off at the main entrance, the Principal was at mid-way point speaking to all the students. I heard the Madam Principal continue with her announcement of a new school policy, 'I will punish any student who is late.' I felt this unwarranted. Therefore, didn't care to know about Madam's sentencing carry out."

I took a breath and saw the look of disappointment surfacing on my brother's face.

"The fact is..." I paused, took in a deeper breath, and continued.

"Heavy traffic on top of dropping off another sibling before me caused another tardy record on my name for 'that' day. Taking the head of the school's warning seriously; I can only surmise, *'Avoid the possibility of being sent to the Principal's Office.'* So, instead of facing the high probability of unwarranted wrath, I left to pursue a sure and exciting fun-filled day. I wandered around and about the streets of Manila. Day-by-day, one thing led to another."

By now, Kuya BB's brown-faced skin has turned flaming red! I better get to the best part. Hurry, talk fast.

"In sharing my *salesgirl* experience, I befriended and assisted a sales lady whose business stand, offers magazines on a particular sidewalk. Oh, don't worry, she took good care of me. After hours of walking and hustling her paper goods, she compensated my sincere effort with some coins. She paid me enough to see my favorite movie, multiple times. I even memorized the lyrics and learned accent of the English actress and singer, Julie Andrews."

No humor would change the frustration illustrated on Kuya BB's face. I had to take a big gulp of air (probably my last)!

"With my daily allowance, I saw more movies... my favorite was 'The Sound of Music.'" Twelve times, the hills came to life for the time being; as the valleys of life kept me buried in despair.

Kuya was in disbelief! His face showed obvious hurt as he listened to his sister's, rapid-fire and inexplicable alibi. He asked.

"Why? Why didn't you tell me about the tardiness from the beginning?" And I answered, "It scared me to tell you, Kuya."

Deep inside, an overgrown fear... shame, the biggest lie instilled from earlier years, had rooted. I wanted to scream. I HAVE BEEN ASSAULTED!

There was no belt spanking; only silence between us.

REFLECTION: Despite my brother's sincere intention... clear devotion, and unending commitment to the co-parenting role (coupled with his many sacrifices for me), my choices would tamper the glass in pursuit for such apoplectic response. Mine was a deliberate act needing attention. For both of us, it was to be a moment of no return for many years following.

DEVASTATING consequences of my choices delivered distrust to Kuya BB's heart. I don't blame him. Inside, I displeased myself and for sure, more so than him. Cold silence in between has distanced us both. It was reminiscent of the stillness, lacking sound; after hearing the crushing words uttered by Auntie Supe's pointing allegations on that harrowing day of deep loss. Nothing more was said. No apologies. No sympathy from our aunt. My father's passing became a regular reminder of, his little girl's—my broken heart. Teasing lies that hovered three years ago by our family driver's, my perpetrator's threatening and degrading looks, lingered and tormented my soul. I couldn't get myself to tell Ma. Now I have betrayed my ally's trust. The sharp pointy and destructive finger echoes for yet another time, loud and clear—guilty.

REFLECTION: I will forever cherish my brother's genuine interest to help everyone in our family. Time, God's gift of healing, provided much rest to my soul for the times of shameful acts made against me.

God protects the hurting soul. He provides divine enclosure as He controls the wheel of life surrounding one's broken heart. God's time, places graceful cushion in over-burdened days, and security with His perfection. His Grace and Mercy is sufficient.

Encouragement:

∽

Psalm 31:14-15
I trust in You, O Lord;
I say, "You are my God."
My times are in Your hand.

(NKJV)

∽

IN JESUS' name, I pray:

Abba, Father, thank you for the gift of time today on earth. Just as You were in control of time then, You are in control of ours today.

~V~
I TREASURE TODAY; YOUR PRESENCE IS HERE.
HELP ME NOT BECOME OVERWHELMED;
INSTEAD, FOCUS ON YOU, TO DO THE WORK
YOU HAVE SET BEFORE ME.

∽

16

THE GOOD, THE BAD, AND THE UGLY

THE GOOD ~ *BROTHERS*

Time has its way of shrouding the hidden parts of the heart. We have been living in the inner city's apartment housing on Santiago Street. Kuya BB turned 18-years-old; and, that means a U.S. military draft letter would soon arrive in the mail. Brother Kuya Rolando is next in line to fill Pa's shoes, and he is not sure how to approach this pending new role. It's too soon to worry about. Though it has been occupying his mind.

Unlike Kuya BB, Rolando's laid back, "Que sera, sera whatever will be, will be," approach syncs up with his very generous heart. Rolando, a special personal ally to Ma, individualized from the two older siblings. His aspiring relaxed chief-in-charge—a welcome change. There is much to say about the passionate marketer. Sales runs in Kuya Rolando's blood. He can sell you anything. If I as much lend him an ear, I will fork any monies hidden in my pocket for a can full of dirt.

Yet, with differing personas, my two older brothers are very close —almost like twins. Two years apart, they were born on the same day and month. As birth rights go, the older is always the leader of the pack. Kuya BB's younger sibling, balanced *their* duo with smooth-operating personality. Kuya Rolando complied, shadowed, and always by Kuya BB's side.

KUYA BB RECEIVED the long-awaited draft letter. Soon after, he flew to Southern California and began basic training in the United States Military's Army Branch.

After, my brother settled in Los Angeles, not wanting to waste any time, pursued employment right away. Robinson's offered him a job as a Window Display Designer at their inner city department store.

As if he never left. Kuya BB continued his financial support, a promise made to our mother. I love seeing Ma receive mail from her oldest son. She doesn't read much, yet a letter with US stamps embellished on an envelope replenishes her soul. Ma's face lights up as she reads his letters, repeatedly.

The busyness of single motherhood keeps her strong appearing-stance. Inside, she longed for one of her best allies by her side. I've seen Ma on her knees praying for her oldest son. Other times, looking weary—just lay alone—on her bed.

Kuya Rolando, in his newly promoted role in co-parenting; presented us, his younger siblings, a gift of freedom. We experienced liberty galore in just about everything. He did not check for any assignments; let alone our whereabouts. Unlike his predecessor, Rolando is more social and has an anonymous personal agenda.

Kuya BB left not knowing the cause of my altered behavior. All reasons he considered, "She's now a teenager." So, I followed the same alleyway with Kuya Rolando, he needs not know anything more about me. The shame that clutches to my soul.

I REMEMBER BEING CHRISTENED, a Protestant, at age eleven. It was not long after my father's death, our family attorney, also a close friend of my parents became readily available to my family. Attorney Ignacio, a widower, displayed friendly connections to both my parents. He spent quality time with all of us back then and now. Ignacio took us out to eat often; and when visiting, toted food for all seven in the house. His busy schedule did not prevent him from taking us to places. Attend his church services in particular.

Ignacio, is a devout Protestant. His church's practices are unique, compared to my family's traditional Catholic religion. Although Ma didn't take us regularly to mass, she made sure her children churched—with, or without her. We obeyed and went along with the family tradition—disconnected rituals. Whereas in this new church, I listened and enjoyed hearing the beautiful worship music lyrics. And for the first time in my life, I heard Scriptures read by the Preacher straight from the Bible. The Preacher shared a surprise statement: "God loves hearing directly from us." Would that include me too? Reading the Bible at home was unheard of. Well, I saw no reading of such. Curiosity brought me back multiple times to attend the Protestant church's Sunday services. I forsook going to my church. No one knew. No one noticed. Because we only went on special days—Christmas, Day of the Dead, All Saints and All Souls Day, Passion Week, and Easter.

Deep in my broken heart, disgrace is at home—needing—hoping for cleansing. Would God be able to help me?

WAS IT MY UPBRINGING, or was it tradition? I found myself inside the confession box, confessing that I had been confirmed Protestant. I found it shocking... the voice coming from inside the box judged me GUILTY!

"Say your penance. May God forgive you, child."

It was devastating. I walked towards the pews. With knees on a kneeler, elbows on the back side of the front row, and hands in perfect prayer form, I recited the reparation for my sin. Tears came down, like a miniature Wailua Waterfalls. Pondering, I asked.

"Why God? I felt good about hearing your voice; words of love."

"Why do you punish me?"

"Do you hear my cry at all?"

"The person speaking from the pulpit said: 'You love hearing directly from us'... and that would include me, right?'" There was no answer. "I thought you knew my heart."

My heart seemed to have slowed down its pulsing enough to dry out the waterfall-like tears down my cheeks. I looked up at the cross. I see a sculpture of Jesus Christ nailed and hung dead on its cross pieces. I asked myself.

"Why do they show you dead when the church talks about you

resurrecting?" I got up and left.

Signs of normalcy have surfaced with such questions I had inquired before. An ordained minister of my church thought of my action rude and disrespectful. "I dared ask such questions." Our unempathetic Priest ignored me altogether. He insinuated that I am a troublemaker of some sort.

Inside, I wrestle with great shame. *Am I really a troublemaker? Did I deserve all those hideous acts—pugnacity inflicted on my innocent body and soul? So many questions God!*

"Why?"

It didn't matter. I have taken a backseat and merely accepted what comes my way.

REFLECTION: Attorney Ignacio disappeared from our lives, and none could recount, "Why?" He was one other father-figure I had hoped for, and again never to be! Appearing to be, peace was short-lived. Stubborn uprooted seed from within a darkened past serves untruthful emotions.

THE BAD ~ *MORE ACTS OF TORMENT*

SOCIAL ACTIVITIES ELEVATED as we celebrated our teenage years. At fifteen years old, I graced Ate Claudette's comings and goings with my presence. It was also a cultural undertaking to watch the younger siblings or cousins for a parent, whatever the case may be. Hanging out, being a part of my older sibling's and cousin's social functions was fun. It was not long, both invited me in on their plans and let me in on some secrets.

Automobile cruising reached its peak level for "fun driving" in other parts of the world; the trickling has just begun in Luzon island. The western world has done it again; ahead of the game. Riding around, cruising in a vehicle—an afternoon delight has gained a popular momentum. Steady invites came knocking at many household doors—looking to cruise. Young and old; boys and girls, have age and gender equality.

Following suit with the westerners, someone soon invited us to join in this latest interest. Their newfound friends invited my sibling and cousin. Friends of friends, so to speak, presented an open invite,

"Let's cruise around the local establishments, within the city limits. Better yet, drive down the oceanfront."

We responded, "Let's cruise!" Claiming, the WE factor, because I am now an integral part of the older girls' social group. Call to mind, passing the boys only group's initiation—becoming the first girl member, adrenaline-charging! Though, I felt strange to be a part of the exclusive, Older Girls Group and somewhat uneasy.

This current dry season, though hot and humid, is perfect for cruising. The excitement lingered long enough, everyone involved has decided on a last-minute ride. After much anticipation—knees on the sofa, looking out the window, I see a well-polished car parking in front of our apartment. This must be our fun ride Cruiser. I see an unfamiliar face sitting in the driver's seat. As always, my curiosity takes lead, though apprehensive. I walked outside to see everything for myself, up close and personal. Wow! All handles and rims are spotless and reflective. Stepping around and admiring this well-kept beauty, I saw my reflection on the metal encasing of the side-view mirror. It was a Kodak-quality image. But the picture-perfect bounced an ugly image of me. I quickly reset, and waited behind the Cruiser.

I watched my two Ates giggle in excitement; and have taken the best viewing seats, both sat in the front with the driver. I hopped in the back with their two newfound friends—acquaintances. I have met them before. Two nice-looking young men, both are over eighteen. Sandwiched in, one sat on each side. I felt so special, perhaps admired. We drove off. Eager to look cool during the ride, my family members asked to stop at a market for a box of smokes. The accommodating driver drove and in a short time, the car slowed and came to a brief stop. We idled for a few seconds; allowing the girls to step out on a "no-stop" curve. The driver stayed and drove us, three passengers in the back, circle around the block.

A sudden rush of fear injected into my whole body. The same agitation I felt back in the old garage; impiety transmitting from both sides. My eyes popped open. I froze. Heart beats rising. Every square-inch of my skin reacts to the *fast-started* beatings of my heart. I felt clammy... as if this entire layer of tissue is producing and protecting my already, damaged heart. Without warning, a set of quick hands lifted my blouse, continuous cupping and squeezing hand motions—groping my breasts —my soul cried out. My legs stiffened straight forward... pulling his hair, slapping his head with his face now buried under my blouse.

"NO! STOP!"

Horrified! I trembled!

*Did I do this? Is this my fault? How did I allow this to happen, **again**?*

I screamed. Then stopped—he stopped. My screaming halted by silence. *I could hear nothing coming from my mouth.* I could hear my inner voice yelling, "This is your fault. You did this!" I could no longer express how I felt. When my awareness returned, I remained stoned-quiet. I could envision the face of "Fonso" as his hands went firmly up my backside. All the while, continued to tremble and sat without speaking.

Several minutes later, grasping the evil actions by these foul creatures, our fun ride turned *torment ride*. A time of pure agony. The circle around ride ended and we're back at the "no stop" curve. My Ates hopped back in the front seat, laughing themselves into oblivion. They don't even know what just happened. One Ate looked back. With my heavy eyelids half-way open, I could only look down towards the floorboard. No questions asked. An undeniable pungent, shame-scent has emerged in the car. The other Ate glanced back to where I sat, saw me, though noticed nothing obscure has taken place, I looked up for a moment... she took her sight back and away from me. *Why did she do that; can she smell my shame?* And, *did she pick up the strong scent of guilt?* I feel so dirty. Thus, I must smell and look dirty.

Silence, all over again. On its side, the crystal clear view mirror forthwith, reflected smudged, dirty, and uglier imagery of me. I left the car without saying a word to my family—to no one.

MIRRORS REVEAL clear reflections of external physical appearance. And often, echo the heart's condition. I avoided looking at myself in the mirror; particularly, at my eyes. No one sees my heart, my eyes—the windows are closed. My personality has changed. I have developed a strange behavior—withdrawn and quiet. No one seems to notice the missing, "rough and tumble," fun girl.

No one cares.

These reflective surfaces have revealed the maturing of my physical body. I have undergone early physical development. Changes that started at nine-years young. Clear signs of my femininity were taken advantage by perpetrators. The attention I perceived and perhaps longed for, as possible genuine father-like connection—woefully, meant for immoral and wicked acts of torments inflicted on me.

Adding it all up, there are evil eyes, lurking and looking for their next victim. Evilness, pulled me into shameful existence. Desiring a father-figure, I let my guard down. The lie: the fault belongs to me, and no one else's.

~V~
LORD, HELP ME REMEMBER, YOU ARE THE TRANQUILITY IN MY LIFE; THE SOOTHING MELODY OF YOUR PRESENCE CAUSES ME TO BE STILL AND KNOW YOU ARE GOD.

THE UGLY ~ *REAL UGLY*

FOR THOSE TURNING FIFTEEN YEARS' old; planning a fun celebration with family and friends, celebrate with exuberance. Not to be in my case as more darkness would befall. And this time, Ma's business associate, and "trusted" friend's act of viciousness identical to my family's so-called *newfound* friends ravaged my body, mind, and soul. Once more assaulted! Absolute disgrace.

I felt neglected and betrayed.

The betrayals of trusted people around were beyond my capacity to deal with. I want out. I didn't remember God's words at any of these recent times. A Minister of God presented God a hopeful ideology.

I don't even think of Pa anymore. Ma doesn't know. My older brothers and sister don't know. Nobody knows, only the victim—me, I know.

. . .

REFLECTION: Confusion became a state of mind. I thirst for truth and clarity in life. Repeated shameful acts began its damaging lies to breed. Living in Bedlam, I suffered many symptoms similar to the mental illness, Depersonalization and Derealization Disorder. I may sound, self-diagnosing; BUT, the symptoms SEEMED to exist in my head. I have learned to disengage myself from the awful reality happening in my life. Believing no one cared, I safeguarded my sanity by imagining—bad things happening are not real.

My mind was on a sure path to an exhaustive end. Unable to focus, I was blanking out. I am a casualty of evil-minded beings—humanity at its worst. Shaming acts doubling its lethal sphere into an existence; hitting the bulls-eye on target into my mind and soul. I am a victim, yet, I couldn't express the anxiety and depression developing inside to anyone. I felt isolated. Evil bled its darkness in a steady and subtle motion into my unsound mind.

God wants nothing to trouble us. Nor, frighten us. He will never leave us or forsake us.

Encouragement: The gift of God's peace.

∼

John 14:27
Peace I leave with you, My peace I give to you; not as the world gives do I give to you.
Let not your heart be troubled, neither let it be afraid.

(NKJV)

∼

IN JESUS' name, I pray:

On my knees, in straightened stance, and fetal formation—always, I long for relief to unload heavy burden. I cast and surrender all worries and fear unto You, Oh Lord my Savior. Your peace is a treasure—lifelong water brook replenishing my soul.

God, You feel our tiring souls—know our troubled hearts, the fear of pain, endless hurts, and deep longing. You are a compassionate God, Who hears our cries and calls! Lord, help us open our hearts to Your divine presence—peace we receive, in beseeching.

17

THE TRUTH OF REALITY

It has been ten years since my brother and father-figure left for California. Life hasn't been easy for Kuya BB, still, his humbling journey had paved its way for easing the ride. Newlyweds, he and his wife, Reign, settled in the heart of Los Angeles. He sounded calm, content, and happy on the phone. Sounding... thrilled! Hearing the "I'm in love" in his voice. I don't remember hearing my brother's voice with so much joy before.

Meanwhile, back in Quezon City, Ma, continued to struggle with life itself. Kuya Rolando and Rex are full-grown adults. Ramon, a teenager. Ate Claudette, now a mother is battling with much ambiguities. Her state of health is more concerning as she persevered to take on the progressing effects of a rare bone curvature. A condition that helped shape my parents assured resolve; the shielding, protecting, guarding, and insulating; not just for her physical well-being, but also her mind and soul—placed secured in a box.

My family's future is despairing in every passing year since I left. Ma believed, their only hope is to move everyone to the USA. She has her sight on California, in particular the City of Los Angeles.

For good (and all), aware of the whole family's dire need, Kuya BB started the mandatory paperwork to assist with the family's move. He went through a long and tedious process to gain the legal documentation. In due course, his perseverance paid off; he received the Certificate of Naturalized American Citizen (NAC). And this result, presented a less processing time period for the rest of my brothers' applications. In perfect timing, each one received their own certificate of NAC.

With Kuya BB's financial help, my three brothers travelled to Los Angeles. Kuya Rolando travelled first. A year later, my two younger brothers followed. Rolando and Rex found an apartment near our oldest brother's. Ramon stayed with Kuya BB and Reign.

Ma, who is a US Legal Resident (USLR), signed an application, petitioning for Ate Claudette. But again, with the lack of personal income as a Veteran's widow, Kuya BB to the rescue, submitted the required document, assuring the US government, he will provide the financial support for my sister's residency. Still and all, the waiting process is lengthy. Hence, Ma stayed behind with my sister and her children. It was a long and challenging wait for both my mother and sister.

With the help of Reign, Rolando and Rex climbed poles as Cable Installers for the cable company she worked for. It was a natural progression for the migrated islanders; from scaling fruit trees to climbing the street poles, right?

Kuya BB registered Ramon to a university known as Uni-High School (Uni-High) in Santa Monica. Known for successfully preparing their students attend their chosen university with no need for an entrance exam. Ramon, one of Uni-High's finest students would celebrate his high-school graduation one year early. It was a proud moment for the Sabella Family.

Settling together with my four brothers in the new world of city living in the USA has given our family many brightened and celebrated days. We are living adulthood and our sibling attachment, intact and tighter than ever. Each one still follows the cultural family protocol taught by our parents. Sixteen years since Pa's death, and we remained a steadfast family.

REFLECTION: In my heart, where I emotionally stood—pitching blame continued towards Ma. If she was less busy, she may have prevented the horrible multiple acts of assault inflicted on me. At 16-years-old, young and immature, I was looking for pure love. Replacing that lost love, when Pa died, Attorney Ignacio disappeared, Kuya BB left; and not trusting anyone, even my Ma. It was so painful being lost that I believe, the decision to giving myself in whole, I would find love through sex.

Jett was in the U.S. Air Force and given an international assignment in the Philippines, stationed at a nearby province when we met. And Ma's friend, who owned a local boarding place for the soldiers, introduced us. His aloofness, impressed on me; somewhat, mysterious. There was kindness peaking through his shy smile. Later, as he met the rest of my family, he would soon befriend, Kuya Rolando. They hung out as much; if not more than Jett, with me.

Time went by fast. During one of my sister's need for blood due to anemia; Jett, who matched her blood type, donated the unit amount required to take her blood cell count to the healthy level. He showed much generosity to my family and everyone seems to have welcomed his presence, including Ma. But, because of my young age, my mother didn't show anymore than, cultural courtesy to Jett. And, I found that reason—be rebellious, the excuse to escape my dark past. We eloped. Ma was heartbroken.

I admit, it was a selfish, inconsiderate, and undeserving, wounding act towards my Ma, and Jett, too!

Several months after the failed attempt to end my life, Jett became my husband. He satisfied a string of faux need for loving attention. The ultimate aim—to get away from the only parent who didn't protect me—motivated marriage. Jett and I married five days before my seventeenth birthday. There was no relative sensation to describe in the day I took an oath before a Provincial Marriage and Civil Union Judge.

Scared and alone, I flew back to the US and settled in Texas where Jett would complete the rest of his military service. Paul, my first-born came eight months after receiving our marriage certificate.

Into my adulthood, I realize how foolish it was to think of leaving and detaching from my birthplace; especially separation from my mother, would keep me safe from the origin of guilt and shame. I was not safe, even several thousand miles of distance. It merely brought reinforcing result; darkness manifested. I was homesick. For what? I couldn't understand. I left home with that driven purpose.

I WAS ONLY seventeen-years old when Paul was born, yet his birth gave me the reason to try harder in living a happy life. I looked forward to waking up and caring for my newborn. My son, my joy, gave me hopeful emotions. Enjoying happiness in our awakening time. Nighttime was an altogether opposite. Locked in my wretched heart, feeling, oh so alone is the ever "hellish" burning shame. I was back to struggling with the demons—my personal tormentors. Thousands of miles away and starting a new life; still, I could not escape my past.

Jett completed his military duties at 22-years-old. Soon after, he moved our family of three to the south. There were developing signs of clear emotional distress occurring; this time, in Jett.

Going to college didn't pan out for Jett. He moved us to Nashville for work, but he labored in odd jobs. In the meantime, I found a job in a factory assembling small electronic parts. Life didn't present us with an easy to follow mapping in the south. We hauled our family of three and traveled to Los Angeles. There is plenty of high-paying jobs with great benefits for Jett, a Veteran, skilled in electrical and mechanical-related work.

I longed to be around my family. Deep buried pain is at a constant feel, makes for continual emotional frailness. There, in California, my brothers could help us ease into city life. Reuniting with the Sabella siblings will be a lovely start. Happiness is waiting for me in the city. Complexity in my life will reset once I am surrounded by my brothers; refreshing my spirit.

Jett and I found a triplex housing in L.A.—the City of Angels, a few miles from my brothers' apartment complex. Jobs seem to have come easily within days of our arrival. Jett found a fitting job in Santa Monica, located twenty miles from the heart of Downtown Los Angeles, where I began work. He joined the city commuters and drove approximately forty miles round-trip to work.

For Paul and I, rain or shine; Monday through Friday, we walked two blocks to the bus stop on Wilshire Boulevard. Eastbound towards downtown Los Angeles, we get off at halfway-point. We walked six more blocks into the residential area where his babysitter lives.

"Let's go son."

Paul smiles. His diaper bag and my handbag over my left shoulder, Paul holds my right free hand tight with his left hand. We talked. Sang. And skipped along the walkways. Often bring me back to a beautiful mental scene of my walk with Pa. After dropping Paul, I'm back on Wilshire, to catch the final bus ride to my work. A workplace in the tallest high-rise building on the west side, built at frontal view of downtown LA. A far cry comparison from working on the farm... though, conveniently located a step outside the farmhouse' backyard!

OUR PROGRAM ON RAINY WEATHER... I switch and place both bags on my right shoulder.

"Jump as I pick you up, ok, Paul?"

"Ok, Mom. I'm ready!"

Stiff like a pencil, he holds his thin body tight, bends both knees; and as I lift him up, he pushes his feet off from the ground. With difficulty, swings his legs upwards towards my left waist; at last, Paul wraps his upper and lower limbs around me.

Although somewhat wobbly, Paul holds our umbrella over our heads. Often, he uncovers us and laughs in pure fun! I love it. So, I ride along with this purpose-driven fun. Intending to have more great time; we uncover ourselves, hold our hands out and feel the rain drops... with mouths open.

"The rain tastes good, huh, Paul?"

He laughs, direct his eyes and jaws with mouth open towards the sky for more. Eyes rolling and squinting from the raindrops. I am with my child under the dark clouds with rain falling, drizzling, showering, and sometimes pouring. Each is a wonderful day we both cherish. And are extended memories of the past; a beautiful time replicated along with my son.

PAUL HAS BEFRIENDED a Filipino boy about his age in our neighborhood. Seeing my son having fun with a playmate, made me very happy. Though Jett appeared content working as a mechanic, he is having a hard time dealing with the angst of city living. He talked about life in an open land, and that simple living is freeing—wishing to be back in the countryside.

I buried myself in the busyness of life. A close relative helped me land the most glorified clerical job with the oil company she worked for. I quickly gathered new friends at work; and, reacquainted with the city lifestyle rather nicely. Working from start to finish was an enjoyable time slot in my day. I looked forward to the workweek, especially Mondays!

APRIL CLOUDS HAVE OPENED and poured its rainwater in abundance, nurturing many propagated seeds from the underground. It won't be long, May flowers will come into full bloom.

Los Angeles sits front row ahead of the neighboring cities in showcasing April showers' lovely yields. Pollinating bees are busy buzzing about—preparing to stage many varieties of flowers. Spring is arranging a bursting view everywhere. And, with this springtime brings forth bouquets—assorted blooms around the triplex. Mixes of colorful presentation to welcoming our second child... *I am overdue!* In which my pediatrician had given me two choices: be induced into labor and hopefully, give birth on April's last day. Or put *it* off an additional day.

"I don't want to wait an extra day! End of April it is."

After about five hours of *exciting* labor, Sam was born. The doctor remarked,

"She is beautiful. Has a perfectly shaped head!" smiling as my prophetic Asian doctor lifted Sam and moved her forward towards my face and said,

"I can tell... look at that round head... she will be smart!"

I say *"exciting"* appropriately, for she is to be the *merrymaking girl* in my life.

THE NEWS of a new niece was an exciting event for each of the new uncles and aunties who could not wait to meet Sam in person. Ten days earlier, Kuya Rolando and his wife, welcomed their firstborn child, K. Joy.

Every visitor asked to see the new addition to the Sabella family, "Where is she?" Proud father, Jett, led each one towards the adjacent living room. Our lowly family room staged the cream-colored wicker baby carriage. Quieting themselves... came whispers. Followed by quick but quiet tiptoeing steps, they head toward the carriage. Then, an "a cappella" sweet sounds of "oohs and aahs" flooded the room. Love-struck expressions surface from the visiting crowd's facials as they introduced themselves to the newborn niece, looking at her preciousness, is sound asleep.

New dad, Rolando, carefully places a carrier with his new bundle of joy by Sam's side. Two tiny human gems comfortably swaddled and in peaceful slumber as their family members surround in a joyful moment.

For all that, there is a clear distinction seeping from the adjoining room; the dining room's closet is calling an invitation. Not for food. The stop-and-go, sorrowful-like sounds, also sounding restrained—a call for help.

Far behind the dining room is the kitchen where the visitors have placed foods they brought. Inside, on the L-Shaped vintage-tiled countertop, showcased Filipino delectable food choices. Tradition called… the family presented a plethora of various dishes from each individual's secret recipe. While several fixed their gleaming attention on two sweet tiny beings, others were catching up with other family-related news.

Except for one hungry new uncle… Rex followed his nose's lead and sniffed his way to the wafting aroma's source. He strutted to the kitchen and came back out with his finger licking delightful moment. Hunger satisfied! Proceeding to re-join the gleaming crowd, Rex passed the dining room's closet door—heard the obvious—suppressed crying coming from the inside. He stopped chewing. Swallowed. Stood still and moved two steps forward and placed one ear flushed on the door; then he listened with intent. And heard more whimpering. Concerned, Rex quietly turned the doorknob and uncovered an unexpected scene hidden in the darkened closet. Like a fetus in its encasing womb, curled inside with head tucked in between the knees… was me, the adorable infant Sam's mother.

The feelings of uncontrolled, intense anxiety—maybe I was dealing with symptoms of postpartum. Best guess—guilt and shame have resurfaced. Tears streaming down my cheeks—whimpering, I struggled to stay noiseless. I avoided Rex's probing eyes. Those slanted eyes looked more spooked, eyelids opened appearing to pop out of their sockets! The palatable pleasantries my brother was experiencing, disappeared. He gently shuts the closet door. I imagined Rex just stood still on the other side of the door and wondered what was *that* scene about? Still, I followed the pattern of keeping the weighty heartache a secret. I waited and continued to silence myself inside. It felt forever. Until the sounds of Rex's footsteps moved further away from my darkened haven.

I was out of sight from the happy group for forty minutes; and, not a soul has questioned my absence when I came into view. That "worthless" feeling confirmed. I avoided Rex.

Meanwhile, feeling the atmosphere; the love, the joy, the celebration continued throughout the remaining day. I smiled looking at the baby pink colored bows on the family room's well-trafficked wood floor. And the thrill, seeing each auntie and uncle taking turns—cuddling the newborn nieces with adoring affection. Unceasing, good bye kisses with inhaling Filipino-style breaths, loving puckered lips laid on the newborn babies' necks.

Ending a tiring celebration, Sam would soon rest back and fell asleep.

CITY LIFE, work, and two children kept Jett yearning even more for the simple country living. Moving back to the south would hopefully, be a recharge. I didn't want to, but agreed. Jett hauled our vehicle packed with bare necessities and drove back to Tennessee by himself. With an infant and young child in tow, I flew and settled in a farther place safe from transgressors, and silent judgments. Fearing the ghosts of "transgressors," and with "judgements," coming from my guilted heart.

Rex didn't share his experience on what he witnessed inside the closet to anyone, including myself. Reminiscent of my witnessing Kuya BB's livened spirit drained dry by the axing words directed at him by Auntie Supe. There was no safe place to hide from the HM's cutting edge, vindictive accusations. I can still hear her voice.

"All of you, are the reasons for your Pa's death." Searing pointing finger towards my brother heeded to a personal undertaking. Repeated imposed guilt.

. . .

REFRESHING, I received Southern freshness attention from elderly folks; earnest, humble, and teamwork always in play. Jett's readiness in donating blood to my sickly sister gave evidence in his willingness to assist others. My heart grew fondness to his servitude trait. He is dependable in helping with the needs of farmers and families around.

The tight family togetherness amidst generosity and service for others is comforting. Country living presented a new regime with familiar camaraderie. Local residence comprised farmers and homemakers. I started with the latter. As farming needs grew—I was in both. Only to find out, homemaking and farming go hand-in-hand living on farm land.

Jett knew some of the details of my circumstances. He married, *that* sixteen-year-old girl he found—blood dripping from her left wrist—barely missing death to try at life once more. Still, our family in a new surrounding was not enough to break the bricks cemented at the front door of my heart. I have buried the past behind a multi-ton weighing vault in which, no human will ever access its combination o'er.

The travesty of my darkened past is interfering in my relationships. Still, unable to talk. Still avoiding the harsh effects of feeling current guilt and shame. And still no one cares enough to ask; not my mother, not my brothers, not my husband; and let alone... them listen?

Doesn't anybody see?

No one sees your heart, Annabelle!

GRANNY, Jett's mother, displays a gentle spirit. She has an overabundance of unconditional love for everyone. The love and affection she gave me—overwhelming. The long lost, estranged love popped back in front of me—thoughtful and hospitable. Here I am in front of a mother who speaks softly, lacking a need for colorful jargon. Incomprehensible patience and reassuring presence, her sincere wish—is nothing short of complete happiness for me. Granny's utmost acceptance of her son's wife was unmatched. Though for me, witnessing her faith was an unwelcome newness. My mind was not shifty—only a heart cemented shut with a warning sign, "There is no one here."

Granny's heart is genuine. A devout Christian, she attends church services located conveniently across from her modest residence; I call the "little white house." With Sundays set for family togetherness—done around mealtimes; the lady of the house has a strategy in place. Every Sunday morning, she rises early with enough time to prepare for the day's family luncheon before she attends the morning service. Each family member knows of Granny's schedule of events. Thus, removing the wonders of where to eat, what to eat, and who is cooking? Her plan works on removing the "wonders" and we get to enjoy the service and fellowship with other church members.

"Hello, nice to see you again." Then smiles for everyone, but my mind is back in the *little white house*. The person's name escapes me—picturing Granny's eating table—completely set with glasses of cold sun iced-tea and delicious home-cooked meal. Maybe she prepped some of her white-bean soup, her specialty. It seem my taste buds multiply every time I imagine this dish... so yummy!

"See you next Sunday..." moving away from the ongoing fellowship; wondering what's for lunch? I have gained a taste for *Granny's delicacy*, slow-cooked white beans with ham bones served with "Jiffy" cornbread.

READING the New International Version Bible (NIV) Scriptures takes precedence over Granny's busy work schedule and household chores. Night after night; supper dishes washed, dried, and put away... in kneeling form she says prayers in the later hours. Evading to display her, I call, "ritualism" she would take quiet time with *her* God in the stillness and privacy of her bedroom. I thought nothing of her rituals. Granny was too nice; there is no reason to antagonize her. I was neither amused, offended, and most certainly, *not a speck curious*.

She never pushed or imposed reading the Bible on anyone else in the family, let alone, on me. I heard the Scriptures read mostly in church services. Most often, the worship segment catches my usual and drifted awareness. For me, learning from *this* good book takes second stage over organ playing and vocal segments.

Singing, more appropriately referred to as WORSHIPPING, somehow lifts me internally. Mind soothing, heightening my spirit. Hymnal books are conveniently available in each pew. With my love for music, in eagerness—I reach for one. My fingers often find preferred hymns. By some means, it drew me to, "How Great Thou

Art's" lyrics. In particular, at the start of its third stanza, "*And when I think of God, His Son not sparing.*" God's Son—not sparing His own beloved Son, died to take away my sin. I felt forsaken, not only by my father's death—as life went on... God did too. God was too much of a "God," too far-reaching by sinful adults, let alone by a desensitized child. Debauchery inflicted on me; sinful act with shameful effects—my child's problem was too small for His attention.

Then there was, the Evangelist and Songwriter, George Bennard who penned his experience—at the last line in the fourth canto, "*To pardon and sanctify me.*" I whispered.

"God, I am shamed and beyond pardon!"

SHAMED—A harsh word, though explicitly offensive had manifested in my soul. Further following a habit of conversing to myself, "'IF' You were there, You would know?" Lacking the desire to understand, tugged me further from the transforming melody, "*Jesus suffered and died—sanctified me.*"

REFLECTION: "IF," with its doubtful meaning, unceasingly and successfully prolonged uncovering the truth my heart ached for. I didn't understand,"He is faithful and just—to cleanse us from ALL unrighteousness" (1st John 1:9). Yet, God who is faithful, keeps His short distance—an arm's length presence, never giving up.

I remember those few fervent moments while on her knees, Ma prayed to *this* same God. As a mother now, I believe without reservations, my mother lobbied to God for her children's well-being.

Granny recognized the spiritual expression of a much greater need; she added my name in her intercessional prayer. However, she never shared personal intercessions with me. I sensed her pure interest. She felt the dire condition of a pleading heart. *Spirit-led* sensory. God chose His servant, Granny, to plant the seed—His love.

Unwavering, His faithful servant would endure many, undeserving riling remarks from me. Vexing further, I pounded on the question: "If God is love, why does He allow others to hurt people?" And more so, "Why doesn't He stop the pain?" Unbeknownst to Granny, I was referring to yours truly, not the people per se. My broken heart. My heartache!

She would refer me to the condition of one's heart.

"God gave each person the gift of choice, Annabelle!" I came back with,

"The hearts of evil people, whom God gave the right to choose!"

"Why, Granny? Why would He allow bad people to choose?" And, "Doesn't He know who the bad people are from the good?" Finally, "What kind of God is He?"

Not wanting to hear what the Scriptures say—I would end the discussion. Get up, walk away and pretend to tend to the children. Granny would hush and lower her head. No doubt, she was praying for me.

God's faithful servant, Granny, delved into Scriptures. Words of God, I have grown to love; verses held deeply in my soul.

QUESTION. Do you have a gem in your treasure chest; reminiscent of a spirited individual overflowing with authentic nurturing care, who prayed with you? For you? They are God's servants delivering to you, His message of love. Their enduring hope and visual trust in God is efficient and effective. "For God did not send His Son into the world to condemn the world, but to save the world through Him" (John 3:17).

Encouragement:

Psalm 16:10-11
For You will not leave my soul in She'ol,
Nor, You will allow Your Holy One to see corruption.
You, will show me the path of life; In Your presence is fullness of joy;
At Your right hand are pleasures forevermore.

(NKJV)

IN JESUS' name, I pray:

Lord, I am grateful for Your servant's devotion, persevered in showing me the brilliance of Your loving presence. Your love was the seed that needed sowing and nurturing. I needed You to wash away the shame placed in my soul. Fruit of the Spirit: love, joy, peace, long-suffering, kindness, goodness, faithfulness, gentleness, and self-control—presented powerfully by a faithful and godly woman. Someday, I will join Your sweet servant—Granny, glorified and in Your presence!

May we recognize and lift in prayer, all Your servants around—identifiable, visible through their fruit—love for others. May we be Your sower to plant the seed of love to those placed before us—in person, on the telephone, via airmail, and even social media. Bless us with a servitude heart by sharing Your healing power towards hurting souls.

WITHIN A FEW MONTHS, we moved out of Granny's house to live on a spacious farmland a few miles outside the city. The lovely ride to our new home gave me a sense of calmness. Acreages line up and down the road towards the place where our family of four will live for a set time. Excitement is defining our ride; and, the anticipation rises as we see the wide entrance towards our new home. Even so the thumping fear inside shook me. My heartbeat rises, this feels familiar! (Yes, from Pa's burial site!) What is it? We drive through.

At the end of the one-mile driveway stood a brick home. Hundreds of acres sprawled in the back, around, and bordered down the prairie is a river. Four-footed backyard residents—well-cared mighty looking horses, freely roam and gallop around in graceful movements. It is breathtaking!

The picturesque land setting took my breath away. Villa Dolores' one-acre compound pales in comparison to the 350-plus acres, our new brick home stands on. As sharecroppers, the landowner gave us spacious living area for our family as part of an agreement—in exchange to tending a portion of land from this immense space.

But, what was that *heart* thumping all about earlier?

I was in total amazement viewing our new home standing brick-by-brick on the prairie, hearing the soothing sound of a moving river water; and, in watching the powerful presence of lean strutting horses, transitory—I overcame that jolted feeling.

∽

HAVING Paul attend school was a hard call to follow. For each of the time he steps up into the school bus; my heart pumps heavy, concerned for my son.

Before moving to the south, Paul went through a series of tests at the prestigious Jules Stein Clinic in Los Angeles. They diagnosed Paul with "DCD"—Developmental Coordination Disorder. DCD is a neurological condition known as developmental dyspraxia. The series of tests given to Paul, was wearing. They questioned me alone, once again, with so many questions; I didn't understand... feeling the interrogations were to find fault somewhere. I felt helpless. I felt at fault. Was the cause because of my young age at seventeen, as a first time mother?

Paul's diagnosis infused a major concern for his future wellbeing. For me, Stein's significant diagnosis is for informational references only. Critical information and a clear starting point to plan for his future. Yet, in weighing the possibilities of Paul not developing, "normal," was less important than finding out how to help my son develop to "his" fullest potential. Medical jargon did not impress me to be still and place Paul in a box. Leaving me with very little hope for a conventional life for Paul. Not happening. The list of signs and symptoms provided was cumbersome. DCD has no cure. You work with it. Various coping strategies are being developed and exercised, still few are available for Paul. The educational system available for special needs' students was a blanket coverage. All students with any emotional and mental health challenges, or other disorders such as DCD; would classify indifferent and placed *en masse*... all together in the same classroom.

Motherhood gave me an awareness for a joyful existence. Though I had a life-sharing experience with my sister who lives with a disability; it did not prepare me for my own child. *I am to be my son's first student in life's curve ball.* Paul was a good baby, a fun child, and a good-natured individual. His slow physical and cognitive development evidenced the signs given earlier by specialists.

"He will live life with much difficulty," was the doctor's ending statement. I remember choking up. A hard reality... be as it may, I felt more hopeful in life than ever before. Though he attended a specific class intended for the special needs, many of his classmates were in need of emotional nurturing or have an undiagnosed condition. Paul toiled and suffered constant bullying. Education provided for Paul fell in the "handicap" section—a universal placement.

REFLECTION: Being a mother, gave me a hopeful emotional sense, *strive* to be better inside... but it was just that, better on the surface not inside; the blemish is the same. Motherhood did not wipe out the spot of feeling shamed! An action to handle for later.

JETT'S CHOICE TO distance himself from facing the truth of Paul's reality in life was hard; I felt alone. Feeling secluded in hopeful feelings for my son, I felt more confident having Granny as an ally. Granny, whose committed passion directed to school children with disabilities is *graciousness* in action. She labored both mentally and physically each school day. Her burning desire to help magnified upon hearing of Paul's diagnosis. Her passion and knowledge—viable instrument in understanding her grandson's needs. I developed a deeper connection and respect for Granny.

THREE YEARS OF PLANTING, cultivating and harvesting dark tobacco crop from sunup to sundown—physically demanding. Extreme physical labor, recognizable as a sure igniter to human aging process. Farming is hard work compared to nothing, I've ever done in life. In my comparing the many corporate hot shot players, I've come across in city life, farmers are chosen players who follow their passion with hard work regardless of its low pay, but blessed with riches— the rich can't play. I say, "Well them folks are workers all right!"

I have the utmost respect to farming's exasperating tasks. There is no case to rebut—early rise with long and often lonesome arduous duties. Farmers of big or small land fall into opus—hard work, most heirs would rather forgo inheritance than till its ground. Most often, sharecroppers don't own farmland. However, their love for farming provides landowners beneficial laboring hands in exchange for a portion of its crop sales. I have come to respect sharecroppers' philosophy, observing Brian Brett's: "Farming is a profession of hope." A strong love affair, hard to grasp. One has to put on their working gloves, step into their tattered leather shoes to understand the profession of unrelenting hope.

Labor intensive, growing dark tobacco requires a long and strenuous process. Grown in four months, it takes approximately 200-300, man-hours to cultivate one acre. So, it's life, shoving fourteen months of 8-hour workday into approximately ten months. Tending to ten acres would mean no weekends and no social outings.

I say, Just give me food! Later, the truth of my reality; I would beg for more. Success defined by the world, not by the poverty I had left behind. MORE, in life. A little social, a little outing; and for sure, a lot of rest! Still, working in the dirt compliments the soiled condition of my heart.

PHASE I: from prepping the planting beds to sowing of seeds, transplanting, worming, and removal of suckers—passion in play. Worming is overtly, the most disgusting step I have engaged in cultivating these plants. Hand-removal then, dropping and stomping would be fine in taking off small *quietly consuming nutrition,* worm; BUT those hardy, 3-4-inches by 2-inches in circumference ones, aren't easily dropped and stomped on. The step requires holding both ends of its wiggly and curling tissues; and with thumbs and fingers on the middle part, is then twisted and torn in half... guts and green fluids would burst out with gusto! And, hard as I tried; sometimes, yucky fluids splatter on my face. I'd be sure to have my mouth closed with such procedures. YES, worming is icky!

Growing tobacco in its initial phase is a definite precursor to the arduous labor stages ahead. From weeding the fields to topping and removal of all the flowers from each tobacco plant... are essential steps in providing more nutrients to its leaves. Imagine working with hundreds of—six or seven feet tall plants!

UNDER NORMAL CONDITIONS, farmers harvest tobacco leaves in the early morning. On the first visual step towards sales, a gathering day, I followed the professional laborers—grab a machete to join the team. Clothed in thick blue-jeans and a long-sleeved shirt, I went to cutting these towering plants. Made certain my calves are out of the way, I slashed—plant dropped. Repeat. And I stopped at half-way through the row; dropped all tools, straightened and stretched. Several feet ahead, are helpers ready to tackle the next step of "spiking" these huge plants.

The tool used for spiking is a coned metal spearhead placed on one end of a stick. Tobacco Farmers carry out this task with precision, avoiding not to split a plant; otherwise, hanging will be inefficient. And because of the urgency ahead of the day's hot smoldering sun, neighboring folks volunteer, with men doing most of the spiking and hauling. Ending with about 90–100 pounds of tobacco plants per stick. This can be heavy—it was for me.

Sun rays could permanently damage any leaves left unattended within minutes. Chances are, a grower could lose a healthy portion of a whole year's worth of work within a 30-minutes, *overdue sun fry*. Farmers are one of the best example of players in team efforts. Seeing any neighbor's needs, farmers in droves arise. Helpers ready to provide long and laborious hours to complete the removal of crops from sustaining permanent damage. Thus, saving a family's livelihood. And, with no pay.

My hands have been in all the processes, so far. So *spiking*, here I come. Without a doubt, I appeared uneasy handling this long and "awkward to handle" hazardous stick with a sharp tip. Yet, I hold my tool securely with targeted plants lay waiting on the ground. I pushed the sharp tip into the bottom part of the tobacco plant; and, *uh-oh*, too low, it splits. This is difficult. My body is already hurting! Conclusion, spiking requires a bit more sophistication. On I go to the next step—lifting those to the hilt, loaded sticks. Ha-ha. You should see those farmers looking at me; the small, frail, skinny as a rail helper. Weakling? Women on the farm stayed at home, and those handfuls on the field—out spiking tobacco leaves, are in pace with the men folks!

My, oh my, two of those sticks—one on each shoulder were enough after a measly, two trips! Feeling like I picked up twice my body weight here!

With careful and controlled movements, we all hustled to bring all the spiked sticks into the barn placing them first on the ground.

Smoking, also known as "fire-curing" tobacco leaves take place in the barn. Our curing barn—a mere ten yards walking distance from the field. Meanwhile, near the field is a pickup truck loaded with a big pile of plants. I volunteered to drive the truck to the barn. Though, I didn't let on about my current condition. Truth, *it* is zapping my energy, and I'm physically draining empty. Still, I reasoned and said,

"It makes no sense to have another person, who could carry those heavy plants into the barn... drive. I am available."

Mind you, I am not an experienced driver. I have driven a handful of times, and to boot... back and forth on Granny's dirt road driveway. Plus, I have no license. But who needs a driver's license on a farm?

At sixty-two inches tall and sitting in the driver's seat, I can barely see the pickup's front hood. Some gaging will have to factor over. I will have to depend on viewing both side mirrors—mostly relying on the team's hollering directions. Quipping,

"What could go wrong in a few yards?"

I was stepping on the gas pedal slow and steady when the loud hollering voices distracted my nervous self. Is it fatigue, or hunger... or a threatened feeling of the over-sized steering wheel—the size of my torso? Three or four yards in front of the pickup's front wheels remain a heaping pile of tobacco on sticks. I slammed on the breaks! My head somewhat veered over. I pulled the hand-breaks. Then, seeing natural marks, up close on the dashboard's vintage leather covering—I shook my head. It was like falling into *kangkungan*, flourishing waterways with fellow squirms. Except, I saw stars instead of "raining" shredded coconut. Instantaneously, I gripped the truck's driver side door handle, opened and jumped out.

"Ok, where do you guys want me?"

No one answered! Every helper was too busy doing what needs doing. Meanwhile, I was seeing visions of several dancing stars!

Three, including myself, helped in handing tobacco-loaded sticks to workers who stood *steady and ready* in tiered format, high-up in the barn. Being careful not to drop price-holding sticks; each plant was meticulously and strategically placed starting from the top of the barn down to about three to four feet from the bottom. This required space is vital for worker's passage, airing; and, prevents the bottom row's leaves from touching the ground that could cause damage. Or worst, catch on fire!

Tying tobacco leaves is the most awaited task, marking the end of the whole laboring process. The next phase before the sale; "tying," in a seated or standing position is tedious and can be backbreaking.

Manual and repeated maneuvering of hands and fingers laboring for long hours. The pulling and gathering several pieces of leaves then tying them together do not look like fun. Sticky, dingy-brown stains from the tobacco have no partiality in prettifying—stressing in cuticles and favoring to go under nail beds.

"No, thank you!"

I was least present at this point. Tobacco is my least favorite of all our crops. Instead, I tended the family's *one-acre* home vegetable garden with my two small children. Each young grower particularly enjoyed digging plump, chemical free potatoes and carrots.

Oh, about that pile of tobacco leaves I nearly ran over—represented a quarter-row of harvest!

"Oops!"

ALONG WITH THE long tough and wearisome farming duties; the condition of my heart continues to spew a cry for help. Busyness is here too. Negligence in my life continues. Even the ever strenuous tasks of cutting, spiking, and lifting of 100-pound stalks of tobacco, were just that—keep busy enough—keep the *cries untended.*

Arduous work in the dirt completed and its harvest hung in the barn for its final step. Nothing like the challenges given by the former "boys only" group; fun and exhilarating! The long periods of hard, grueling physical work produced more destructive resentfulness in my heart. Again, the toxic feeling of negligence surfaced and magnetized in rapid ways—propagated its damaged roots.

I played my role well as a team player. Three years of non-verbal complaints! No time for sweet sleep and complete rest. There was no outside dining. And no movie watching. Nothing, but work clothes and the same church clothes to wear. Was I complaining? Or, finding an out from all! Later, in my reasoning, people handed pity on me. Allowing those around—believe the poor sufferer played by a brokenhearted pro.

FOR MA'S USLR status reporting schedule, Ma flew to California. Ate Claudette fell behind. The process of petitioning my sister is taking a long time. It was necessary for Ma to report her status in person to the US. She also plans on returning to Manila, back to my sister as soon as Ma completes the required reporting.

So much has developed—Ate Claudette had given birth and is now a mother of three. Although, concerned for her physical condition, I am thrilled for my sister.

It was a perfect timing for Ma's travel to California, she plans on visiting me here in the south and is eager to meet her... whom she refers to as: "Stateside—born-in-the-US," grandchildren—Paul and Sam. Going into our third year of farming, I am one month away to giving birth. As planned, Ma flew into my "neck of the woods" to help with the day-to-day family care and other activities. Her arrival placed more than physical relief in the pending days ahead—her presence permeated nurturing sentiment to my exhaustive living.

Each day presents a heavy workload for Jett, who is in every way involved in farming. As his sole dedicated helper; I am working in the dirt where needed, fend for our two children while preparing for the birth of our third child.

SUMMER DAYS ARE PASSING. Tying of tobacco leaves is fast underway. Day after day, Jett, and the helpers are working long hours, motivated to move on to the last process—selling.

The greatest anticipation of the year—I gave birth to baby number three. De is beautiful. She feels beautiful and smells beautiful. My sweet newborn took my troubled mind away into a blissful time. Looking into her innocent eyes is a reminder; love still exists somewhere in my broken heart.

Ma, "Lola Dolly," the Lice Exterminator is in the house! She received grand-naming by her first grandchild, Paul. Lola Dolly, who battled and won the war against my lice-infested hair using vinegar and *kus-kus*, is ready to tackle, come what may. Her message is unwavering. Healing ahead comprises of natural remedies. Am I ever ready! Ma's belief in health and wellness is exclusive. The principles and practices of effective natural methods she has used all her life—embedded into mine.

I have been experiencing repeated inexorable muscle spasms concentrated in my calves. Like a surgeon's hands and fingers held up, are oil-drenched hands. My personal masseuse, the Amazonian Lola, rubs up and down my calves un-knotting the effects of lactic acid build-up from walking and working in those long hours in the dirt. More so, it was her *ole* time method of easing discomfort from breast engorgement, I felt the most relief from post birthing.

Ma took two flats (cloth diapers) to make a tie by tying the pieces together. Age has not weakened my mother. As the muscled woman I've known, she placed the tie snug across and tucked around my chest, as tight as possible. She flexed and muscled through, pulled the cloths tighter—then asks, "Can you take it tighter?" I couldn't make a sound. She didn't wait for my answer; instead, tightened the tie more. I groaned!

"Hay naku po" (OMG). I looked like a halfway-tied... felt like a mummy! I could hardly breathe but wait... it worked. Relief at its best!

Those affectionate moments of caring touches instilled a deep longing from a needier time in my childhood. Am I feeling the love? If it could, a part would surface from its depth and unveil the truth. Yearning to expel the darkened terror that hurts and kills—*Ma, I have something to tell you,* but I never said.

Days and weeks would pass so quickly until one inexplicable thought came on the day of Ma's flight back to California. I had a strong, strange yearning to leave our current residency. After Ma left, I made one phone call to my brother, Kuya BB. As sharecroppers, we were cash poor. Though we lived lavishly in the landowner's brick home, surrounded by the beauty of natural surroundings—rose an unsuspected eagerness to leave. Eager for calmness, hoping to soothe my troubled mind.

∽

WHO SAYS I couldn't do it all? Not that anyone has dared to ask. My family didn't know what I had become. Weighing gravity of my appeal, the ongoing financial hardship and long physical labored days supported my reason for moving back to California. Our growing family had endured a range of uncertainties as sharecroppers. Instinctively, I took on the low road. Toddler Sam, baby De and I, flew westbound and settled in the City of Alhambra. A suburb of Los Angeles, the quaint city sits five miles east of Los Angeles. Paul rode with Jett hauling our limited household belongings.

Kuya BB owns a three-bedroom home in a semi-affluent neighborhood of Alhambra. It didn't sit on hundreds of acres, but the backyard is plenty big surrounded by flowering shrubs and fruit trees. Two uninhibited and fruitful avocado trees provide cooling shades during the hot Summer days. Plenty spacious—this home has a fun layout. We leased the home with no reservations, hoping life would be different and sweeter in suburb-living. Our new hillside three-story home with a fenced-in backyard. There's *that* thumping again! I ignored the mysterious beating of my heart.

Sweet life served on a silver platter came with a whipping whirlwind. A new power was developing inside my mind; I wholly entertained.

A working wife and mom, I am—still feeling—oh, so empty. I feel the need to be of value. Most women in the 70s who seem to share my sentiment, are on the bandwagon. No ride will leave me behind! Showing my ability to do all things, I hopped on the wagon ride and added a full-time college student stat. During which, I held a demanding full-time job placement. Hours were long. I subconsciously exhausted body and mind, in hopes to fill the void, and avoid any added confrontation from my dark past. Setting my plan in motion.

∼

~V~
OUR MINDS CALL FOR REST AND WITHOUT—BODIES FALL BEHIND AND LEAVE SPIRITS DRY.

∼

Encouragement:

∼

Matthew 11:28-29
Come to Me, you who labor and are heavy laden,
and I will give you rest.
Take My yoke upon you and learn from Me, for I am gentle and lowly
in heart, and you find rests for your souls.

(NKJV)

IN JESUS' name, I pray:

Our souls yearn for rest, but not as the world defines respite. Living in tumultuous worldly lifestyle demands only more unsatisfying desires, laboring to catch breaks for our weary existence. We long for God's rest. Our minds call for rest; without, bodies fall behind and leave spirit dry.

18

FATAL TOUCH

*L*OVER OF PLEASURES. Money is no longer an issue as it was during our farming days—humbling yearly pays in tilling ten acres of land. Labor beyond my understanding. Undeserving. Sunup to sundown grinding work produced our family of five—an unmanageable annual income—not enough to cover living expenses. I saw our arduous work with little future. A family affair that had taken most of our day's time in strenuous work. I was glad we're out —I'm out.

Most profitable companies in the early 1980s were generous employers. Human Resources vie for top candidates. Applicants with references for high performing work history, compete with those who have certificates in higher education. And, I have references. Referrals from being: seamstress to farming to factory worker to corporate America, I am your worker! I can learn anything. A team player, I accept any challenge.

I landed a position as the Senior Clerk, Marketing-Allocations and Price Department in one of the most sought-after business establishments—an oil company. Atlantic Richfield Company, offered unheard and hard to match, starting salaries. Sugar-coated offerings; sign-on bonus and pay increases based on high-performance reviews. Top performers could garner up to one-third of pay increase. I received a "28" percent salary increase in my first review! The oil company I worked for provided cost-of-living increases to every employee, not once but twice a year!

And so it was, I bought everything *we* wanted. Current trends in apparel, shoes, and purses—I want it, I bought it. The children lacked nothing. Jett was less excited in my recent purchasing mania. I was feeling more of worth now. We have "things" to show for it.

"You'd be a better mother if you didn't work," Jett uttered.

"What are you insinuating?" I asked. He seldom spent time with the children.

Not a word, he just looked at me. His statement sounds like a challenge? I accept.

Perceiving to be an absolute matter... a challenge. Game on—I hit the training floor.

I can be a good mother. I am a good mother!

REFLECTION: God is awesome! I did not see His unrelenting hands working mightily! The plowing, tilling, planting, weeding, and pruning happening right before my eyes. He arranged and nurtured my life in His divine manner. In the grounds of my heart, God Father in Heaven planted His Word through His trusted servant. He brought my mother back to help recap loving moments with her caring touches. Straightway, a third angel, De, appeared wonderfully in my life. Amid three years of hard labor, He provided a very comfortable home. With an acre home garden filled with plant-based nutrition. Complete with practical medical needs provided by our landlord—a physician—blessing each family member with remarkable good health. And surreal surrounding reflecting His Majesty!

How could I be so blind to not see God's mighty work? Citing, the blessings parallel my childhood upbringing—too far gone.

However, we spent more time in the field than we did to nurture "us" as a family.

OUR FAMILY'S schedule accepted the madness in a daily run. Upgrade in the materialistic lifestyle brought the ever-growing duplicity into our marriage. Brewing inside our hearts is mixed emotions. Jett's unrelenting and controlling moves to stop the undesirable in his life—

targeted me. Inside, I believe he resents me for an inscrutable desire to come back to California. I was inconsiderate in leaving behind his love for farming. Raising tobacco is not something I'm proud to labor as a "farmer." It causes cancer. I'd choose not. While the gravity of darkened past has progressed beyond temporary pleasures, I became vulnerable to outside stimulants.

With this major challenge thrown at me, I perceived testing motherhood was the most incriminating one. Being a good mother meant, going a new direction from my upbringing. Outfitted with maternal DNA's laboring energy; I can prove to be better. As "Supermom," I will not neglect my children. Financial budgeting will be efficient. I will serve food three times daily. Not the once a day "ketchup on white bread sandwiches," if at that. The Filipino that I am, I prefer white rice and Spam! Paramount, unlike my predecessors, I can identify and ward off... those potential perpetrators around my children.

Finally, feelings of neglect; not just for me—for the family. Three years in working the dirt have caused a charade of unmet duties. I am stuck living in lice-infested life. (Those lice, aargh!) Drama, a livelihood plague sucking blood from my dehydrating heart.

Dark begets more darkness in play. Spirit and body despairing and exhausting, I needed more energy to tackle the day. And to help boost more vitality, I was given a free sample of white powder stimulants. This "pick-me-upper" drug worked the brain and helped conceal the true condition of my heart. A covert place to be and no one would know!

One could reason for the truth... being, I felt rubbish. Jett's ego bruised. I felt neglected, again! We are two damaged goods needing divine intervention. My petition for treatment produced one marriage and several personal therapy sessions, but soon ended by Jett's unwarranted reasoning. We were two heavy-weight boxers in a ring. My whole experience with him had toughened me more. Though, I begged him to do "this" fighting in private. There was no begging at this point.

He weighed at a solid two-hundred pounds and I, at ninety-two. With gloves tightly on, we fought, screamed, cried, pointed our fingers towards each other. I reciprocated to his continued verbal explosions, able to dodge most of his ramming cruelty as the young audience of three watched.

. . .

REFLECTION: For years, I justified that when you hurt others; you give them the right to hurt you back. I acknowledge a hurting heart, inadvertently hurts others. The travesty, I believed—deserving those harmful acts targeting my guilt-ridden young soul. In the center of our distresses, existed a cry for forgiveness. Forgiven. Abusive conduct may be a learned behavior from an environment. Why didn't I recognize clear signs of a deeply troubled mind beforehand? Later in our marriage I learned, Jett, endured years of painful emotional and physical abuse in his youth. And my gut feeling, he has been lugging this learned behavior. Looming, awaiting an application!

In similarity, I showed no signs of an unsettled mind at first. I did so! I tried to end my life. Yet to Jett that suicidal act gave a message of true love instead. He believed the attempt to end my life was because of him. My desperate plea for love drove me into darkened ways resulting in unhealthy relationships.

Shamed feeling made its way to accepting deserving punishment, *I deserve punishment.* Although not my doing, my perpetrators convinced me to believe... the fault was all mine. Meriting continued oppression. How? Re-direct—mistreat those around me. Take the attention off me. Challenge me and darkness within rises to the occasion. Not from that lighthearted girl who took a challenge from the "boy's only" group. From a heavily dejected spirit able to spew darkness so powerful, I merely followed like a puppet on a string.

LIBERATED by the world's standards and the need to survive, I focused on my heart's desires. To keep busy working, caring for the children, and dodging Jett's automatic pillory was my daily goal. Insanity was too much to bear. Just enough white sprinkles for my lost soul gave instant but temporary relief. In time, the numb feelings attracted a slay. Jett's looming shadow released in the frontal view of our most loyal young fans—made for three more broken hearts brought on by our actions!

An evening of forceful physical battle came between my intoxicated husband and myself, his anesthetized wife. Physical aims and hits landed on its target. I see our most loyal fans watch in horror.

Paul, in extreme fear, physically intervened and wrapped his small forearms around his father's massive shoulders. Paul takes over directing two major players on stage... yells,

"Please get us help, Mom!"

I hesitated. Jett won't hurt Paul. With eyes bulging, Paul yells at me once more,

"Go!"

"Knock, knock, 'Please open the door!'" came on my neighbor's front door.

The door opens wide; and, I other residents seated in the dining room, each face freezes in unwelcome surprise. I burst in through—dove under their eating table and whimpered,

"Please help."

Within a few minutes, the local law enforcers arrived. One scan. One view. One order.

"Your family needs the obvious—brief separation and respite from this difficult night."

The police officer strongly advised... the children and I leave the house for the night; but, ordered Jett to stay home.

One sibling is nearby. An older brother could accommodate, comfort, and if need be... hopefully, protect us. I called Kuya Rolando and informed him of our grim night. Rolando, the ever-helpful brother,

"Shall I pick you and the children up?"

"No thanks, I can drive!"

In grave state of mind, I rushed to pack our blue Ford truck with just the clothes we have on and De's diaper bag. Four policemen were leaving the house as they watched the children and I, drive away. The night has settled. It's vice movement of a darkened day is in full motion. Driving towards the entrance to the 10-San Bernardino Freeway. In shock, still shaking in fear, I merged onto the freeway going eastbound. Thankful, traffic is flowing in the early hours of the night. Headed to the city of West Covina. There, we will have a refuge in Kuya Rolando's home, 12 miles away.

I felt safe in our family's pickup truck, the reliable vehicle that labored on the farmland and hauled our belongings two-thousand miles. I felt safe inside the truck driving.

Déjà Vu! Remembering the day of a heavy rainstorm back at Villa

Dolores. I felt safe inside Pa's vehicle—when a "man-angel" reappeared to save me.

Here I am in a similar safe haven... a vehicle for safety... trying so hard to focus on driving. From my peripheral vision to the right passenger window, I saw Jett's face peering through his vehicle's driver's window. Is this a nightmare? Am I imagining? Has fear added in facial form—in hatred?

Familiar expression of anger, he motions me to pull over aside. Upon seeing his father, Paul begs me not to stop. Foot steady on the pedal, I pressed further reaching over 70-MPH. Jett's car gains on my blue truck. Seeing faces of fear on Paul, four-year-old Sam, with De's car seat squeezed in the middle, I exited off the freeway. I drove over the freeway and popped in frontal view—is the "easy order in, and easy out" popular hamburger establishment filled with hungry people in line. Soon their famished anticipation for satiety turned troubled. Worried in not knowing if I might crash the truck in front of several others receiving their orders. I slammed the breaks and stopped within a few feet in front of paled and trauma-stricken faces.

Jett's car screeched and with harassing intent, stopped close to the truck. At once, he got out and walked towards Paul's side. He reached over and took De's car-seat with her in it. His sight redirected at me —orders us.

"You all will have to come home if you want to see the baby!"

Unknowingly, a frightened customer called "911"... a new set of police officers arrived within a few minutes. City of Baldwin Park, a neighboring town, a new set of police force, moved around assessing the incident. One officer took, De, away from Jett and handed her back to me. There was genuine concern on this officer's face; his unsolicited advice directed to me.

"Before any of us can help your family, you need to act," and continued.

"File a report and restraining order. Or, live in craziness filled with anger... *facing fear each day!*"

The officer, looked at me... as if he saw something inside me. Feeling sorry. He walked away.

I did not report such happenings. I am part of this. I can fix this insanity.

• • •

WE ARRIVED at my brother's home. Jett pulls up behind but stayed in the car. Still emotionally stirred, I was unloading the kids from the car and saw my brother by the door. He stepped towards the truck; his sight sweeping on all the children. Nothing to unpack, Kuya Rolando motions everyone to go inside. Paul held Sam's hand and De saddled on my hip. Seated on the living room's plastic covered soft velvet floral-printed couch, I see Ma displays a mother's concerned look. She hurts for me—for her child.

Somewhere between the crazed brain and pained heart, I believed now—the perfect time to tell her. However, there were only tears shared. Ma hugged me saying nothing. Just then, Jett walks in; still loaded with vexing gestures, heavily stepping towards where I stood with De's arms and legs wrapped securely around me. I feel my toddler's body shake as she sees her father approaching. She buries her face on my chest and tightens her limbs' wrappings around my torso. Jett's former *hang-out buddy*, Rolando, shunned him. After seeing my condition up close and personal, standing anxious with hands in his pockets, looks me over again and lowers his head. My brother tried to stop me from going home that night. Kuya Rolando is not one to interfere, but his nonchalant persona turned worrisome for me.

And without looking at Jett, he walked closer and said,

"Just stay, Annabelle! There's plenty of room for everyone."

In fear for the children's safety, adding concern for Kuya Rolando's involvement—to no avail and low-spirited, I drove home with the children. Jett followed my drive back to our house. Drowning in deep sorrow with three innocent children sinking with us; we are two broken people needing divine intervention.

Once home, the darkened morning brought extended desperate plea. Neither, slept through. From fetal position, I got up and was right back in the front war zone. Jett gets up and on the double; jumps downstairs, runs back upstairs and six feet from where I sat heedless; entombed in his left hand an *identifiable* object. He brings the piece of metal barrel up and pressed *it* against his left temple.

"Shall I end my life too?"

Fear struck all over my body. Who will stop the madness? Who will save my children?

Our hearts, all five—drained of hope. My littlest one, too young to process. It hurts to see the visual hot mess we have placed her in. All three innocent hearts are breaking. I pleaded.

"Please, no, don't!"

∼

MEANWHILE, unhappiness and drama were developing within the Sabella family circle. Divorced from Reign and remarried—Kuya BB's new wife, appears to hold the opposite view of his supportive ways. He veers into her lifestyle. Looking like, chaos and separations are gaining momentum into each of my sibling's own unstable ways. As if we were all back on the same ship—not a fun voyage. Instead, cruising in a boatload drama-filled.

We moved out of Kuya BB's home and moved to a nearby single-family dwelling close to the children's public school. In tow are our hearts' baggage's filled with nurtured hurts and pain from the recent past. Packed with unresolved and abusive acts of loathing towards each other. Even a brief physical separation only infused more distrust brought on by disgusting behaviors with each one.

In the midst, meeting other people presented temporal happiness. Possibilities faded out. Still with no change, there was no hope for the future. And as we continued, insanity proved once more—attacked each other. Heavy-duty guilt and shame feelings would prevent us from possible healthy relationships with others.

When needed, my dark past spews an edge. I have a shield. The thick, numb feeling inside does not see or hear any reason when husband attacks. We each live for self and day-to-day, each one lived on edge. Our children displayed obvious signs of destructive emotional insecurities! Young minds' connective tissues to understand are tragically being seared—unable to develop in healthy ways.

Human parental intellect often wishes to do what appears "right" for the children's sake. Albeit, injurious activities continued. Full-blown drama and darkness indwell at home. My independence and rigidness invited for more of Jett's uncontrolled and attacking behavior. Until that forceful blow, was to be his last, inflicted on me. With a heavy heart and only one bag in my hand, I cried out towards my young broken-hearted children.

"I will be back for you!"

. . .

REFLECTION: As a parent, leaving the children behind in a crazed environment was one of the biggest mistake I have ever done. Even with fear for my physical being and life loomed overhead. The misconception their father will not hurt them took place. So as its dire representation of the log in my eye—I left all three with fearful feelings of abandonment often reinforced by their father. "Your mother is a bad mother! She left you." The perception I had as a child. I felt abandoned when my father passed. Ma was too occupied to see the signs of a victimized being within her very own child. The grueling lifetime of surviving its painful consequences, my calloused heart entrapped with guilt and shame gave way to the enemy. The adversary's cunning ways—powerfully effective and appeasing. The enemy is in a celebratory stance for achieving success as my fleshly desires soar towards its highest self-will.

We have an incessant adversary who continues to infuse lies infecting the world. The prince of deception scripted in the garden. "Now the serpent was more cunning than any beast of the field which Lord God had made. And he said to the woman, 'Has God indeed said, you shall not eat of every tree of the garden?' And, the woman said to the serpent, 'we may eat the fruit of the trees of the garden; but of the fruit of the tree which is in the midst of the garden, God has said, you shall not eat it, nor shall you touch it, lest you die.'" (Genesis 3:1-3). "Then the serpent said to the woman: 'You will not surely die for God knows that in the day you eat of it, your eyes will be opened and you will be like God, knowing good and evil'" (Genesis 3:4).

Jett has taken the same bite I took—we believed the same lie. We gained nothing but sinfulness. And sure as death is upon our marriage.

In truths, only God is good. So, only He knows all that is good. God is the originator of goodness; "And God saw everything that He had made, and behold, it was very good. And there was evening and there was morning the sixth day" (ESV Genesis 1:31).

God's holiness gives us a full view of His goodness. His goodness motivates the disposal of many blessings into our life; the goal of His deep compassion, awesome kindness, and overflowing generosity.

The good news—God gave us redemption in His Beloved Son. While evilness, pain, and isolation gut a soul; Christ Jesus, our Savior's blood have stamped us—"Redeemed and Justified." He is the goodness restored in our soul. God's grace and mercy does not have a stamp with insufficient funds—always, in abundance. We need only to repent of our sins, acknowledge Jesus is Lord, and His blood stamps us "cleared and sufficient."

∼

INSANITY IS the new norm in our life. For the interim, I moved in with a single female relative who exuded a fun life moving around freely. I now adhere to my own established standards allowing me to navigate through each new day as signs of improvement. The missing link—a fun livelihood that could work for me. For the children's wellbeing, I dared step back into Jett's abode. Checking in on the children means facing an ever angry, prideful, and Machiavellian persona's wrath.

Unmoving; I am wearing the same issues, same piercing flaws, same anxieties, same exhaustive tactics, and the same useless reaction. Described as insanity. Ruthless. I see him digging in secret places stashed deep in my emotions while gripping damaging weaponry ready to inflict pain. There was no visible sign interesting enough to find. Pride, looks as though, has taken over Jett's focus. He knew about the multiple offensive actions inflicted on me; still unable, and too prideful to grasp its weighted gravity placed in my life. Not once... he offered an apology.

The adversary is exercising his absolute power amidst chaos. Ultimately, I attracted the exploit from another bruised ego that would tilt my spirit over the edge. And so it was, the children were not around for our agreed evening visit. When Jett's desperate mindset delivered a fatal act; re-cutting through the unhealed laceration of my spirit. Reliving atrocities once more—the assault is real. And the "mother of all bombs"—exploded. Jett inflicted the final blow into my brittle heart. Exploding any chance of deliverance to pieces.

∼

REX AND KUYA ROLANDO, co-founded a lucrative cable contracting business. With Rex's skills in business operations, coupled with Kuya Rolando's marketing master, together they built a profitable business. In completing their management staff, I accepted the position as their

Administrative Assistant. And working side by side with Rex gave a sense of protection; he beheld somber scene from that cold dark closet. I wonder if he too ever thinks about that afternoon?

Our familiar team-working, skills tightened our sibling connections giving each one confidence in performing our tasks. We enjoyed friendships in the workplace. Financial success for both management and its workforce. Alongside, extended involvement outside routine work environment with employees and their families. To most who deal with me regularly, my life on the surface appeared great and desirable. My managers' trust and belief in me grew stronger; and, they left me alone doing my job. Others say:

"Annabelle knows what she is doing. Organized, fair-dealing, rule-abiding, busy-working and happy doing so!"

I had so much independence but at a dangerous level. No one knew my hidden thoughts, not even Rex. I was teeter-tottering between doing good from bad. I was developing a growing addiction to white powder stimulants—cocaine!

Cache of temptations surrounding are easier to entertain when cries for relief attracts these luring options. Soon, I was in a classic step upward. The euphoric feeling of false value infused by hefty servings of energy powder, gave me un-natural power. Improbable sensation; I stand loosely on top of the world experiencing good sensations of physical attractiveness, confidence stance, and have visible courage. I am of value again! To appear focused on everything... I say, this is good! Investing in the *feel good* substance is lucrative in so many ways.

Alas, my life is unraveling. An IMPOSTOR has taken over my body. *She* makes me think and do what *she* wants. I have no control over the matter. All matters. To keep me deeper in the mud, my ambitious life's bluffing dealer (AKA Satan) reaches for my heart and exposes shamed emotions—holding me as his hostage for a bigger ransom—DEATH.

The ability to perceive right from wrong had disappeared from my awareness. And what went unnoticed is the administrative position entrusted by my brothers as the company's *scrutinizer* has taken a back seat. My accountability to self is gone, and I had lost conscience of rational. Soon, I alluded to having the "let's be happy" mindset with sprinkles of powder.

Rex has noticed my shifty demeanor. Diminished scruples added to my declining image and language used were enough proof. I tried to complete the unfinished attempt to end my life decades ago. Nothing bothered me at this point. Within a few months, the numbing effect of pearly powder had taken roots. It's lying effectiveness replaced a life with *its* sole solution—physical death.

One more darkened night came. After finishing up at work, I drove straight to my regular drug dealer to help drown my deep sorrows away. This trip was willful.

"I WANT TO DIE!"

"Here... some cash, give me more!"

Several hours later, I was "brought back to life" by a familiar voice. Harsh vocal tone woke my *drugged* eardrums.

"Get up!"

"Rex?" glassy-eyed, I whimpered. A quick scene of me crying in the closet came to view. But, this time... he seemed upset!

"Is that you, Rex?"

He didn't answer. Rex looked at me with disappointing eyes.

I had fallen asleep on my "righteous" supplier's couch still dressed in my work clothes. Rex drove me back to my apartment. I was so deeply buried in my guilt and shame. My brain couldn't discern the veracity—the reality is far gone. Truth! That morning was Sam's first day back to school, and I had HIGHLY forgotten. The only thing my sweet daughter wanted is for me to take her to school. I failed her.

It is unlike Rex to say cutting words, let alone sharpened ax thrown directly at me. Out of angry desperation and disappointment, Rex's final statement was ruthless.

"What is this about? Do you want to die?"

"Yes! Yes, I do!" but didn't say a word. He continued.

"If you had died today, Kuya BB would have nothing to say at your grave!"

My brother Rex's unyielding words pierced through my aching heart. Hearing our older brother's name mentioned played a note I haven't heard in a very long time. Kuya BB presented a soothing tune of hope when he shouldered Pa's responsibilities, complete and with no reservations. Desperately, I yearned for security. A cry for help at home was unheard when my brother left to serve in the U.S. Army. I cried silently at the sudden disappearance of family confidant, Attorney Ignacio. Repeated horrifying sexual assaults to my body destroyed any hope for a loving security in my future. Spirit broken—hope disappeared. I felt shamed. And so severe, I felt abandoned and isolated.

The status of being separated was a sure springboard towards a very taxing process in dissolving our marriage. Countering later, the divorce was not my choice. It was Jett's. He sternly gave me the ultimatum.

"We will not have a trial separation, let's get a divorce!" he was firm.

"All right then," I nodded in agreement.

His face tightened, looking puzzled, and surprised by my response. He didn't think I'd go through with his bluff. Jett was likely thinking he could still intimidate me with his controlling ways. Be ruled by his overpowering demeanor. Deep down, I know that we are both victims of hurts and pain. Yet, I felt nothing—it was a justified way to put the blame on someone who has hurt me. On him.

REFLECTION: Who is the common denominator in this fiery circle? How things stand, *I placed center.* I stood on its stage unable to vocalize the much crucial and troubling script. Failure to recognize, let alone verbalize my inner feelings was mine to change. My choice.

I needed to talk for a very long time. To feel real once more. Feel and touched in a healthy, loving way. Wishing I have someone I can trust to help solve all my shaming guilt. Who can I trust? I have destroyed the trust of my loved ones. Who can trust me?

My inability to talk and feel left me incapable of trust.

Lord, help us see the faces of crying souls. Of cries longing to be heard —desiring to be loved, kissed and touched. Of cries seeking forgiveness —to be free from false guilt and shame. And, extend Your healing love to shattered and broken-hearted souls around us. In Jesus' name, Amen.

Encouragement:

Proverbs 3:5-6
Trust in the Lord with all your heart, and lean not on your own understanding; in all your ways acknowledge Him, and He shall direct your paths.

(NKJV)

IN JESUS' name, I pray:

Oh, such beauty to behold, knowing You are God. To trust and obey when there is no other way but to surrender all of me at Your precious feet. You are the lifter of my heart, placing me higher than the skies. I am a bright star shining—Your brilliance to flickering others. Who can know me better than You Who created me?

19

TAKING CONTROL

I have taken control. It's clear, change is waiting at the end of the road. Spiritually and physically, my marriage had ended. In my mind, was meant to be.

REFLECTION: Getting married in my early teens and becoming a mother four months into my debutant year, 18—Paul would be a sign of God's faithfulness. Nurturing God's creation—feelings of worthiness that carried for a brief period.

Describing my first child Paul comes coated with sugar and molasses topping a chocolate cake! By not touching on the sweet goodness of "a brief period in time," tucked in my heart, is like not remembering Paul at all.

Thinking of Paul, who embodies simplicity and joyful attitude—whose hope shines brightly around. I wish to have my son's spiritual persona, full of meekness. With obvious bravery and gallantry. Just as Paul shows modesty, he has faith.

Scripture says:

"Now faith is the substance of things hoped for, the evidence of things unseen" (Hebrews 11:1). God is the lifter of Paul's soul. God shaped him with humility. Who can question a wonderful creation who relies on the Heavenly Father?

Jesus' humble Spirit displayed God's creation in Paul's humility.

Encouragement:

～

James 4:10
Humble yourselves before the Lord,
and He will lift you up.

(NIV)

～

IN JESUS' name, I pray:
Placing Your loving hands under Paul's heart, lifting his spirit with Your humble presence keeps him forever in Your bosom, directing him eternally by Your Spirit of love. Keeping me, his mother, comforted and peaceful, knowing You are His good Father in Heaven.

SNAPPING BACK TO TAKING CHARGE, "If it will be, it's up to me." I have concluded and trust that my standards are better than anyone else's. Believing, I can, and will handle all these problems by myself. Applying the self-defense mechanism I had built from long ago. This, my stoned-wall spirit, is a back-to-back militia. Equipped to charge at the commando's order.

I gave the order, a head-on battle between me and myself with a stronghold 3rd party, not wavering.

TIME PASSING SEEMS slow at first. For many months I faced a heap of decisions. In house-keeping, work office relocation, drilling days of dealing with the children's emotional well-being, and clear signs of developing personal health issues. No matter where and how I turned with all available time invested, I bear nothing but dead hope.

Feeling boxed in between the engine and its caboose, I rode on the rails of life's hefty servings of brokenheartedness. My focus was on the now relief. I need it now! Choice producing, *my way solutions*.

• • •

REFLECTION: *My way solutions*, continued to fail me for so long. Stronghold of lies had me exactly where I was. But I remembered—God's words do not go void! From the first time I heard Scripture readings from an unpopular Protestant church in Manila to humdrum Bible Studies given to members of a genuine, modest church in Tennessee; were, spirit-filled encounters.

THE WORLDLY SOLUTIONS had produced more complexity in my life than I had bargained for. I have drawn a solid dividing line with a permanent marker—splitting our family. Tearing apart two sets of families. Close friends pressured with an uneasy choice of whom to place their loyalty. And most often, to avoid further heartaches, one would stay great distances away from their original friend... rather than pick a side. Siblings from both parties were hurting for all involved. Perplexed on what to do, most kept their comments zipped shut.

Our children were the most affected in seeing both their parents battle, resulting from their own feelings of abandonment. Hurtful language cutting through innocent hearts. Being forced to choose which parent to defend. Who to stay with? And which one to love on? Viewing hurtful scenes... they, too, are spiraling down towards more hurts.

The fear of inflicting more harm and indecisiveness on the children, though emotionally painful, I backed off. I find no logical reason to say anything more to our young children. Instead, I kept the full truth to myself.

REFLECTION: Remembering those flashback moments in which my parents kept their disagreements away from view, resulted in some sanity for their children. I aimed for mental health. I needed filling of His Holy Spirit. Of His courage and strength to carry on.

Retreating from the insane behavior I have been engaging with, came easier.

Encouragement:

∼

Isaiah 55:11
So shall my word be that goes out from my mouth; it shall not return empty, but it shall accomplish that which I purpose, and shall succeed in the thing for which I sent it.

(ESV)

∼

IN JESUS' name, I pray:
Sweet words of encouragement from God Himself—Spiritual food for our dehydrating life is nourishment for our starving souls. Patiently, He is waiting for our response. Eagerly and lovingly stands but by a few inches—ready to pour out His amazing and everlasting love.

COMING up with the list of solutions was an easy task. Starting with my perception of what is right from what is wrong. *Right*, is the accuracy of my belief based on what I feel to be true. It is fitting to assume what my view is. It begins on how things feel inside. The reasoning was mine to give. My standard and mine alone.

The abusive behavior has taken an analogous effect. As I became numb, Jett's set-in-stone process of filtering my, as he often referred to, **"bad blood,"** continued! The contemptible reactions, slicing looks, demanding tone, and degrading smirks were no match to my anesthetized heart. He didn't grasp the atrocious effect that all offenders, including himself, have achieved. Oppression towards me had reached its peak level. How high? I can easily see Mount Everest below.

I had submitted to everyone else's desires, demands, and wants for too long. Not to be outdone; trained by life's billhooks, whips and chains—I charged forward full speed, holding nothing back and attacked with intent to annihilate evildoers.

∼

OVER TWO YEARS of battling is sapping my vitality at a pace I can't keep up with. Energy begets more energy! Getting fit and healthy suited my personal solutions. I signed up for a gym membership at a local establishment. The now active lifestyle established in my youth continues to show healthful outcome. It proved to be a break towards my wellbeing. During the many entanglements in my marriage, getting physically fit showed signs of a healthier mind and body. To be mentally tough. Be physically strong to endure the punches, literally.

Looking to build stamina, I took an aerobic class at the new local gym. Exercising in a group setting is new. A newness that brings the change needed. As a young child, I could play outdoors all day and if needed, labor arduously most days. Aerobics' physical movements for more than an hour, don't fall on Bibe's challenge tab. Not then, not now.

Members recognize Joseph, a group exercise class instructor for coaching physically demanding workout classes. So, it is fitting that I, the Queen of challenges, try this *hard* class. No argument here after two tries; I've concluded, his workout is a "bit," challenging.

With a friendly demeanor, Joseph, always enters his class sporting a confident smile and greeters reciprocate with happy beams around. He leads a fun-choreographed workout session often ending with members' grateful cheers and delivers great anticipation for his next class. His passion to help others achieve physical fitness is clear in his driven coaching style. He has balance. An attractive, alluring spirit that always seems to have members flood him with personal inquiries. Joseph speaks every word with passion and clarity. Easy terms he uses, even I, understand. He is a definite attraction for everyone who takes his class… especially for me.

I sensed projecting out of Joseph a similar trait to my father's soft persona. Confidence in humble astuteness. Recognizable, skilled in his field and gifted in teaching. I admire his calm mannerism—an attribute long missing in my life.

MOVING TOWARDS IMPROVEMENT, my personal therapy sessions were valuable in giving me starting points. In particular, Ms. Therapist made an explicit suggestion: "Draw up a plan." Though listing critical priorities in my life became cumbersome. She warned of reacting hastily. "Jumping out of a burning pan into the fire," per se. Visualize desired changes and "make your plans."

For me, "jumping" would be like full-grown tadpoles. Those tough, black greenish-colored, leaping creatures in bulging eyes—leap from one rock to the next. Jumping across puddles into larger mere where fresher and greener-looking vegetation flourishes. Where food is plentiful—flying residents are in abundance. I was jumping around looking for the "fresher and greener" side of life. Food for my hungry soul and water to quench my thirsty heart!

Is it I that needs changing? "For things to change; something has to change!" I have heard of Norman Vincent Peale's famous quote: "Change your thoughts and you change your world!"

How do I change, my thoughts? I hear, "You did this to yourself; bad girl!" The thinking process... from bad to good?

Self-development books were plentiful and so my journey back into reading, fully ignited.

REFLECTION: In the many years of choosing what material to read; flipping through hundreds of pages in self-development books followed my time with the Lord in His Word.

~V~
READING IS KNOWLEDGE GAINED; A REMEDY FOR THE WEARY.

COLLECTIONS OF QUOTES from many poised, passionate motivators, fully spirited leaders, and selfless individuals are available. One great legendary motivational speaker, the late Zig Ziglar's inimitable panache is one "Cat" person from the many I try to copy. Jim Rohn, an enthusiast is a motivating force to thousands; I now follow his practice of leaving an after dinner dining tip "like a rich man," though strapped for money! I love it, "tip like I am a rich girl." Inside I felt wealthy—attitude pushes up your altitude higher. And not leaving your children in a mess—invest hours of praying in kneeling form.

A LIST OF GREAT "CAT-PERSONS" I try to duplicate:

- **Barbara Johnson's** humorous style is honey in my flavor-lacking world.
- **Elisabeth Elliot's** passion for purity drove my deep desire to be pure—her forgiving heart moved my hardened heart towards accepting God's forgiveness, forgiving myself, and extending forgiveness to others.
- **Dr. James C. Dobson's** lesson of tenderness in having a "Tough Love," a hard call, yet, may be the only "call!" In two of my favorite books I learned more about my husband, son, and brothers in "Bringing Up Boys"—as I understood exactly how God created me in reading "Bringing Up Girls."
- **Charles Colson's** intelligence with humility, aid in understanding my faith in the Living God.
- **Frank Pastore's** daily radio show took me to advance education in motion and emotions; how complete I am in God, Who is the head of all principality.
- **Josh McDowell's** boldness and courage—engendered the evidence, proving our Messiah, Jesus Christ—exists. Resulted in my deeper desire to dig for more.
- **Ruth Bell Graham**, helped me identify others housing broken hearts.
- **Billy Graham's** life story is altogether amazing; his love for God—led millions to Christ.
- **Joni Eareckson-Tada's** extraordinary show of endurance in suffering. She keeps in the race—fighting the good fight; whilst, helping those who are in need.

And so many others, whose names I have written in my journals—my inspirations forever.

• • •

FINALLY, now that I am applying my own solutions, order in the house is imminent. Factoring on personal experiences in the past and present and using what I have learned would be the best outcome. Established by my own standards, I now hold the solution—my very own, moral compass.

Don't challenge me, I've been through a lot! My life's resume summarizes, "Over Qualified." Born and raised in a third-world country, I lived in close quarters with nineteen, co-inhabitants. Hunger was a great felt. Long hours of arduous labor don't scare me. I am a survivor of death-defying natural disasters. I have dealt with loved ones appear and disappear from deaths and departures. Over and above, I can scout those *would be perpetrators*!

Ultimately, the madness in life has affected my health to the point of near death. I had occupied three different hospitals' ICU patient rooms. Diagnosed with COPD-pneumonia, each time I fought hard to heal. I wasn't ready to die. At the first diagnosis, they placed me in an oxygen tent for treatment.

Seeing through to the other side of the transparent tent, was Rex's smiling face. My brother's happy expression didn't match his head's side-to-side shaking movements... made me revisit a sizzling dialog he mentioned recently:

"Ate Bibe!" then the following question after his comments continued.

"When, will you take care of the 'problem?'"

"You're only killing yourself!"

Unable to pull much air from infected lungs, soft answers struck the mother cord deep inside. I want my children!

"I don't want to die!" I meant it.

"My children need me."

Though I occupied two more ICU hospital rooms in the following months, there was no obvious change in sight. Insanity seems to rule! Who can purify... this, my infested thought process?

REFLECTION: It was back in one of Joseph's group exercise class, when I asked him a lead question. I inquired for a book recommendation —a nutritional related reading material. He did. That led me to inviting him to meet me for lunch. To thank him in person for the informative and helpful material he had given me. *Yes, I had intentions.*

His confidence, humorous ways, and calm demeanor have been weaving in and out of my mind. And his physical looks... undeniably, handsome—attractive in every manner of speech. If you know what I mean! He attracts the goodness from people. That means goodness lives in him. We saw more of each other.

JOSEPH, took the second and third times to help nurture me back to health. My children didn't know about my illness, but their father did. He kept Paul and Sam from calling when they wanted to speak with me. He had personal reasons. I didn't want to add worries—none of my children found out. I wasn't in the state of acceptable persona to battle further. More detrimental was that my children were made to believe I was too busy to care!

Even the incessant, testy, child-custody court appearances couldn't drown my strong desires to take care and protect my children. For four years, nothing stopped us from pursuing the same result. Each wanting to gain physical custody of our children. Our inability to agree on the physical custody of the children, resulted in the court order of a Court Mediator, Child Psychologist to our case. The Mediator will interview Paul because the girls are too young; then, will present his findings and recommendations to the court. Determined to claim the same results as I; Jett, the petitioner, used manipulating dialog, only hurting the children's innocent minds further.

Using the children's well-rehearsed interview; finely tuned by their father, an innocent appeal. His father instructed Paul, exactly on what to say to the Mediator that would give the picture of me, as an unfit mother. Further devastated my son's mind. Paul gave the word-for-word —a statement—his two sisters' desire, is to live with their father. I felt so deeply hurt for my son... the coercion destroyed his spirit further. However, I know my son's deep longing to please his father. To feel supported and connected. For his father to be proud of him. Paul has long yearned for his father's acceptance... just the way he is!

The court issued a joint custody order in favor of Jett. With the notable solid verbal warning: "There will be 'No' physical discipline imposed on all minor children."

We lived by the court's order. As simple as that sounds, it was most distressing. Knowing the children are in an unhealthy surrounding—torment to my soul.

How do I place order in the house? As guilt and shame continue to pile on, reinforcing *that* feeling of being a failure.

Selfishness.

Dishonesty.

Prideful.

And weighted disagreeing methods played out. Each of us players alter the true point of our moral compass with its needle shaking profusely—unable to settle.

Encouragement:

Daniel 2:22
It is He who reveals the profound and hidden things; He knows what is in the darkness, and the light dwells with Him.

(NASB)

IN JESUS' name, I pray:

Inside, I was wrestling. Restless in following my own standards! I know that You, oh Lord, slowed my mind and strengthened my soul. All secrets belong to You. In time, and for a greater purpose; to reveal is Yours.

James 4:6
God resists the proud but gives grace to the humble.

(NKJV)

Twenty-four seven, I was on the go, facing daily distressing challenges of life. Oh, how I wish I could take each step effortlessly as I did climbing the infamous *Aratilis* fruit tree. Driving round-trip—working and single-parenting full-time. At home dinner preparation and clean-up. Brown-bagging lunches for the following school day. During the night hours and weekends—overseeing school homework and activities. Grocery shopping, do laundry on weekdays and the rest on weekends. And oh... the driving—if only I have a personal driver! (An Uber or a Lyft, maybe ;)

WEEKEND DRIVING WOULD SAP the rest of my borrowed energy. Jett has picked up interest in a woman living further away. He moved in with his new girlfriend and took the children with him with no regards to how the distance would further strain our travel time... in particular, my travel time. To loosen up some precious time, I completed other chores on weeknights. Free to be me—even for a short time. All along in the subterranean of my sub-consciousness, I was visualizing an emotional rest.

A child's heart is pure and honest; even during a chaotic life. Little De's words of wisdom before entering the heightened court order of providing transportation on weekend visits to their father, she comments:

"Mom, you haven't tried 'it' (driving) yet, and you're so worried." She was right!

REFLECTION: God used a child's candor to hand-deliver a message: "Have faith, and trust in Me." I didn't recognize His voice then, but He was vocalized by my daughter's words. God was nourishing a seed planted in the grounds of my soul years earlier. All the tilling, weeding, suckering, and de-worming of a diseased soul were taking place.

"I am the resurrection and the life" (John 11:25). The Messiah is in my life—rides with me even in slow-moving traffic. Driving to Orange County on a Friday evening often keeps the traffic at sloth-like speed. It would take more trips before tuning-in to radio stations. Music then, only kept my mind adrift. No permanent solution around, only "The passing pleasures of sin" (Hebrews 11: 25). I was not interested in the perpetual answer. I rejected the things of God because I focused on "the now". Wanting relief now.

Rejecting of the Holy Spirit—the unpardonable sin was incomprehensible. But the Gospel of Jesus Christ in His Holy Spirit instilled more than a curiosity to understand. The Savior was Who I needed. God is so good. He is faithful to complete His good work, started in me, and in you. Allowing the wrestling of my soul's weariness, emptiness, and loneliness to deepen. He leads me to the Cross.

~V~
YOUR SPIRIT IS FIXED ON MY SHAKY SOUL, O LORD;
HOLDING ME IN STEADY FORM.

SIMILAR TRAITS to my late father, Joseph has a set of attentive and heeding ears. He has enduring abilities accompanied by an attentive heart. Hearing every word shared. He listens to the dire cries of my soul. Early into our relationship, I tossed Joseph into the sounds of a crackling fire. I talked. There, he was standing by my side, with ears open. Being heard is more personal and relational for me. Years of despairing and wishing—now someone listens to my broken spirit. Yes, hope is now breaking through. Revitalized by the freshness of facing pure and intentional eyes focused on my inner self.

Willingness is an attitude of the heart—a window to true intent. This man is right. I am so lucky, Joseph's interest towards me and my children are well-meaning. Unlucky, it reeled Joseph in by the master of bitterness—and became the target of fault. No longer was the validated dissenting marriage's painful past justified, as Joseph became the target and the major *reason* for the divorce. Concerned for the children, Joseph kept silent. He was studying child psychology and understood the struggle.

A familiar choice. A selfless choice.

Encouragement:

TAKING CONTROL | 161

Matthew 11:28-30
Come to me, all you who are weary and burdened, and I will give you rest. Take my yoke upon you and learn from me, for I am gentle and humble in heart, and you will find rest for your souls. For my yoke is easy and my burden is light.

(NIV)

∽

IN JESUS' name, I pray:
Great is Your faithfulness! Jesus, may your Spirit of strength be in those who are burdened, giving rest to their tired souls. "Like a deer pants for the water brook, so do our souls pant for You Oh Lord" (Psalm 42:1).

I WITNESSED WHAT SELFLESS, love is very early on through my parents. Both Pa and Ma shared their provisions beyond giving financial support to relatives. Righteous characteristics I graciously appreciate and try to follow.

Ma was living her life in full commitment, loyalty, and respect to an unfaithful man—her love for my father was incomprehensible! After my father's passing, she entertained a potential partner in life, but could not match the glowing presence exuded around her truest love. The many years of witnessing my mother's love imparted to my father, is a model of selfless vow.

Joseph's pure intentions stand out. I dated no one before my marriage, though recent experiences have equipped me to detect a troubled mind. My eyes see no symptoms of such. Without a doubt, he and I have similar standards. Joseph defines health and wellness in its sincerest form. A choice heralding a healthy mind. Moreover, he respects my space and supports motherhood! As the court order ended, we stayed together—adhering to our own standards. My justification is that I am in love and happy. So God would be okay with such happiness.

. . .

162 | A KISS WITHOUT ANY SHAME

THE STANDARDS I HAVE, only accomplished basic personal needs. I am looking for someone who could meet all of my needs. Who could fill the emptiness of my heart? My need for a human savior. So much telltale about Jesus, still He appeared to be beyond my reach. My experiences with those "chosen" individuals in robe attires, traditionally conveyed from the holiest of holies—a total confusion. Amending my repenting, young, passive soul by completing the recitals of penances. To receive redemption, I would have to prove my worthiness for a savior. Walking onto those holy grounds placed in front and center stage usually behind the speaker, I am often reminded of a "Savior" hung *and* nailed to the cross. He *is* dead. How can he save me? I have to be pure and clean before I can be in his presence. Pure, I am not!

That's it, I will paint a redeemer of my own.

Sounding self-seeking, yet in reasoning—if I had been more self-centered, maybe I would not have been an easy victim. Not again. I know how my savior would look like, act like, smell like, and he would be my go to Genie. No need to pray, "Just do as I say!"

Encouragement:

∽

Matthew 27:51
Then behold, the veil of the temple was torn in two from top to bottom.

(NKJ)

∽

IN JESUS' name, I pray:

Anyone can find You, our Redeemer, our Savior, and Lord; Jesus Christ's complete and unconditional love in Him alone. Let us come freely through torn pieces of the veil, surrendering ourselves to Your Spirit of rest and peace. May Your Spirit deliver each person's brokenness into Your healing hands and experience—refreshing of mind and soul.

• • •

WITH HIGH HOPES, I applied the imaginary brush strokes to fill the emptiness in my heart. And as my heart receives the varied brush strokes applied, I imagined the undeniable likeness of my redeemer. Designed with all the attributes that would enable him to love me, unconditionally!

REFLECTION: My One and only Redeemer waits ever so patiently as He moves each puzzle of my life, creating His masterpiece!

20

GUILT VS. SHAME

*E*ither way, human conscience gives off a clear response—with a right from a wrong method. Vice versa! In suffering from guilt and shame for years, my feelings of both have settled to an acceptable level. In which, there are no alterations necessary—setting my standards in stone. Allowing only for the acceptable reactions.

Anyone who disagrees with the set of standards I created, has no role-playing in my life's bravura stage. I have survived living in guilt and shame. Guilt in allowing *it* to victimize myself. Getting along with the boys and desiring only pure fun brought malicious meaning to my offenders, who robbed me of my innocence and left me to rot. In deep emptiness and longing for my father, I was an easy catch reeled into the hands of perpetrators.

The guilty bearing has been in hidden sight into my adult life. Piling up are feelings of guilt from harmful actions. I now inflict on others. Yet, there is something inside I could not distinguish between the inner or outer sense. They conflict my conscience. Are these wrestling senses connected to a greater presence—a spiritual being? God? Can God love everyone, even someone like me? Is there any truth to this claim?

What is the truth? And claimed by whom?

REFLECTION: I have been battling with making the "right" decision for a very long time. Even following my set of standards came with uncertainties. Wrestling with a very strong clamp in my life; guilt and shame anchored deep in my soul. Ever-growing conflicts surrounded me. My siblings were dealing with similar challenges. And none has opened-up either. God is faithful to the prayers of His Saints. He allowed moralistic paths for *the* set of standards to get through. Continued tussling, bustling, and tensing placed me in a desperate fight for change.

In learning there is false guilt and true guilt, FEAR has taken its acronym to its fullest potential; in "False Evidence Appearing Real." My perpetrators falsifying their heinous doing... the fault is mine alone. Fear infiltrated my out-of-order conscience, I believed this lie.

The assaults done in obscured places have caused me to feel ugly. I was in obvious solitary confinement. My dire need to disclose brokenness was vanishing for fear of other's acceptance and judgment. Perception of my innocence is vital—I believed, just in that acceptance, I will heal. But, I didn't know how. Where to begin, and who to confide?

Encouragement:

∼

Psalm 119:104
Through Your precepts I get understanding;
Therefore, I hate every false way.

(NKJV)

∼

IN JESUS' name, I pray:

Truth is harder, yet liberating. Empowering light eclipse dark's safeness. Jesus, the voice in the dark—One truth that lights the world —Sovereign in all creation. There is One and only true Son of God, One true King, Lord of Lords—Jesus Christ.

May Your truth redeem a darkened heart with supreme excellence, ruling power, and divine presence—the golden key unlocking the door to a broken heart.

∼

The imaginary canvas reveals my redeemer. He is beardless, unlike the Jesus represented by mere brush strokes. Perfect in appearance. Smiles in confidence. And just like my Pa, versed in higher education. My brush strokes produced a savior with absolute love at the center. I want to touch and feel his love always. Filled with admiration, I looked at the finished work of art; a spirit-filled, "Visual-Augmented" piece. Where shall I find such a person?

REFLECTION: Pure insanity! Again, I pursued the change from a human being for redemption. Standing in front, is Joseph, who displays a comprehensive bodysuit of qualities—the best candidate. There is no father-figure available nearby to sit on the godly throne. My brothers are all married. One has re-married. Each one has a busy and intricate life paralleling mine.

Prayer seems to pop up in my mind more times than I can remember. In the past of dire lost and need have me calling to God. These days, I have been in a zoning state—conversing. Not to myself... I think... with God. Odd feeling—there is some kind of higher dimension around my surroundings. Snapping back to reality. The worrisome problem continues over my children. My two innocent young daughters are out there—vulnerable. Missing the girls evermore when they are out of my secured beehive-like protection.

Deep in my heart, I wish to be wrong about many things. During a period of uneasy thoughts of *time will tell*, it came—sooner. Hard evidence lay waiting on the judge's table. The same judge who presided in the prior ruling saw the evidence submitted and found the petitioner in contempt of court and ruled in favor of me, the respondent. The court granted a joint physical custody of the girls with more time in favor of, me, the mother; and, granted Paul's request to live with his father. Coupled with a regretful acknowledgement by Your Honor, followed his ruling with an apology handed.

"On behalf of the court; I apologize for the misgiving."

The Judge aimed, the gavel landed on my side.

I felt relieved. And yes, the much-needed healing is underway.

. . .

REFLECTION: Led by the formidable advice of his new girlfriend, Jett agreed to placing Paul, in a Group Home Facility. Where he lived for most of his growing adult life. Red light signal flashing; alerts and more alerts!

I am somebody's daughter, a victim of abuse. Deep anger, hatred, resentment, and bitterness from long past have damaged Jett's ability to distinguish tactical works of the world's chief adversary—Satan.

"Do not be deceived, God is not mocked; for whatever a man sows, that shall he also reaps" (Galatians 6:7). Lord, I pray for Your mighty protection for our little children and those who are under the care of another. May You cover each one with the divine protective layer in their awakening and slumber periods.

May Your loving kindness convict each offender and Your Spirit of conviction awaken dead souls—to walk in the brilliance of Your forgiving heart. May each healing and newness be the salt and light of the world for You. In Jesus' name, I pray. Amen!

JOSEPH, my ally's presence, provided the atmospheric sense of security during the difficult times in the courthouse. During my embroilment in each court day, I felt Joseph's genuine strength and solid support on my back. His gallantry—unwavering. His presence giving me a sense of security. I felt at ease. This person has my back and for the right reason—he cares.

The children and I moved out from one of Kuya BB's home into a house nearby which included a separate dwelling in the backyard. Joseph took his residency in this one-room structure behind the main house. A humbled dwelling as we decided "staying together" may not be best for all involved. Though Joseph continued to provide much help in our everyday life. He shared everything. Emotional, financial, and father-role support poured out.

Most evenings, Joseph tutored De in class assignments—often, they discuss other matters of her day in school. She talked, he listened. One of Joseph's great attribute, he listens. Seeing her tremendous need for a healthy father-role relationship, I thanked God for Joseph's pure intentions. He is an educated person who encourages achievements in both education and personal growth. Both girls have lived a troubled life; drained with decision-making on who to choose, mom or dad? Sam's and De's minds, bodies, and souls are wearing.

Is that hallucinating state of my mind thinking? Those imaginary lines on the canvas—forming life? Here to protect us is the "Knight in shining armor."

JOSEPH IS FAR FROM TIMID, his love-in-action; noting his interest for the children and I, is genuine. In good time, he purchased a townhouse in a nearby city and we parted ways. With the minimal child support I receive, Joseph offered financial resources for me and the girls. His support went through the roof. Aware of my wish to own a home, his generous notion was spot on. Love-inspired in motion, he wrote a check for the down payment needed to purchase our first townhome. This three-story high living quarters with spacious floor plan, allowed plenty space for Sam and De, each a bedroom of their own. A master bedroom with its walk-in closet, lavished bathroom and a shower-tub combo big enough for nineteen, co-inhabitants! Ha-ha. Right! Not to mention, an enclosed pool for the owners.

What closed the Real Estate purchase deal? Our new roomy residence is a short-walking distance to the girls' high school.

Joseph's commute from his Baldwin Park condo to work in Santa Monica was long, even in the wee hours of the morning. Yet, he made time for us. I appreciate his sincere desire and great effort to help with the girls in school and at home.

A captain of an East Los Angeles City college volleyball team, Joseph embodied passion in athleticism and love for education. Surprised? *Don't be, Annabelle,* if you are in the crowd of parents cheering for one of De's many long distance runs. Or, Sam's Drill Team tryouts and performances—Joseph takes the lead. He is at every event for both Sam and De. Smack in the midst, he leads the coaching and louder cheers. Embarrassing on some occasions. Ha-ha. He was a towering support for the three of us. An invincible loving presence unrecognized. Joseph enjoyed and loved every moment of tutoring De and watching her excel in education.

On the family's entertainment side of things, we enjoyed playing board games, going to activity engagements, live concerts, and plays.

Joseph has taken us on fun-filled road trips. From California's Central Coastline, Arrowhead and Big Bear mountains to Arizona's mystical Sedona Resorts—he never pulled back from sharing all he had. What a treat! He makes himself available, should De or Sam need to talk. Though not always in agreement, Joseph listened with an open mind, heart, and ears. All the while—Joseph experiences mudslinging. Sadly, given plentiful to the children—verbally published libel by the accuser.

Looking to be... those brush strokes on the canvas have come to life. Joseph can provide all of our needs—equipped with patience, and vigor to tackle those I cannot. I was lucky. A divorcee with three children, several years his senior—I hit the jackpot!

My burning questions: "Will Joseph be able to clear away the guilt and shame buried deep inside my soul? If he could, how?" He is but a man!

DAY AFTER DAY, I witnessed Joseph's unconditional love in action. He makes sure we have food on the table. Food varieties similar to the Sabella-family holiday celebrations back at the Villa Dolores bungalow. There is no lacking in food.

The travesty of hunger is a daily reminder, how lucky that I live in the U.S. I understand food crisis and poverty still exists all over the world, even in many parts of America!

Choices of bread and ketchup are plentiful. Nowadays, this semi-filling sandwich is not at the top ten of my preferred food selections. There is a plethora of choices from poultry, seafood, and beef. Ice cream is my favorite dessert, vying for a spot in the freezer box. Plenty of lunchmeat choices: from smoked ham, honey-turkey, and yes, roast beef too. Local farmer-grown fruits and vegetables at nearby spacious city spots. And oh the milk, in heavenly abundance! I might serve you labeled beverages at meal times. The probability that you'll have a glass of clear, crisp, cool water is greater. Should anyone want ice in their water, there is plenty available! Sam and De both love Capri Sun drinks—the sisters' favored drink, an item placed in their daily school lunch bags.

. . .

REFLECTION: Thank God for the U.S. Governmental support available to individuals and families needing aid. Thanking God further; that we live in the USA. We are so blessed to have the opportunity! It is humbling to experience hunger when preceded by abundance. I remember when steamed white rice topped with boiled bitter-melon or charcoal roasted eggplant, garnished amid sautéed fermented anchovies (my personal favorites)—would grace my hungry stomach.

My heart swells with so much gratitude in having access to complete nutrition, three times or more each day. Work or jobs in the western world in various professions are available to a wide range of ages; offering business opportunities attainable to those who desire to do so. Young and older workers afford to provide food on the table for their families.

Encouragement:

Matthew 6:26
Look at the birds of the air; they do not sow or reap
or store away in barns,
and yet your heavenly Father feeds them.
Are you more valuable than they?

(NIV)

IN JESUS' name, I pray:

Oh Lord, the provisions You serve us daily are plentiful and overwhelming. Thank you for jump-starting my life in a humbling beginning; where Your continued blessings of family, food, and secured comfort of home are more than sufficient. Help keep me forever grounded in Your ways instilled from long ago.

SAM AND DE have settled into their new schedule. Family and friends they longed for, have welcomed both in sweet open arms. Two broken spiritual structures have begun the first step towards repair. Relief in seeing healing is underway; I have embraced the busy surroundings, seeing happy faces. For the moment, I cherish their renewed presence. Deep down, I was jumping in gratitude. Sam and De have waved their white flag... a plea for years—both lives were draining out to levels of danger. Both parents helped damage their sense of security! Who can they trust, not their mom or dad!

Though, the relief seemed temporary; I thanked God. Where does one go to find a giant cutter and loosen the strong bondage of guilt?

Encouragement:

∽

John 3:16
For God so loved the world He gave His only begotten Son, that whoever believes in Him should not perish but have everlasting life.
(NKJV)

∽

IN JESUS' name, I pray:
I want to live; free from the bondage of sin, complete liberty from guilt and shame. You, oh Lord my Savior Jesus Christ is the One Person Who can wash my sins making me pure with Your sacrificial blood. Please transform my self-centeredness into Your likeness; filling a deep void, help me be like You.

21

MEETING GOD'S GRACE, FACE-TO-FACE

*T*wo years of adjusting, re-connecting, and nurturing are in steady stride. The busyness of our day has evolved to welcome pleasantries; work and school periods have interlaced in healthful ways. My spirit is calming. Having the girls around is a major factor and Joseph's solid commitment is helping remove uncertainties—loving security in my life. My heart longs for Paul. Feeling restless. I feel something inside... not thumping... a stirring towards God.

Looking for God in a building, I set out to attend a neighboring church. Traditional upbringing is a mapping I can start in search of God. Remembering my mother's instructions: "Dress up and go attend, mass!" Seldom, I wear a dress. But going to church is a special time.

Santo Domingo Church's structure is massive and magnetizing. Built in 1954—the Spanish-influenced architectural beauty emits holy sensation and welcoming atmosphere to the surrounding cities of Quezon City. The church's design is breathtaking. Along with the expanded mass schedule held inside its centuries-old structure, provides an awesome regal view drawing thousands of worshipers.

Yet in my search, I found God nowhere in, or around the Los Angeles Metropolitan area churches. This *Jesus*, alleged to save lives still appearing to be lifeless on a cross. Most say, "His lifeless body represents His sacrificial suffering. His death. His life for the sin of the world. He died so we may live!" I don't understand. I need a living *Person*! Curiosity building up each day leads me to deep yearning.

Life has been chaotic, unstable, rash—my spirit is bleeding dry. Not wanting to perish—I opened my heart and asked. Redemption; not by just anybody—by the Living God. Please, release me from the bondage of guilt and shame. Free to live. Sounding beautiful as God's grace and mercy I have heard about. Words of encouragement surfaces: "God so love the world..." that means me too. "That He gave His only begotten Son..." (John 3:16), our Savior in Christ. A gift with a promise of *everlasting life* to those who would believe in Jesus Christ.

Encouragement:

Mark 15:38-39
The temple curtain torn in two, from top to bottom.
And when the centurion, who stood there in front of Jesus, saw how He died, he said: "Surely this Man was the Son of God!"

(NIV)

IN JESUS' name, I pray:
Everlasting life! A promise to behold; completed when on that day at Calvary, Jesus uttered: "It is finished." I believe in You, oh my Lord and my Redeemer. The torn curtain gives me direct access to the holiest of holies anywhere, on any day.

LOVING my children without conditions is harder than persuading myself *it* to be. I avoided facing my reality. In looking at my reality, it's no wonder my existence is cloudy. I didn't want to face any more smudges.

Teenagers are tough. Someone once said: "Raising babies and young children are physically draining; raising teenagers is heart-taxing." Just ask Joseph... and he'll add, "Especially teenage girls!"

There is little in life's experiences that could have prepared me *suit-*

able as a teenager's mother. Yet, I believe raising girls are tougher. Now, this may not be as fair as one would think. The matter, Paul is a Special Needs child is no comparison. As my teenage lifelong struggle with remorse would be an unfair platform. Maybe, I held my bearing in mimicking my mother's style. I was in fear of similar hurtful things happening to my daughters. WHAT IF THAT HAPPENS? And, WHAT IF THAT PERSON HURTS HER? More dreadful feelings piled on the mountain-heap pile of FEAR? Remember, False Evidence Appearing Real, hopped on the road with me again.

MUSIC AND DANCING MOST OFTEN than not is a happening fun time for Joseph and I. Though, there were exposures to *worldly* fun; we joined in as the wave of disco dancing advanced. No sooner, it's phase developed the same way as those "fun," I tried before. Liquor does not agree with my light-weight, any more than the white sprinkles long gone. In my sobering phase from the pleasures of life, I hopped on a purposeful pursuit for my Savior.

Something drove me to search for a traditional church but felt exhausted. It was during this tiring pursuit we receive an invitation to attend a church service.

Encouragement:

Jeremiah 29:11-14
For I know the thoughts I think towards you (Annabelle), says the Lord, thoughts of peace and not of evil, to give you a future and a hope. Then you will call upon Me and go and pray to Me, and I will listen to you. And you will seek Me and find *Me*, when you search for Me with all your heart, I will be found by you, says the Lord, and I will bring you back from your captivity.

(NKJV)

MEETING GOD'S GRACE, FACE-TO-FACE | 175

In Jesus' name, I pray:

Thank You, that my search has led me to Your promise, oh my Father in heaven. You have loosened the shackles of guilt and shame that have tied me for so long. And for *bringing me back from my captivity*, blessing me with Your absolute love.

I met Joseph's youngest sister, Kathie, about the same time we dated. She, too, is a regular in the aerobics class. While dealing with the emotionally draining court battle, she was a breath of sunshine in my life throughout a darkened time. Kathie is fourteen years younger yet her intelligence and wittiness have me tagging alongside her happy world. Her smile lights up my day—the sincerity of heart displayed. Akin to her older sibling, Kathie, makes me laugh in her humble mannerism. We learned of each other's painful pasts and we bonded in fitting ways. For a brief time, we worked together in a corporate office setting. Together, we attended family events and partied amongst many friends. Los Angeles' own Circus Disco place was a regular venue to meet, dance, and party the night away.

Carlos, also an Aerobic Group Class Instructor and one of the family's group of friends, has been dating Kathie. The committed triathlete, Carlos, lives his athleticism with passion. His outward appearance would come across—conventional. Though, his chic ways could pass for a high fashion brand model—debonair for sure. Yet, beyond his chic ways, I see a humble guy. I am familiar with eyes which speak of a different world.

A world full of life. Carlos came from an impoverished country. He and I know where we came from! What we have experienced and seen! Both speak our "back home" languages, he speaks in Spanish; and I, Tagalog! Still, we understand one another in deeper ways.

Unbeknownst to us, Carlos and Kathie have been attending a Christian church in a nearby city. Something enlightening is noticeable about their presence—a *Spiritual* newness. Both have been sharing the good news. The *Gospel*.

My endless curiosity for a Savior readied me to accept Kathie's invitation to attend Calvary Chapel's, Sunday's service in West

Covina. Their chapel's services start with praise music sing-along; an enlightenment. They read and study Scriptures straight from the Bible. There is something similar to her description of the chapel's services... worship time and reading of Scriptures, with the pastor conducting Bible Studies. Fellowship after. The chapel's praise music and reading are parallel to the Protestant Church I attended back in Manila.

"Is Raul like a Priest?" I quipped. Kathie answered.

"A Pastor." A title I have heard of. But not "Calvary Chapel."

I WAS FEELING RATHER nervous while preparing for the much-expected and long-awaited church activities. A thrilling sensation similar to meeting a royalty, I dressed up in my best dress. Sunday church service is not new to me. I have attended a nearby Methodist church before. In Tennessee, my interest in worship music by a congregation of fifty members followed a Bible Study. Though, the study seemed a waste—yet God's words spoken then are now taking roots.

It's Sunday and the girls are away visiting their father. As usual, feelings of antsy-ness during *these* visits, wrestles my heart. Kathie picked me up with ample time to drive down West Covina. She hopped on the 10-Interstate Freeway going eastbound. As Kathie shares the goodness of her morning, I hear her vocals change. It was bothersome, though I did not know why?

Something struck me with a powerful darkened video re-playing of *that* night—the night I was driving with the children to my brother's home. *What is happening here? And, why is this happening? (Is there anybody listening out there?)*

Where is this re-reeling of darkened past coming from? Trying so hard to focus on our conversation... as my body shakes and pushes off chilling thoughts out of my head. At that moment, we heard a loud popping sound... POW!

Kathie veered off to the nearest left shoulder as the car seemed to have rode over potholes on the road. I stepped out and seen the left rear passenger tire had blown out. It is now thirty minutes before the praise music begins—we'll be late. We have no mobile phones; neither could call for help. I felt disappointed with the possibility of not attending the service. Is *this* strange force trying its best to keep us from attending? In particular, me from attending!

Kathie and I went to work to replacing the blown-out tire. Within ten minutes of digging through the car's trunk for tools and spare tire, a road highway *help* arrived. Two experts in changing flat tires... workers in orange vests completed the spare tire replacement within five minutes. We drove off waving to two speedway angels. I say, sent by God! *Evil force, you are NO MATCH to God's plans!*

Worship has started and for the first time, I felt an indescribable peace. Amid our morning challenges; God is faithful to bless our day. Pastor Raul is uncompromising, bold in his message, straightforward —he shared the Word of God with passion. God is knocking at the door of my heart.

Pastor Raul invited everyone to receive God's gift of salvation.

Encouragement:

∽

Revelation 3:20
Here I am! I stand at the door and knock. If anyone hears my voice and opens the door, I will come in and eat with that person, and they with me.

(NIV)

∽

IN JESUS' name, I pray:
You are faithful, Oh Lord; to see me through those darkened days. Never knowing You were by my side—carrying my heavy load, collecting my tears, and stands waiting at the door of my heart.

"FATHER GOD, I believe in Your love for me. I have faith in Your only begotten Son, my Savior Jesus Christ's sacrificial love. Forgive me of my sins. With my Savior's blood, wash away all the guilt and shame. Make me a new woman of God. Pure in your presence with a new heart, a new mind, and a clear conscience. Add my name in the book of life, forever. In Jesus' name, I ask, Amen."

. . .

I HAVE FOUND the truth in God and He had set me free! Our Father Who art in Heaven, through Christ, I can be in His presence; a treasured privilege. Oh, how I feel so, so loved by the God of the Universe. I know who I am—assured by His Holy Spirit. Every minute of my day, I am greeted with love—*A Kiss Without Any Shame*. His Word gives me unyielding security, great wisdom, mighty strength, courage in living, conviction to do His will, and confidence in His truth. I am never alone.

SPEECHLESS, I accepted the Pastor's invitation quietly in my heart. My Savior and Lord Jesus Christ, all by God's grace and mercy—I am justified—redeemed by His precious blood. Inside—I rejoiced, unable to describe the awesome relief and peace I was experiencing.

The knowledge—peace is from God Himself—not from the world I have clamorously looked to for decades. *God's love is liberating.* Feeling on fire for God, my days of feeling guilt and shame are gone. I felt lighthearted. I glimmered in God's grace. I wanted to shout out; I found love! *When you finally accept God, that final moment... it's real, it is Spiritual.*

GOD IS LOVE.

IT SEEMS like it's been a lifetime of struggle to find and accept what is good and perfect love. Jesus has given His love everlasting the reality in my life. It is taking time to absorb God's forgiveness to include understanding, why He'd forgiven me? Someone has poured much into my heart; stress freeing. Yet, I have so much to learn about God's great love. For now, I am enjoying the feeling of *genuine freedom*.

Carlos and Kathie have been attending a local Calvary Chapel in the City of Montebello (CCM). Joseph and I found the new chapel's Bible Study format refreshing. With its location fitting. We joined the family in our new Spiritual venture. No one knows my prayer of repentance; not even Joseph. Though the cell door to my heart has opened, I am still seated and immovable. Not puzzling! For decades, *it* was my protective shelter away from the darkened and cruel world.

We attended Bible Studies on Sundays and mid-week given by Pastor Pancho. CCM's modest building structure is in open view on Taylor Ranch Recreational Center. And the humble footage sits resembling the "Little House on the Prairie," grounding with its own converted barn.

I can visualize the Family Ingalls from the "Little House on the Prairie." Each one sporting smiles as one-by-one came skipping, running or slow stepping down the hill—picking up a flowered weed. Relating with Laura, the Ingall's second daughter is a spirited tomboy. She overflows in vibrant energy. I see her in challenges duplicating mine on a screen.

On Sunday's and Wednesday's services, the chapel comprises 70-80 members and guests. CCM's quaint setting feels homey; with the ranch's main structure used for the Adult Bible Studies and the up-cycled barn for the Children's Bible Studies, stories, and related activities.

After several weeks of attending and hearing the Word of God, Joseph and the girls' demeanor appear to be changing. Visible changes. Physical signs of comfort, relaxed-like, similar to the sense of relief I celebrated in private... surfacing from all three. Feeling joyful and for its sweet moment, I am thankful for this physical and emotional newness in each one. In the girls.

The sky's clear Summer night showcases assemblies of stars; spurs an atmosphere of openness. In the midst—listening to the Pastor's message, I became distracted by an inner tugging... "Acknowledge Me before others." For me, that meant accepting Him—here, in front of the humble congregation. Following the message, Pastor Pancho invited the congregation. Appearing his sight, was on me. He asked,

"Are you tired of being sick and tired?" Is he asking me?

"Please come forward to receive Jesus Christ as your Lord and Savior and... "

Before he could finish the second part of his invitation; with intent and ready position, I stood up from my chair. He finishes,

"Please step forward."

Like a first-time, "Bride-To-Be," I walked down the aisle towards where I visualize... no, I see my Lord Jesus awaits.

Two huge fans placed on the opposite sides of the room thrust hefty loud-sounding air around; rendered my lightened strides—

floating on air. The cotton Summer floral knee length dress I wore flowed about in its natural way. My decisiveness in choosing the floral-printed dress—jumping out of the closet that morning—spiritually intentional. Colorful imprints of various types of blooms over pure white background. Somebody, perhaps the "Spiritual Stylist," helped dress me, His Bride. Helped prep my soul's re-birth in public view.

I continued to smile ever so brightly absorbing each step forward in overwhelming anticipation—to claim those long-awaited loving kisses from my Father in heaven. Given with His divine love; *a kiss without any shame.* His heavenly presence waits for my public acknowledgement of my faith in His only begotten Son's sacrificial love. Jesus shed His blood for me to wash away all the impurities of guilt and shame. As I face my gracious God, face-to-face for yet another time, I repeated every word said from the pulpit. Recited in accepting God—repentance of my sins, to give me a new heart, a clear conscience, and help transform me into a new creation as He puts my name in the book of life forever. In front of many others, I received Jesus Christ as the Lord of my life. Amen!

REFLECTION: On the outside, others see tears of joy roll down my cheeks. What is unseen inside, is *that* little eight-year-old girl now beaming with joyful gladness as I bid farewell to brokenheartedness—gone forever. My shattered heart, mended by God's love everlasting. "In this, the love of God was manifested toward us, that God sent His only begotten Son into the world, that we might live through Him" (1st John 4:9).

Again, "Through Him!"

I've lived most of the forty-years through the eyes of hurting individuals. God has given me eyes to see. Through faith in Jesus Christ, joyful living is possible. Verse 10: "In this is love... He loved us and sent His Son to be the propitiation for our sins." I have been looking to replace the love lost in my father's death. Lacking the appeasement graced only by Father God in His Son. It is no wonder; no humans around fit the bill. Likewise, I had not known the depth of the following passage—Verse 19: "We love Him because He first loved us." So, the image of God's love is in me, in all of humanity. Hence, the image is His love.

Encouragement:

~

1ˢᵗ John 4:15
Whoever confesses that Jesus is the Son of God,
God abides in him, and he in God.

(NKJV)

~

IN JESUS' name, I pray:

I believe Lord; You are the only begotten Son of God Who has washed away all my sins. Your love shines in my world. May Your Holy Spirit help me abide today, always here, and into eternity. I ask for Your heavenly protection from all temptations: my flesh, personal desires, and from this world's prince—the adversary. Direct my path and grant me Your wisdom, courage, and boldness to live the life worthy of Your calling. Jesus, please provide me Your strength to carry my cross and follow You.

~

I WAS twenty-eight years old and unsaved when I first informed Ma of those darkened harrowing moments. Ma responded by asking,

"Why didn't you tell me?" I saw tears running down her cheeks with empathetic eyes fixed on me. Her sincere repentance of true guilt and concern radiated through.

Though, Ma, was sorry for what had happened, I had not fully forgiven her. At forty-years-old, I am feeling relieved knowing, as God has forgiven me; I too can forgive. First, to those people who inflicted unwanted touches, mental and physical assaults, forceful hand-whacks, with lasting invective words. The lie in believing my perpetrators' own deep-rooted pain and anger feelings was the green, GO light signal given when they tore down my innocence.

My spirit wrestled with guilty feelings of abandonment. A created mindset induced by Pa's passing and Ma's busyness; mirrored through my parenting. No one is good but God—I fell short. Remembering how hurt and angry I was; yet, unable to do anything, I succumbed into isolation. Separated from the family and unable to live in full liberty.

When Peter asked, "Lord, how often will my brother sin against me, and I forgive him? As many as seven times?"

Jesus answered, "I do not say to you seven, but seventy times seven" (Matthew 18:21-22).

I say, oh Lord, this is impossible!

With God, nothing is impossible! That's it. All these times, I was relying on self to make things right. How again, Lord? Start by forgiving my mother and others, including, Jett.

In crucial time and only by His divine intervention, He placed me face-to-face to those who hurt me. I forgave. And by the grace of God —I sought forgiveness from others, including Jett. To each one, I offered:

"I am sorry for hurting you back!"

Then, I asked my children for theirs:

"Please forgive me!"

God cut the cord that had me tied in Satan's lies—**releasing** me from the bondage of sin, forever.

REMINISCING moments about my father appear far in between these days. But, when those times occur—all are vivid. My love for my mother existed—buried in deep blame mode—I kept an emotional distance. My uncaring detachment elongated to last for a long time.

The innermost joyful experience in forgiving Ma allowed me to see more hidden treasures—appreciating the many functional and personal skills I have developed all these years—taught and guided by my first teacher!

Setting us both free to receive God's healing and relish life together. Heart open, I prayed for Ma's salvation.

My mother did not know about our family driver's malevolent exploitations, nor about the family friends' immoral assaults including her ill-minded business associate—wrought on me.

Encouragement:

Colossians 3:13
Therefore, as an elect of God holy and beloved, put on tender mercies, kindness, humility, meekness, long-suffering, bearing with one another and forgiving one another,
if anyone has a complaint against another,
even as Christ forgave you, so you also must do.

(NKJV)

IN JESUS' name, I pray:
The uncontainable joy I now have, overflows. Abba Father has brought brilliance back to my life through Jesus Christ, Lord and Savior of all. "And His countenance was like the sun shining in its strength" (Revelation 1:16).

~V~
I SEE YOUR HEAVENLY BRILLIANCE SHINE THROUGH THE CRACKS OF MY PAINED HEART TRANSPIRE HEALING TO MY SOUL.

REFLECTION: It is easy to comprehend what the Lord said to Abraham: "Walk before Me and be blameless" (NKJV, Genesis 17:1).
James 2:23 says: "(Abraham) the friend of God."
Friends—I have a few at work. Joseph is a supportive and closest friend. More gathering of friendship from within the church. I am a friend too! Yet, to understand "the friend of God," is beyond my current status as a Baby Christian.
What does it mean to be God's friend?
I want to walk with God and spend time in His divine presence. I am so busy Lord. You know my schedule. Where do I begin? My family is important. Health is key to keep on pressing. Sleep is vital in cleansing

the waste and replenishing healthy brain matters. Remember Lord, the girls are turning into teenagers! I have just enough time to clean the house, do laundry and shop for groceries. Managing and operating my time to the maximum allowable twenty-four hours in a day.

There were too many important others. Work outside the home, spending time with family and friends, deadlines for more projects. Not to mention saying, "Yes" to everything and everyone needing my attention. Most often relying on my humanity's "old woman's" (old self) own wants and desires, in my wisdom. Which resulted in nothing more than wanting more.

"What about Me and you?" asks my Lord.

22

SEE GOD'S IMAGE

Though most activities remained unchanged in our household, I bask in His glory knowing God is in control. Joseph, my *knight in shining armor* has received God's gift of salvation in Jesus Christ. Praise God. Because of this, we are now both *babes* in the Lord and thirst each day for His divine presence.

Reading the Word was limited to attending Bible Studies, I needed more time to be with God. My longing to be "The friend of God!" is growing. A phrase unreserved and open to anyone. Each day, I thirst for His living water—satiating my dehydrated soul.

Acting in obedience to God's divine instructions, Joseph and I committed our pure devotion to God. Though he visited us often, *we stopped sleeping together—we stopped physical intimacy.*

Living in the busyness of life challenged my desire to be in God's divine presence. There is little time to be a friend. I need to make time. And, to do this, I need to re-organize my priorities.

CHRISTMAS EVE HAS ARRIVED and we still have gifts vying for wrapping time. To celebrate Christmas in its peaceful state, Joseph invited me out.

"Let's go for a drive to the Santa Monica Beach and have a picnic lunch!" with cheers in his voice.

186 | A KISS WITHOUT ANY SHAME

A small block of mid-morning quiet; hmm! To do something different; a "spur of the moment" kinda thing, I would enjoy that. Still, there is so much to do! Then I imagined... Annabelle, this would be like: take me... as in, "Calgon, take me away," instance.

The Holiday Season is here with mounds of last minute items added on top of a long to do list! Joseph insisted on the picnic plan. I jumped on the opportunity and said,

"Ok, let's do this!"

To help prepare; I brought out the paper goods, silverware, cloth napkins with the red and white checkered tablecloth. As Joseph places each picnic item in a wooden basket, I was looking out the kitchen window visualizing how to pack this stuff in my car! When, to my delightful surprise I see a white limousine parking outside parallel our garage. (That's my knight, alright!) Inside the elongated vehicle is the day's chauffeur in his complete formal suit attire, topped with a hot-pink baseball hat. I was right... *wow, my date, is working to impress me!*

Ooh, fancy!

I love being more feminine in these romantic expeditions. Wearing a cropped T-shirt and red color (this shade is more feminine-looking, right?) sweats—Joseph held my hand and led me into the limo. More, oohs!

This Christmas Eve Day, 1992, is a joyous time for me. Being a "born-again" with new beginnings at hand. Celebrating Jesus' birth— His hope, joy, and love is outshining everything else in my life. Revealing God's love as He continues to mix and brush bright hues on the canvas of... this time, my heart. Stroke by stroke, the transformation begins.

THE LIMOUSINE RIDE WAS EXQUISITE. Though, I was excited... I wondered, why a limo? The driver found a place to park. Now, it's our turn. Finding the perfect place on sand-covered grounds, Joseph guided me with careful strides down slippery rocks onto the beach-front. My mindset has taken a U-turn, and for the moment, I am in amplified sensation. The setting was so peaceful and surreal. The report of clear weather provided a perfect setting with the mid-day sun glaring through the cool ocean breeze. Since we are in the latter month of December, snow on the eastern mountain tops is visible.

Stimulated by this spectacular scene, I slowly breathed in fresh air then blew out and said,

"A beautiful 'picture-perfect' day!"

Joseph, in his usual sweet romantic ways, chose the perfect spot for our picnic—the cool dry sanded area felt refreshing and close enough to appreciate the mild ocean waves. For convenience, is a mere few yards' walking distance back to the limo.

I laid the red and white checkered cloth over the cool sand. Touching and feeling tiny matters between my fingers; rubbing and feeling—called to mind a touching moment. When my father placed me down on a beach front after fishing me out from a near drown. I felt God's presence; unexplainable.

For the first time in so many despairing years, there is hope, **He Offers Peace Eternal** in my life. I have been enjoying the ocean breeze and was entrusting my day. It's hard to explain God's promise; "Peace that surpasses all understanding guarding my heart, mind and soul" resonates more each passing day.

I was enjoying a peaceful state; eating away the perfectly cooked shrimp, white rice, fruits with vegetable and cheese tray. I did not notice that Joseph had stepped away. After a bit, he appeared from nowhere and was soon back in sight. I couldn't help notice his bare feet gauging careful steps as he came closer. He sat down, opened a bottle of bubbly champagne and sat beside my calmative state of mind —I noticed an expression of discomfort on his face. He smiled. I smiled back thinking: "Who can resist that engaging smile?" and those pearly white teeth! Big happy smiles always does something to my head. I lose my place, up inside my skull—I get siphoned in by the expression. *Now, where were we again?*

He pulled his legs closer and forward towards me. *Okay, now what is he doing?* He pulls his feet closer and showed a pair of cut-up, scraped skin, garnished with salty sand at the bottom of his feet!

"What happened?"

While carrying multiple items in his hands, Joseph lost his balance (and dropped not a thing!), slipped down over sharp and slippery rocks. *Yikes*! A high rise building safety warden that I am—Joseph, a clinician himself—we poured the celebratory champagne over his *seasoned* feet.

• • •

JOSEPH TOOK a breath and rearranged his composure. Appearing preoccupied. *Are you revealing something here Lord?* His behavior is odd —ignoring my suggestion to seek the obvious need. His bottom feet's deep scrapes and cuts appear to need immediate medical attention. Instead, he turned to his side, grabbed two wrapped items, turns back to position. Looks at me, then hands over one elongated shaped box. Still exhibiting discomfort on his face, Joseph recomposed.

"Merry Christmas Eve!" next he paused, looked at me, and kissed me. At that moment, he said,

"Open it."

I smiled and complied, thinking, O K A Y! this is weird. He's in pain and instead of finding medical attention, hands me a gift. In my head, *you know this can wait later or tomorrow!* I played along and opened my gift.

The box housed a deep eggplant purple (my, err—our, favorite color and vegetable;) champagne crystal flute with clear-colored stem. My face gleamed.

"Wow. It's design reminds me of a Calla lily—beautiful and I love it!" I thanked him.

Joseph turned the valuable glass around to show the inscription —"*Me.*" I was so touched. "*Me.*" with a period, is my insignia—used on greeting cards and letters I have written him.

A merry Christmas eve. The day gets better. He opens the other wrapped box as he says:

"Merry Christmas Eve to 'Me.'"

He moves in closer to show me the inscription on his glass, "Marry." Oblivious, inscribing merry as in the "Merry" Christmas is appropriate (how embarrassing my college graduate misspelled the word). I verbalize:

"Me"... and "Marry... " and finish with, "Yes, Merry Christmas Joseph".

I don't get it, but hey, these flutes are stunning. Joseph paused, and somewhat sizzled for the moment, just staring at me. I'm still looking... *these glasses are beautiful!* At that time, Joseph moved his glass crisscrossed against mine and said,

"Read it!"

Intrigued, here comes my conversational "Friend." I queried.

Read it? Why? It's two words, one misspelled, ha-ha! "Merry Christmas me" already! OK—together the two words read, "Marry (and) Me." Thanks, my Friend.

Unaware, I was gazing through him! I could hear his voice, though, I didn't comprehend what he was saying. He held the glasses together again and voiced out,

"Marry me."

My gaze has dampened with tears as my lips quivered. Heart beating in delightful speed! I am both speechless and motionless. He assisted me to stand as he kneels on the sand, looks up at me with loving eyes and asks again.

"Will you marry me?" and he gives me *that* smile!

My starry gaze is becoming fixed now and I can hear him speaking. *Where did I go? Where am I? Who am I? Did I have a mini-conference with my Friend, the Lord Jesus Christ Himself? I'm back now—I'm here!* Tears rolling, lips trembling, full focus on my Joseph.

As Joseph waits for an answer from me, I noticed him adjust his hand around a fabric covered small box. He places his flute on the red and white checkered sand covering, carefully.

My eyes jumped out of their sockets!

Like a child on a Christmas Day morning, I grabbed the deep purplish-blue velveteen covered box from his hand—opened and pulled the ring out and guess what? (Let's sizzle here for two seconds —la, la, la!)

Yup, I did—me, myself, and I, placed the gorgeous princess cut, sparkling diamond ring on my own finger! I continued to stare at the ring. Is this really happening? Then I felt Joseph's hand on mine and finally understood his question...

"Yes? Annabelle, will you marry me?"

"Yes... yes, I'll marry you."

"Oh, my" is what my now Fiancé, might have thought.

We both impressed the day; hilarious, enjoyable, and memorable! One of the best and blessed day ever!

~ DRESSED IN PEARLY WHITE LACE ~

THE GENTLEMAN JOSEPH IS, he honored me, his "Bride-To-Be," by extending his pure intentions to my dearest loved ones. Before Christmas Eve day at the beach, he had asked the girls for my hand in marriage. In the rare times of seeing my son, Joseph, later informed Paul. Seeing my children's happiness for me; each has loved Joseph for his positive reinforcement in parenting style.

Nine years of enduring the backlash, we see life hopeful. No one will mess our minds in mindful threats and treatments. God supersedes the wrong-doing that was. Shows His grace and mercy each day; and, secures our everlasting future through Jesus Christ.

Pastor Pancho married us at the Calvary Chapel in Pasadena before a hundred plus eye-witnesses. Family members from both sides took part. The girls were my Maid of Honors and Carlos was Joseph's Best Man. Paul was present and happy for us. Joseph's parents, sisters, brother, and close friends were members of the wedding party. The wedding group also included my brothers Kuya Rolando and Ramon; Rex escorted me down the aisle and gave his consent for marriage along with Ma. Missing, was my brother, Kuya BB. Though I wish to have my *father-figure* see me in joyful time of life—deep in my heart, I understood why he didn't attend. In Kuya BB's place, we enjoyed his two sons who joined in the wedding festivities.

Walking down the aisle in a pearly white lace wedding gown was an exclusive and beautiful moment as God presented me pure to Joseph. There are no words to describe—glorious feelings of joy. God has graciously blessed us both in marriage. The hope for the future is secure in His mighty hands.

We returned home from our delayed honeymoon filled with God's love and faithfulness. His word is truthful and promising.

Married couple, Carlos and Kathie, teen-sat De and Sam, while we were away on our honeymoon cruise. We were welcomed with gracious news. Days before her fourteenth birthday, De accepted Jesus Christ as her Lord and Savior. I say, hallelujah! *Praise God!* We, along with the "Teen-Sitters," have been praying for the girls—a wonderful answer to our prayers. I am so relieved as I hold on to God's promise of redemption; my "Littlest One," has the Holy Spirit's protective layering.

Encouragement:

∾

Lamentations 3:22-23
Through the Lord's mercies, we are not consumed,
because His compassions fail not. They are new every morning;
Great is Your faithfulness.

(NKJV)

∾

IN JESUS' name, I pray:
Lord, Your loving-kindness never ends. Each morning brings new joy to my life. Your over-flowing love and compassion have healed my broken heart. Great is thy faithfulness—showed each moment I stand before Your divine presence. Stay with me Oh Lord; my portion—I hope in You.

∾

SAM AND DE are lovely in physical looks. Both are over-the-top friendly. And, wear smiles enough to melt any high-schooler's between the ages: 15 and 18-year-old boys, I call... *"mid-man."*

Sam was in her high school's dance drill team and De was in a long distance running team. The sisters are outgoing individuals. It is in their cuteness, creativity, and athleticism, they draw in many *mid-men*. Both have many friends, but it was the slew of *these nearly men* that had me spinning—like a top spinner! Each time I meet one of these *middy-men*, I sense some kind of hot fluid breaking through my veins. Not krypton nor its varietal, blue krypton. The Hulk likeness inside was turning my blood into a color green! I had to get down on my knees, praying often—I am tamed.

Sam attracted friends with bright neon colored hair and *off* hair styles. Human connection made difficult for me by their outlandish hair do's and apparel styling. In proximity, I have an uncanny ability to spot a minuscule, cell—anything! Get your facials close enough and my eyes will see each level of your skin's three-layer deep tissues. From one's hair follicles to sweat glands along with dark un-aerated blood flowing through one's own veins. Should I try hard enough, then visions of your third layer skin... where facial fats and connective tissues live, rise higher. I see you! Remember—I am Sam and De's mother! X-ray vision enabling me to read through most people I meet. God is good to give me discernment; His wisdom.

"God, help—'not me'—please, help 'these' *mid-men*!"

"Help me, a *born-again*, 'Filipino-Mestiza' mother, show love all around; even to these, 'Middies.' Lord, forgive me and help change the way I pray." (For their sake!)

Encouragement:

∼

1st Kings 3:9
Therefore, give to Your servant an understanding heart
to judge Your people
that I may discern between good and evil.
For who can judge this great people of Yours?

(NKJV)

∼

IN JESUS' name, I pray:

Lord have mercy on these *mid-men* flocking, encircling my daughters' innocence. Give me your Spirit of discernment, envelope my girls with Your divine protection, allowing me to minister to young souls. Help me see past facial and physical appearances, to see Your perfect creation in each one placed in front of me.

MOST FILIPINOS ARE KIND-HEARTED and hospitable. Many can forgive with ease and are generous at heart. But, stressing on BUT, a strong likeness to any other Spanish bloodline, *ahem*—Filipino-Mestizos are, hmm, can be *locos or locas* (crazies). Please know, there is no deliberate disrespect here—no pun intended. Yet, I saw first-hand how Filipino-Mestiza mothers operate. My very own mother and aunties were not one to reckon with. Each of us, fourteen compound youngins from back in the bungalow where I grew up, prolonged life through total obedience to our elders.

If God is to be the top priority in life, my obedience to Him is first in order. Praying always that I recognize each young man or woman brought into our home bears goodness. Exhume God's love placed in their hearts. God made humans in His own image. God is good. *Why start by seeing the bad first, Annabelle?*

Setting me up to find one, I read: "For all have sinned and come short of the glory of God" (Romans 3:23). looking for the bad resolves only to my disobedience.

"For as by one man's disobedience many were made sinners, so by the obedience of one shall many be made righteous" (Romans 5:19). Lord, remove the natural woman in me and replace views of averageness with Your greatness in others. Help me see Your graceful image in each one of these young souls, in Jesus' name, I pray, Amen.

~V~

LORD, REMOVE THE NATURAL WOMAN IN ME AND REPLACE VIEWS OF AVERAGENESS WITH YOUR GREATNESS IN OTHERS.

∼

23

PRIORITY NUMBER ONE

*E*veryone is in God's priority. Jesus gave His life that through faith in Him, we receive salvation. "Who for the joy that was set before Him endured the cross" (Hebrews 12:2). I pray for subservience attitude.

How does one follow and walk with God? I *ask* to be His friend!

Joseph gave me a Bible representing the words spoken by Jesus in red color. On Sunday services, I follow through as Scriptures are read from the pulpit—and back to follow-up, reading in mid-week. Twice a week for an hour for each service, we study along with our pastor.

At home, reading Scriptures word-per-word takes about twenty minutes. Less than an hour from one hundred sixty-eight hours in the week. Hmm, I need to sleep and eat to survive. His Spirit asked,

"What about Me and you?"

God has redeemed my life back to Him and is now transforming me into His likeness. Living in the set of standards I created kept me away from the truth for so long. Why would I remain in disarray—ineffective ways? Newness is at hand. It calls for my obedience upon which—to grow in Him is to spend precious time with Jesus. Follow Him. He is where I am at present.

In remembering Pa's loving hair strokes and kisses on my forehead, recalls the commitment made by him. In this, reciprocating to my father was made easy. My deep love and trust in him—without fail, made our togetherness, more delightful. My father brushing knots off my hair was not a favored fun; though, in each moment, the discomfort is near non-existent! *Why?* I loved Pa. He loved me. Our quality time together—paramount to us. Overcoming discomfort with tender ease. Understanding Pa's unconditional love and commitment secured my place in the world.

My time with Jesus is a touch of heaven. To be in fellowship with God; my confidence in life is in Him. The Holy Spirit has forewarned paying attention to the priorities that I have set in my life outside of God. He led me to read the Word of God; one Scripture at a time. Each night, my quiet time for thirty minutes, I receive God's daily instructions and confirmation. Assurance of His love. Courage to continue my walk on the narrow path with Him. Have confidence, knowing He is in control. For correction and protection by His Spirit. Receive His strength to carry on. His wisdom to identify the opposition—Satan's lying works. He equips me to say, "*No,*" and gives a commandment; "*In the name of Jesus, get away from me Satan!*" Experience His blessings, possible only through the nudging and empowerment of the Holy Spirit.

I tore all the standards I have set in my self-centeredness in *post* knowing God. I am now re-defined by a new set of priorities placed in the following order:

1. Spend time with God.
2. Go before His presence.
3. Read His Word.
4. Worship the living God in spirit and truth.
5. Praise Him, from Whom all blessings flow.
6. Be thankful for everything.
7. Repent—ask Him to forgive me of my sins.
8. Pray in supplication and for others.
9. Hear His instructions.
10. Apply His corrections. Each day, His Spirit empowers. All day, through my faith in my Lord Jesus Christ, by Grace; and face-to-face, I talk to God Who is my Father in Heaven.
11. Nurture my relationships; my husband and children first, then friends and relatives next.
12. Be God's servant at work and at play. Ministering to others.
13. Service to God at church; and,
14. Give attention to those whom God places in my life.

REFLECTION: Jesus, there have been so many thriving changes since You came into my life; You, oh Lord, remain the same. Seeing and delving into Your mighty Words have empowered me in so many ways, I never understood this to be possible—miracles in life. You know. You hear. And You keep Your promise. Reading Your powerful Words took eight years to complete; starting at the beginning—from the book of Genesis to Revelation—the study of the last. The victorious Christ revealed in His glory.

I don't linger nor wonder anymore; for I am loved by an everlasting love. "I am famous in my Father's eyes, make no mistake, He knows my name" (beautiful lyrics sang by Francesca Battistelli, and co-written with Mia Fieldes, and Seth Mosley). Jesus' blood shed for me. Because of His blood, there's no more wrestling with guilt and shame. His Spirit lives in me. Full of Grace, the Lord is with me. My confidence is in Him, Who knows my name.

∼

AFTER DE'S met up with the Lord, she prays with intent for His strength and guidance. She is diligent in staying pure. And, is selective with friends. Joseph and I have no problems with her choices! De values education so much, she forwent family vacations to attend High School Summer Classes. Imagine my thrill on this matter. *Hmm, perhaps, she could be a lawyer.* Incisive, bold questioning and rebutting are her norms in discussions and disagreements. There is no argument from mom. *Study, and study more De!*

In the meantime, Sam has distanced herself more from me since declaring my faith in Christ to everyone. I see... that she is falling deeper into the lost world. Evidenced more when we established the new set of rules.

"Rules, rules, and more rules." Since I have been *born again*, and being made over, my spirit longs to grow steadfast faith in the Lord Jesus Christ. I have tried very hard to transform part of my *Filipino-Mestiza* mothering into Evangelical ways.

REFLECTION: In praying for patience, I now understand the saying: "Be careful when you pray for patience!" Testing came. I received a grade "D" for patience. Today, I am teeter tottering at a close "D+ and a C!" There is no promise of promoting to an "A" divine grading. Improving my patience is to trust and obey; to go through the process of God's priorities at hand in my life.

When the subject of friends comes up, both girls have home-schooled with the set of rules. Mom and Joseph's RULES in spending time with friends at home or away from:

- Number 1 ~ Friend meets Mom and Joseph. Get to know one and the other.
- Number 2 ~ Bedrooms are off limits to boys.
- Number 3 ~ No overnight stays by boys.
- Number 4 ~ No overnight stays with friends.
- Number 5 ~ Events attendance with an adult chaperone. Note: We approve of School Overseers.
- Number 6 ~ You want a potential date, "*mid-man,*" pick you up; do you? He must meet the following criteria: have met parents (emphasis, Joseph and I) at least three times prior; provide complete name; current registered auto license plate number and California Driver's License information. Yes, two forms of ID's!
- Number 7 ~ No drugs and no alcohol.
- Number 8 ~ Observe curfew hours.

I had a Filipino *back home* upbringing, much different from California's city living. Joseph, born and raised in Los Angeles, balanced out our proposed rules. After hearing the rules set up about friends at home or away, delivered De's eye-rolling gestures. Adding infamous sighs in between her usual questioning and rebutting. There was no visual proof against our rules from Sam. She merely smiled.

"We have set the rules. Follow or hole up in your bedroom. It's your choice."

To be honest, I want them to enjoy and relish high school—a period I squandered away by getting married at age sixteen. Mushy inside, but with a strict outward appearance. By abiding with these rules, their activities with friends would continue, *only,* with a stamp of parental approval.

THIS *"OUT WITH A FRIEND"* night hold a warm temperature. De is prepping for yet another invite to fun dancing with friends. An invitation different from before. She is going with a *mid-man*—a friend from school who will pick her up. We have met. Joseph and I like his respectful ways and humble mannerism. We felt comfortable to let De go with him.

She steps down from the upstairs' bedroom dressed in her favorite color—bright yellow Asian-designed apparel. De looked so pretty. She looked stunning!

Our townhome's kitchen window faces the main street. Below is a wide driveway where visitors could park for a limited time. The same area where our limousine parked on that beautiful Christmas Eve Day. Several steps across is our garage door where I saw De's friend from school parked his shiny black *Bavarian Motor Works (BMW)* sports car. Out came the driver, my daughter's friend, not a date!

"Well, well, well," I muttered.

I grabbed and pocketed a pen and paper sitting on the kitchen counter and stepped towards the front entrance. Joseph had just opened the door and there, he stood ready. From four feet behind Joseph, my eyes saying, "I see you." Thinking, hey, that's a nice suit. De introduced the "Beast," I meant, her friend. No sooner after our introduction, Joseph was in pleasant conversation with the couple. No, not the COUPLE, I meant… them two. After the usual manner of greetings and small talk, we followed with well-wishing and precautionary word of advice.

"Have fun and be careful."

Led by De, they stepped outside, tailed by Beauty's mestiza mother, close behind their short steps down and around to his "Beemer!"

Hard as I tried, I couldn't hear any of De's chattering, only my heart's fast beating. No one around could see my heaving chest—causing me to pull the paper and pencil out of my pocket in quick motion. De seeing me step straight up to the back of her date's car, looks away in embarrassment. I was non-verbal, but De understood my *facial language*, "Don't look away like: Mom, I forgot the rest of *'your rules.'"*

Darkness has settled in the parking area. Standing under a faint light bulb by the garage doorframe, I squinted to focus—zoomed in closer. Seeing what I needed—using the short-hand method, I scribbled *this* Beemer's license plate's letters and numbers. It was obvious; there is a clear message here—*dress to impress*. He wears a vested-suit, coupled with this fresh out of a *hand-washed—hand-waxed—hand-shined* auto service. The jet-black sports car is an impressive looking set of metal. Assisting De in the car, he looks at me with a smile—he offers his promise to take care of her. He takes several steps around towards the driver seat, with eyes still on me. Our eyes still connected, I stepped towards De's friend, bent my knees lower so I could look him at eye level, and remarked.

"I see you take good care of your car—it is so clean and shiny. No visible sign of scratches or dings. It's beautiful!"

He smiled, acknowledged these spoken facts, and thanked me. Then hearing the ignition cranked, I looked to see De's facial expressions through the open-wide driver side's ultra clean window. It was clear from the look of her smiling face, I'm hearing a ventriloquist-like questioning, "Are you done yet, mom?" I bid them,

"Have fun..." chin down, eyes up, gazed at him; and gave a hand wave, the green light to leave. He drove away in slow motion as if he knew I wasn't done. I hollered a few words. Though words said echoed and evaporated into the night's warm temperature, my daughter's DATE heard me. I know this because I saw this nice warm and gentle "Beast" look at me through the car's side mirror.

"Bring De back the same way!"

De came back on time. Yes, in the same way she went out that evening.

IN THE FOLLOWING years of transformation, I hit the ground on testing my faith and obedience. When trials came, I delved into God's Word. The test of my belief is difficult to ride through, but Jesus said: "I will never leave you nor forsake you" (Hebrews 13:5). In Him, He allows only what I can endure. In testings, growth came; enabling me to carry through the next trials ahead. Trusting in Him is the only action I pursue. He has shown the beauty of His correction and is molding His masterpiece.

I can learn to love others. My heart is open but needs to open wider to accept others as they are. To surrender everything and everyone to God. Having the ability to love others, manifests His mastery in me.

I have forgiven everyone. Even those who have not asked. By forgiving those who hurt me and ministering to those who house brokenheartedness, placed me in close fellowship. My fellowship in Jesus' sufferings—I can endure. Focusing my sight on Him who knows my heart's desires and wants. "I have not, because, I ask not" (James 4:2 NIV). His Spirit guides me in what to ask God. Is it mine over His desires? Or are the desires His for my life?

I asked God to change me as He pleases. To see more good in others. Whether one believes in God, seeing His image in everyone including my husband, children, extended family, and friends, even strangers; I see more good than bad.

To make things clear, I didn't want to include the bad people. God keeps *those* people He does not want in my life, close to Him as much as me. In today's world, this works for me.

He empowers as He uses. In, avoiding others because they don't suit my way of life is tragic. His Spirit nudges saying,

"He or she is in front of you, Annabelle, because I, God, stage every play; and the person may need ministering; and, or serving, even if they are 'those' bad people."

Not that God needs me to do anything. Nor needs help from me. He looks to grow my faith in Him. Praying for our loved ones is reassuring; praying for our enemy is true love from God. My obedience—apart from Jesus, I can do nothing.

I HAVE SECLUDED myself for so long because of the stipulations I placed on many undeserving individuals. It is only, I... I am responsible for my isolation. Giving my conditional love to others with certain expectations resulted in missed joyful moments. Unconditional love for others; and, to be in His likeness, is a far reach. Especially for me.

How is God transforming me into His likeness is beyond my ability to understand! Everyone wants an everlasting life filled with happiness. I had all things available to mankind. Yes, family, health, food, shelter, even money. Yet, relationships with others come with provisos.

"Buts," and "Ifs," go hand-in-hand with imperfect individuals. Praying for God's wisdom—His will. It was not self-knowledge or self-will that provided the missing link to my happiness.

How do I find healthy relationships?

The question I ask of myself is, "Am I capable? Better yet, am I spiritually healthy?"

I understand my mental health is still mending. My spirituality in begging to be more like Christ, I am hopeful, because of the changes He makes daily. Healing takes time, but His goodness is complete.

~V~
AVOIDING OTHERS BECAUSE THEY DON'T SUIT MY WAY OF LIFE, IS TRAGIC.

∼

It was not long after I met Joseph, that I was introduced to Carmen.

A close friend of Joseph's wanted to meet me, and so a date and time were arranged to meet up at a nearby shopping center's parking lot. *Wow, meet at a parking lot... hmm! I can't wait.*

I hindered my inborn friendliness inside for decades and freed only for my personal use. It was a time of hiding deep feelings of many regrets. I can turn its conditional dial to: a nice, *nicer* or NICEST persona—brought about by the other person's temperament. Any kindness from me would depend on a person's attitude.

I had just stepped out of Joseph's sedan, when I saw a van rolled in closer to where we were parked. The blue and white VW van stopped within a few feet from where we both stood waiting. The driver stepped out smiling... I was shaking his hand when my peripheral vision pulled in an image closer. (Imagine, me distracted!) Coming from the passenger's side... out came a Rita Moreno-like, silhouette. This woman was styling a thick reddish wavy hair. Rita Hayworth, isn't too farfetched to Carmen's physical appearance. She walked away from the van and moved with outward confidence. Albeit, Carmen's smile was the trigger touching my innermost. Not to mention, her pearly polished teeth were an obvious backdrop aligned for her gracious smile. We shook hands. Our eyes connected. She appeared to be nice and friendly. I reciprocated—I too, *can be...* nice, and *was* reactive. I see, deep inside Carmen, is a heart— relatable. Our connection was immediate.

Carmen is thirteen years my junior and just two years older than my son. We share similar childhood. An only girl growing up with three brothers. She appears to have a healthy lifestyle and happiness seems to follow wherever she trots about. Nice and friendly, Carmen draws people near her sincere smile sending caring messages without uttering a sound.

REFLECTION: Our lives have interlaced from what others would call Best Friend Forever, thus "BFF." I now reveal the truth. Carmen is more than a BFF, she is my SITA—Sisters In Transformation Always.

Interesting that we would undergo similar life experiences! Believing now, God answered, "Yes," to my prayer for a female friend. He sent a would-be BFF flowing with empathy. Sita, understood my past—we would embark into spiritual growth together as Besties! Our lives would mirror each other as years passed on. With God's faithfulness, He gifted us both with Jesus' unconditional love.

Hallelujah, Jesus!

Carmen and I are a Team—Prayer Warrior Princesses for over twenty years; together, in our alone time and group settings, we pray for each other. For His divine intervention for our children, siblings and relatives' salvation in Christ, grandchildren's wellbeing, and for our friends. We are steadfast and loyal to the truth, to the Word of God. We trust in His ways. Holding each other accountable. Sometimes we are nice, often nicer! God gave me a healthy Sisterhood in Christ with Carmen. Many a time, I talk and she listens.

MY PRAYERS ARE BEING ANSWERED. Healthy associations are emerging. Genuine personal interactions with loved ones are reforming in healthy and meaningful ways. God is in all of our lives as we lift others in prayers. Even if I don't see, God is moving the puzzles of our lives every day.

Encouragement:

∽

Psalm 37:4
Delight yourself in the Lord,
And He will give you the desires of your heart.

(NKJV)

In Jesus' name, I pray:

Lord, thank you for giving me a desire of my heart in my "BFF" and prayer warrior, Carmen. Your blessing of a true friendship with a pair of listening ears—hears and prays for me and mine—comes as an angel by my side.

24

FROM SALESGIRL WITH LOVE

I bask in His glory each day. Life's roller coaster rides often are scary and fearsome. Despite, they're most often exhilarating and fun. As God promised... I am experiencing life in abundance! Wishing in the past years' life would settle into a ride along—in human and spiritual unity. Never ever changing. How would that be?

IN REMEMBERING GOD'S GOODNESS... the West San Gabriel's Young Men's Christian Association (YMCA), sits across the street from our townhome. This convenient location for our family's activities is a mere four-minute walking distance where Joseph works out and teaches a group exercise class. Where De and I, take self-defense evening classes and Sam works as a part-time life guard. Personal interests, hobbies, and recreations that fit into our busy schedules.

Several weeks after my public declaration of faith in Jesus, God led me to a woman in despair.

I had just completed a killer step aerobics group exercise class when I remembered... we are having company for an early dinner. So I rushed towards the exit door. Outside, I stopped at the top step by an overgrown bush and rummaged through my gym bag.

"Where are those keys?" mumbling... at that time, I was quickly distracted by a familiar sound. Recalling my time in the darkened closet... an upsetting lonesome place to be in.

I stopped moving and listened. The obvious sobbing sound was coming from the other side of the dividing bush. Curious—I continued to listen. I closed my left eye to help focus my far-sighted right eye. One-eyed vision zoned in through the bush—a silhouette appeared on the other side. With both eyes opened, I stepped down, and went around the bush.

There she was, seated on a bench with both hands covering her forehead and facing down—crying softly. I walked over and asked,

"Are you okay?"

She lifted her head and revealed tears flowing down her face. She looks familiar. Does she need help?

"Is there anything I can do? Are you hurt?"

Her face nodded. I scanned to see any signs of physical harm. But, I see none in this moonless night.

The exit door's faint light reflecting across and through the bush enhances the now darkened atmosphere. I can't seem to extract a name from my memory bank. We have not talked, yet I have seen her familiar face before. For sure, she is a YMCA member. I checked around the bench for space to sit down. Seeing my eyes wonder about, she scoots to free-up space. I sat beside her. A muted illumination appeared where she had repositioned—exposing a youthful face, appearing to be ten or more years my junior. It wasn't long after I sat down, and she spoke.

"I am so confused... I have made a mess of my life and I don't know how to help myself." Then looks at me with pleading eyes.

"Who can help?"

"Please help me!" entreated her soul. She continued.

"I'm about to go crazy with all the wrong things I've done. I tried, and it isn't enough! My family is suffering because of me. Life is hopeless and is no longer worth living."

Every word she said set a familiar feeling within myself. I took a deep breath. What do I say? This ministering is new; requiring a pastor's expertise here Lord! Still, I know what hopelessness feels like —wanting to end life. My lungs expanded with more breathing. I didn't probe for any personal information, instead, came simple words in my contralto voice.

"I know Who can help!" Somehow, a huge amount of air pushed from my expanded lungs ejected a powerful tone.

"God is your 'Helper,' the 'Healer!' and He is available to you right now!"

Her crying rhythm slowed. Sensing... she wants to hear more.

Wanting to comfort her further, I placed my hand on her upper back, rubbing—she quieted and stopped. Still feeling helpless.

"How do I get God's help?" she asked.

Oh Lord, she didn't just ask me that question, did she? Tugged by the Holy Spirit, "*She did!*" Since her attention focused on me, the tone of my voice came down a notch as well settling for natural contralto range.

"God loves you and is available to forgive you of your wrongdoings—all of your sins through faith in His Beloved Son!"

Inside, I felt His loving forgiveness all over again, such a beautiful moment. She, too, could have the same by choosing. I continued.

"God's Son, Jesus, shed His blood for you, for all of us; for all mankind."

"Do you want to repent?" seeing her face nod, I gave a loving direction.

"Ask God for forgiveness and invite Jesus Christ into your heart as your Lord and Savior?"

Eager eyes fixed on mine and her heart opened wide, she said, "Yes, I do!"

After asking God's forgiveness, the repentant lady acknowledged and invited Jesus Christ into her heart as her Lord and Savior. Equipped with a new heart and a new mind, she left with a peaceful smile displaying a huge sigh of relief. God has freed her from bondage.

I WATCHED her disappear into a hopeful future. We did not cross paths since. I never saw her again. I wondered, *was this an Angel of God's? Not necessarily a real human-being? Was I being prepared for future experiences as this?* God used me, His servant—to lead a troubled stranger, His child—into His Kingdom. Feelings of *kingdom-come* came to life. I understand the liberating and loving emotions. It's Jesus! He occupies hearts.

AND SO IT HAPPENED, motherhood placed me in a trying time of life. My daughter De, left God—her first love, and went with high expectations from the world.

She entertained a huge lie, likened the prince of darkness, who now has her in the palm of his hand. The experienced dark *persona*, targets and destroys purity of deceived girls. Wickedness and lies to include an unloving environment now filled my daughter's life as she lived homeless with this destroyer of love. Aimed on demoralizing and devaluing her with no expiration date.

Each day she endured revolting full-on; verbal, physical, and emotional abuse. Then coerced, this is the way "love" is. Each day became cloudier in passing. Doubt, in saving my adult-child, *my littlest one*, from distress is forming in my heart. It binds my hands. No one can say or do anything to convince her otherwise. I can hear the *old woman* inside of me say,

"Exterminate the problematic lice-like creature!"

THERE IS no vinegar strong enough to annihilate, nor large enough *kus-kus*, to scrub this spiritual infestation out.

I wrestled and felt a deep longing; burning pain for my child, heart-handled, likened to the darkened ways. Demonic rouse by the prince of darkness himself. The same hurtful hands who finds and destroys young hearts and souls. I see and know. I feel. Oh, how I ache for my little one.

How can I solve this problem, expunge it? I sizzled with this idea though not sure how?

I have forgone my physical health, worst—time with God fell back. I was going into panic mode. How do I save *my littlest one* from this brute? My obsessing mind wants to get rid of the problem—how? When all I hear is *exterminate*! Be rid of the lice!

"What about Me and you?"

God never fails. He thinks of me always. God has pulled me out of many death-defying-like storms. This too will pass.

Aware of my daughter's dire situation, Kathie informed me of a group, Prayer Warrior Princesses (PWP), from our church. Faithful women of God, including Kathie, have started prayers for other girls.

They would include De's name in their *prayers and fasting*. I accepted the committed group's invite to join PWP's weekly devotion and since I work, *it* would be from afar. I understood, my long distance participation is scheduled during lunchtime on a designated day. Starting on the first Tuesday back to work, with some measure of fasting, I set up the lunch hour to walk. Walking, praying, and praising God for who He is in my life. For who God is in De's life.

Meanwhile, back at home, I returned to making time with God. The daytime, *once a week of walking and praying* evolved to a daytime worship, "in spirit and truth." Monday through Friday twelve noon is lunch time with God. Short of four miles, I walk round-trip each day on the side streets of Pasadena City. Warm up and speed walk for thirty minutes. With a half-hour to spare—back at my admin chair for cool down and leg stretches. Spiritually replenished and physically refreshed, I consume a nutritional snack in the last twenty minutes of lunch break. From time to time, I get invited to Friday lunch by my office peeps. An opportunity to reconnect back with co-workers, I'm happy to comply!

Green street lights worked to my advantage. I hop on to the pedestrian side and onto the sidewalk. Each *go walk* signal from the intersection of Los Robles Avenue and Cordova Street—walking, praying, stepping along; making a U-turn at Hill Avenue by its Pasadena City College's student parking number 3.

My body remembered the many years I walked at lunchtime at the heart of Los Angeles City streets. Back when my personal intended goal is to reach Clifton's Cafeteria for lunch. The well-known eatery was Los Angeles, downtown's regulars' favored dining place. Oftentimes, permanent *street residents* accompanied me in the dining area.

Little did I know, street walking exercise in the past would prepare me for the many walks of my lifetime—endurance to stay in the race built then was in preparation to keep me in a long and difficult life's relays. I stayed the course.

Encouragement:

∼

Hebrews 12:1-2
And let us run with endurance the race that is set before us looking unto Jesus, the author and finisher of our faith.

(NKJV)

∼

IN JESUS' name, I pray:
"Jesus, who for the joy set before Him, endured the cross, despising the shame, and has sat down at the right hand of the throne of God" (Hebrews 12:2)

I have Your divine mercies, knowing my faith in You kept my feet on the ground, walking and talking during all those thousands of steps. You kept the green light going and my footing upright.

∼

REFLECTION: Three more tortuous years and several more heart-breaking encounters would pass. In our trust to God's faithfulness; praying and fasting, He answered our prayers. In time, my daughter came back to her first love—back to the Lord Jesus—releasing her from the bondage of sin. Praise God for His amazing faithfulness. Grace and mercy abound.

By divine appointment, De, now too, a PWP herself became one of my prayer partners. Face-to-face holding hands, via texting, sometimes in e-mails, FaceTime as well and apart—God shines His graceful mercy in inconceivable brilliance on His children. God "shall supply all of our needs according to the richness of His glory by Christ Jesus" (Philippians 4:19). His peace that surpasses all understanding guards my mind and soul, (Verse 7) through the tormenting journey.

Through this storm, God blessed us with so much love; in a grandson!

∼

SABELLA'S six progenies have blessed our mother with seventeen grandchildren and twenty-one great-grandchildren. Ten of the latter group have met Ma before moving back to the Philippines.

In the past few years, Ma has become self-absorbed and difficult to care for resulting in her caregivers to quit. My mother's mannerism has slowly changed. Uncharacteristic, she has become somewhat self-regarding. Ever so regarded as the "Queen of Hospitality," she disregards her own children's good intentions to help. A husband and wife caregiving team have taken over Ma's care, and since then, her health has taken a downhill turn. The lingering effect of dementia has resulted in many mishaps. An advantage her new caregivers took much to enjoy... my mother's cash, and credit funds. Monies handed to Ma, most often ended up in the caregivers' pockets!

My father's loyal wife, who never remarried, perished to loneliness with its partner's *guilt and shame*. I know my mother tried her best in those years as a young widow with six children. Her generosity took her to poverty, and a few came to her rescue. Even her family and friends failed her. Truth—I had a hard time dealing with their abandonment. The fact, survival in the third world country is just that; the last man standing gets the prize—survives.

I believe Ma felt betrayed and abandoned by adored ones she helped care for. There's that word again, ABANDON! Looking in the mirror, the Holy Spirit convicted and humbled me to see the true condition of my heart. To be honest, even after forgiving my mother, I too, found other priorities to tend to. Ma was not on the top of important *to do* list. Oh yes, I visited her at the townhouse provided by Kuya BB. Work and family as justified excuses, did not go unnoticed. God knew where my heart was, and is.

In the many years, my prayers of salvation for the entire family included my mother. I pray for change.

"Lord help me love my mother more. I know I can never love her like You do. Please help me show her, she is not alone. And no matter what, I will always love her."

God's faithfulness prevailed, yet again. I had a sudden burst—deep desire to care for my mother—an unexpected and profound interest to do so!

"Whoa! Jesus, you are unbelievable." Jesus is happening.

Yes, He is transforming and moving my heart to love on Ma.

AFTER A TIME of persistent urging by my two brothers, our mother, is heading home... back to the Philippines. I felt sad. Never mind... I clashed with my brothers' decision—I was out-voted. Together with my siblings, we completed plans for Ma's move.

The Sabella brothers were mindful to giving our mother traveling comfort. With my siblings' generosity; Rex, and I will accompany Ma in Business Class air travel bound for Manila. Kuya Rolando and other family members gave her monies in twenty-dollar bills as parting gifts. She counted her money, rolled them tightly and placed securely in her pant's pocket.

Diagnosed with a drop foot condition, Ma is wheelchair bound. As a Special Needs traveler, the airlines granted Ma's request for a seat assignment closer to the lavatory. I sat to her right by the window and we settled in our seats. Weeks of preparation, followed by a four-hour wait to our boarding—I liquefied in the Business Class sitting place—emitted a long... "Sigh!" At last, we're seated.

I felt peace as the plane lifted off the ground. Looking out into the darkened night; in silence I asked, "What is Ma's future, Lord?" I paused, and stared outside into the dark, listening. From my peripheral vision, I see a stretched arm interrupting my pause, handing me a primed menu. Noticing Ma's eyes focused on different food selections; choices of Western, Filipino, or Japanese Kaiseki, dishes. She wanted all three dishes. Rex and I chorused in.

"Only one Ma."

Our mother had performed many cooking miracles in meal prepping days in the Villa Dolores' wet kitchen. One chicken miraculously provides the main ingredient, and enough for three more dishes. My lunchbox in grade school days included: soup, main entrée, rice, and fruit. It's fitting she would ask for all! Not surprising, Ma would settle for some western cuisine.

Flight Attendants are service-oriented towards elder passengers with special needs and their travel comfort is a prime concern. Sensing my mother's restlessness, they came often kneeling by her aisle seat asking for anything else she may need. These activities went off and on into the wee hours of the night during our seventeen-hour flight.

My entire body is screaming for rest. Even so, seeing Ma restless kept me, "restless." Isn't she exhausted? I am exhausted! Trying as hard to stay awake, I kept on dozing off. All the details for an international move have drained my whole body and now, my head—vegged. Every neurons—limp. Sometime between dozing off and awakening moments, muffled by the airplane's jumbo jets; I hear voices, whispering. Hearing the quiet-spoken words from my beloved "seat-mate," I fought hard to listen. A stewardess responds for the umpteenth time to Ma's whims and wants.

After I blinked multiple times to replenish tears into my tired and dried out eyeballs, came a familiar script. An attendant is kneeling by. My retinas received more lights and sent my lenses to see a rerun. Ma's loosely fisted right hand—slipped *something* into the attendant's hand and whispers,

"Take *it*!"

I did not ask, instead, shook my mother's shoulder and said,

"Please stop... this is the third time... you have given both attendants their 'tips,' for the same type of service. Asking for more glasses of ice cold water when you don't even like ice in anything!"

I looked at Rex, seated across the isle from us (how convenient) and stretched my puckered lip pointed towards Ma. He smiles and closes his eyes. Still looking at Rex as if I could nudge him from where I sat.

"Really!"

"That's it?" my patience dropped hard to the lowest level.

Ma's parting gift, used as tip money; Rex sat up from his pretentious sleep—muttered words to our mother. I am not sure if she stopped. I was too tired to see. Later we discovered, she gave away all but one cash bill to the attending flight staff attendants. Upon our flight's conclusion, the generous traveler slipped the *last* bill into her baggage handler's helpful, willing and open hand. That's our ever generous Ma!

However, I realized with her altered mind, the logical skills no longer showed value in money. We are from a Third World country and we think twice before we hand out any money... any amount.

MY BROTHERS HAVE PROVEN the best care plan in bringing Ma back home. She now lives in one of Ramon's townhouses and appears to be adjusting well. I chose a living unit fronting a courtyard, displays various tropical plants and flowers. Re-designed to emulate the former townhouse she lived in a Los Angeles suburb. The unit's structure shares many similarities to Ma's old residence; a wise choice, hoping to comfort her in a similar surrounding.

Finding the perfect home for Ma wasn't an easy task. I have been praying to God, implant in me His super-natural love for my mother. Prayers are being answered, my feelings have developed lovingly towards Ma. But God had more things in mind. God placed Ma and I in a journey towards humility and trust. In moving our mother back to the Philippines, I had an initial plan to stay four weeks. Ample time to help settle her down.

I guess planning made God laugh—my plans went awry. Wanting to meet the four-week's deadline, I kept on presenting each potential place to be the perfect residence for Ma. Just the same for each one, she had something unfavorable to say. Leading in her comeback statements, always, was her deep desires to go back home to Los Angeles.

"I want to go back to LA. I want to go home, Bibe!"

She wanted nothing more than to go back to her old residence—her apartment—her home. There was no place in the island good enough. Even her sisters and close relatives could not convince her of such a place. God showed that I was doing this all wrong.

"Remember your prayers to love on her, Annabelle?"

With my *heart open wide*, I followed on the narrow path—listened and served, obliging Ma in loving patience. Jesus showed me His ways. Allowing me to experience un-pleasantries during this time—a genuine fellowship with the Lord Who is close to my heart.

In the days leading to a decision for which is to be her permanent residence; I slept on the floor by Ma's bedside. Planning began, and somehow, I wanted to observe her surroundings. How would she feel? What would she see while lying on her bed? There were only several furniture pieces available in the sparsely furnished townhouse. A sure benefit is a hospital bed, though a purchase order for one would take several days to complete. For the interim, I have assigned the daybed available to Ma. Ramon offered comfortable accommodations for me in his home, but I declined his hospitality to be by Ma's side. She needs my all-day presence. I was no longer surprised by my responses. God is leading my yielding heart.

Our first night came slow and steady. Amazing hours that held me closer to Ma—to be in the moment with my first *teacher* in life. There are no framed acknowledgments hanging on the walls. She does not hold a Bachelor's Degree in any high-ranking formal disciplines. Ma, Dolores, in my book, holds the Master Trainer in domestic skills and commitments. My mother, who taught me pretty much everything about forgiveness, generosity and its partner, service to others, is one Cat Lady to copy. The trainer who led a stellar example. Never-ever saying: "I told you so!" Didn't nag. Didn't have to. The consequence speaks for itself. Dolores lived her passion. Doing so in loving confidence.

Laying on the thin mat placed flushed on the floor against Ma's bed frame, I see the pair of once-busy working hands, appear stiffer. Inflicted with rheumatoid arthritis, her fingers struggled to inter-lace with mine. Instead, I carefully squeezed my fingers through her tightened joints. We held each other's hands, cherishing the moment.

There, I picture. No! I see what her surroundings are like. Feel like. Still, who will be around? Who will care for her—love on her when I'm gone?

"Jesus will! Annabelle."

She pointed her curved finger towards an oil-painted canvas.

A strategic placement by the siblings' conglomerate design. I say, *brilliant*. The family picture hung on the wall at the top of the first set of stairs facing the living room. This eight hundred living square footage, a multi-used area—is also Ma's bedroom for convenience. Directly across from where we laid is the picture of Pa, Ma and their six children. Creative work of art. A custom oil painting from an original picture taken with Ma and her adult children about twenty years ago. Ramon had the custom oil painting redesigned to include Pa. The talented painter, Wendell Cristobal, painted an image of our father to the right of Ma. The scenery, in which, I felt Jesus' presence. We fixed both our eyes on this amazing oil painting—our hands still interlaced. God's overwhelming peace surrounds the mother and daughter who have re-connected.

Though Ma's caregiving staff is nearby, my childhood co-habitant, cousin Ate Alice, graced us with her humble and servitude heart. Ate Alice welcomed us home from day one of our arrival and has not left our presence. The compound inhabitants, greeted their sister and Auntie "Loleng" (Dolores' nickname), with open arms. Each volunteered to help care for their sister and aunt. As in the past, teamwork is at play. In the following days, one or more co-inhabitants would show up, visit, and remain in company. Often, their stay would last for days—helping with Ma's home transition. There have been occasions of having the family sleep in "sardine-like," set-up on the cold, tiled flooring—with me huddled around Ma's bedside. These familiar sleeping arrangements from the past—a loving time.

Oh God, I have been sick with bronchitis twice during my stay, still and all, Your divine presence and loving ways are overflowing. *Whatever You are doing, keep on doing!* My joy is overflowing with spirited intention—deepening desires to love more on my mother. Six weeks later, I left for Los Angeles. I was in tears leaving Ma behind—tears of peace and comfort. God has assured me she is in several loving accomplished hands. God provided for all her needs; answered my prayers, and transformation is in play.

~

My annual visit with Ma came earlier in 2011. I planned to fly out in late May and return mid-June. Rex and Ramon, who have taken part-time residences in Quezon City, joined in on my visit.

Kuya BB travels to Manila two to three times a year. During these visits I have seen my oldest brother. The deep longing to tap into our former relationship rises when I see Kuya BB. Still, his choice to stay clear from me remains a mystery. We have small talks now, which started about thirty years ago. From time to time, I see Kuya BB in San Gabriel where Ramon stays during his visits to the US—we engage, but only in small talks. Sometimes during conversations—something ignites a choleric reaction from Kuya BB and I would walk away. I have not stopped praying for him—for each of my brothers and sisters —all eleven, every day.

Seeing Ma in a calm mood is relief to my soul. She now has Aleck, who loves Ma like a grandmother and has taken the lead in caregiving. She took on a sincere interest; the responsibility in getting to know her patient, she called, "Lola." At first, Ma was resistant to new caregivers who have no blood relations to her—would throw any reachable items at the newbies. Aleck and the other caregivers, in fast movements, dodge the many flying items. After two years time, Ma's agitation turned into a loving and nurturing relationship with her lead caregiver.

This June was a short visit with my mother and the travel back to Los Angeles arrived sooner than I was ready to leave. My family went out for dinner to celebrate Rex's birthday the night before. Rex has settled comfortably to a lighter petition for his birthday celebrations and is satisfied to dine with family. Ok maybe a gift, or two. Precisely, a new pair of shoes would suffice! Kuya BB was present and treated everyone that night. Looking at him from four chairs away, I asked God, *When will You answer my prayers for Kuya?* Scanning the seats, I added, *And for the rest?*

After an early breakfast on departure day, I spent the rest of the morning packing and getting ready for my travel back.

God's Word resonates.

"What do you have for me to do, Lord?"

Encouragement:

∼

John 14:13-14
Most assuredly, I say to you, he who believes in Me,
the works that I do he will do also
and greater works than these he will do,
because I go to My Father. And, whatever you ask in My name,
that I will do that the Father may be glorified in the Son.
If you ask anything in My name, I will do it.

(NKJV)

∼

IN JESUS' name, I pray:

Twenty-five years later, I am still in awe with God's goodness. I can see the image of God in all His creations. Channeling through us, God imparts love and peace to His children with open hearts. The Gospel blesses us through Spiritual prosperity and through godly stewardship; we impart the good news of inheritance to all.

∼

Rex, his wife Carmen S., and Ramon came to have lunch and spent last-minute bonding time together with me. Kuya BB came to see Ma. He knew I was leaving, but his knowledge of my departure is not of great importance. But, the truth... it is important to Kuya BB—he just doesn't know that yet!

Ramon's personal driver arrived earlier, since traffic is anticipated at a lengthy bumper-to-bumper presence towards the airport, and to beat the road to the airport's chaotic "metal-to-metal" transportation presence. Leaving earlier is highly recommended. After arriving, the hurried driver took my luggage and packed it in the van. I walked towards Ma's bedside. I held her hands and looked at her peaceful smile as I prepared to say my goodbye—she looked especially lovely. A co-inhabitant's daughter, and caregiver, Josilyn, combed Ma's God-given platinum-colored hair. She styled Lola's hair in a cute ponytail. Ma's bright orange-yellowish house dress complimented her extra bright smile today. I leaned over and stroked her hair back a few times, giving soft kisses on her forehead. I whispered into her ear.

"Remember, Jesus loves you, Ma!" then I looked back into her eyes.

With her grayish-bluish eyes (a family trait in aging) fixed on mine, she spoke softly back in Tagalog.

"Oo, alam ko naman! Humihingi ako sa Kanya nang patawad para sa aking mga kasalanan." ("Yes, I know! I am asking God for His forgiveness for all my sins!")

Oh, that... nudged hard by the Holy Spirit's queuing, I responded to Ma's comments.

"Do you wish to ask for His forgiveness now?" I waited for an answer.

"Yes!" she nodded.

My God, You blew my mind to loving pieces! As all the angels in heaven are jumping for joy!

At about 4 p.m. PHT, Philippine time, Ma entered God's graceful presence—pure, white as snow, by the cleansing blood of our Lord and Savior, Jesus Christ. She has been reborn. No more pain of losses, isolation, and the heavy burden of guilt and shame. Her bright and peaceful smile, looking ever so lovely signaled; a *heart open wide*. Nearing 93-years old, Ma remembered—she loves God for He, first loved her.

We celebrate our unique connection beyond mother and daughter, each time that we talk. Seeing each other as God's child when we're in front of a laptop.

REFLECTION: God's image is love! Believe, even amid our memory loss, in crisis, and pain; in isolation and trials, in suffering; our Lord's loving presence is with us.

Seeing me on a computer screen, helped in my mother's remembrance of me. In the few times, when asked who I was, Ma would respond: "Don't ask me, you know who you are!" We laughed together during our screen-to-screen encounters. Often, with the same question asked, she would respond: "Bibe or Annabelle!" God reassured me, Someone knows Ma's name, and is etched in the Lamb's Book of Life.

25

KISSES OF LOVE

FROM DISCOMFORT TO RELIEF—Most mothers would agree after birthing a child follows enlivening relief! Though the shadow of death wasn't lurking around—in three birthing occasions, I felt the imaginary presence of two enormous hippopotamuses coaching. One stood near the top of my head and the other at the bottom of my feet. The one at the top kept my head still with its four webbed toes and coached, HOLD! Whilst the other below pulled my feet towards his much-filled rounded belly (a male because of the larger imaginary size) and commanded me to PUSH! This went on **forever** with sips of air and ice-chips in between. I know some of you can relate. Yes?

Please know during pregnancy, I enjoyed every moment of my meal-times. I reasoned that everything I consumed was nutritional. Calcium in milk and ice cream. Needed carbs in chocolate and cookies. Fiber in Casava cake. Liquid in sodas. And so on and so forth! Thank God, *this* birthing, too, would pass. After many weeks of lugging and balancing my weighty load, it ended… in twisting and untwisting a pretzel-like body from many hours of labor pain. Ahhh! There is no other word—better describes, RELIEF, after delivering a baby. With baby in my arms, joy funneled in. I experienced and saw God's miracle in face time value. I gave soft loving kisses on my baby infant's forehead. Seeing my children is a reminder that God is always by my side.

Pain and suffering are similar, in that physical pain is synonymous to the emotional suffering of my heart. I thirsted for love. Emotional agony produced various pain beginning with my heart. Most often, unable to breathe, my enlarged heart would function in erratic ways. Thus, producing abnormal activities—heart murmuring. The good news, by having my *heart open wide* to God, He released the heavy burden wrapped around my soul. My spirit experienced the promised newness. Jesus is the Living Water Who quenches and continues to satiate my thirst.

"But whoever drinks the water I shall give him, will never thirst. But the water I shall give him will become in him, a fountain springing up into everlasting life," (John 4:14).

THE PLANNING for the Sabella Fashion Group's 25-year celebration is wrapping up. With this, the "Who's Who," of Manila's top fashion designers have received a personal invitation from its owner, Ramon Sabella. The formal gala attendees will include loyal suppliers, retailers, and clientele. A grand celebration that will include a message of gratitude. For this, Ramon invited me to lead the lavish festivity in prayer. And added, he will dress me up in formal style; who could resist? More so, what got my attention is the word, "prayer."

"Ramon, did you say, prayer?" I didn't wait for an answer. Instead, asked again.

"You said, 'prayer,' right?"

"Yes," Ramon confirmed.

"Thank you. Yes! I'll do it!"

I am beyond thrilled giving honor and thanksgiving to the God Almighty for all the goodness He has blessed Ramon, his Business Partner, Joel Cristobal, and the entire Sabella Fashion Group employees!

REFLECTION: Uni-High School in Santa Monica handed Ramon his High School Certificate of Completion in the eleventh-grade. Not wasting any time, he attended higher education classes; but could not ignore his passion for creativity, he left college to follow his dream.

He drew his plans. Laser-eye focused, Ramon succeeded to

becoming one of the top managers at the popular Thrifty Drug Store; where he learned hands on, amongst other skills, Retail Management. How he started? At the last minute, the interviewing manager was quick to hire and assign Ramon as the day's "Ice Cream Scooper" to fill in for an employee who had called in sick! Soon after, he was training for management.

Meanwhile, he worked as an apprentice for Ruben Panis, one of Beverly Hills' respected fashion Guru; a Filipino "top-flight" designer with such clients as, the Gabor sisters, Rhonda Fleming, and other high profile clientele. The drug store's leadership took notice of Ramon, *this* young passion-driven manager, and offered him a director position. He began preparation to become the company's first Asian Regional Director in Southern California... when... passion struck, mighty strong. He turned in his resignation. Ramon sold his yellow Mercedez sports-car and packed his bags... bound for Manila.

That was twenty-five years ago.

I ARRIVED Manila in early August with enough days to acclimate and prepare for Ramon's exciting event. Thrilled to be a part of a huge celebration and more so, an opportune time to visit Ma.

Celebration Day: many of the expected "Who's Who," dressed in beautiful formal *bling-bling* attires have arrived. The Sabella Fashion Group was in the company of a loyal clientele spanning twenty-five years. Blinding crystals and sparkles all over—enough to light up the ballroom. Each "wannabe diva" slow-stepping, gaits in a maze-like direction along embellished formal dining tables, parading their custom-designed formal wear.

Am I in the filming of My Fair Lady? Almost. Minus *fascinators* (cocktail hats). Seated—the night's Queen Diva, herself—Dolores Sabella. Ma, the mother of the visionary president, sits alongside her two progenies: Rex with Carmen S., and myself. Dressed in bright formal attire, the *lady* in a beautiful red gown is off the chart! Each invited guest takes adoring looks from far away. With crafty planning, guests move up close and personal by the seated Diva—all lookers are satisfied even for a mere second glance at this CLASSY LADY!

After the guests have settled in their seats, the servers spread around to assist with the grand-looking dinner tables. This sets the tone for prayer. Ramon made his way to the stage and announced my name.

"Here with us today, is my sister, Annabelle. She will lead us in prayer."

Applause—the whole ballroom attendees—applauding!

I turned around and saw my mother, the master trainer, seated by me, smiling and looking with intent. I recognize that look. Seeing as her stiff hands came together clapping, gave me *spiritual nudging*. I stood up. Then looked back at Ma, to seek approval for my "pose." The Queen Diva, the proud parent… gives me a nod. Trying to mimic this mighty *cat lady* dressed in red, with high heels on, I glided—cat walked towards the back of the stage.

On the steps was, the Event Director, Louie. He handed me a stock paper and printed on is the prayer. "What… prepared prayer by someone else for me?"

MY EXPECTATION WAS to pray freely and boldly. Unveil the good news of salvation in Christ. Thank each key staff member. Extend mounts of appreciation to the many loyal clientele. Lift in prayers the future of the Sabella Fashion Group. And to give God all the glory—from Whom all blessings flow. I did not feel anxious… God wants something greater than my expected plan.

I ask God, *what He wanted for me to do?* At the end of my quiet query with God came a clear answer. Then His Spirit spoke.

"Remember when! You were amid dire needs!"

Pray for each one present in the room—for their personal salvation. For conviction. For each of their families—good health. For provisions —home, food, jobs, and clean water. His Spirit of protection from the prince of lies. Pray for those God places within my vision (that night). Wow! Did He ever placed those who needed prayers in front of me!

I stepped up on the wide stage, dressed in jet black floor-length satin formal gown, flowing as the Spirit moved me. Inside, I thanked God—praying He gives me His Spirit of love and understanding for the surrounding people. I looked at the exquisite stock paper… and ever so, lovingly recited the printed prayer.

Soon after, God provided the times for me to pray personally for those guests He placed before and around me. I prayed in silence before and after dinner time—everywhere my steps took me—to each person I met. In greetings. Even during a photo shoot. Seated or standing up—for many friends, past and new acquaintances with strangers alike—I prayed for each one.

"Lord, bless this person here with me. May I in all: each handshake, meet and greet embrace, eye connection, much laughter; my words be pleasing to You, imparting Your Spirit of love to each one. In Jesus' name, I pray, Amen!"

My prayers for everyone was complete.

I rejoined my family. Together, we enjoyed watching the array of fashion designs paraded before us, great vocal entertainment, and the evening's nourishment—a delightful spread beyond expectations. Later, I thanked Ramon again for the unique opportunity in leading God's imparted two-part prayer. Directed by the divine hands of God —each human heart—lifted to our Father Almighty for continued blessings in life. Thanks be to God.

SPENDING time with Ma has been comforting in seeing the loving care others give her. Yet, I have noticed her quiet demeanor. Perhaps her visual perception has declined.

After arriving back home to the US, I planned for a regular time to see Ma more often via the Internet. I came to realize while spending time with my mother during my last trip that her mind is slowing down more. Our screen-to-screen conversations have diminished down to my mother's head movements. Always, our talks are accompanied by her familiar, *Sabella-branded smile*. Beyond Ma's facial expressions, I recognize Ma's differing smiles. I know when she is feeling good or bad, happy or sad, well or sick—saying nothing. On good days she would say, "Annabelle," sometimes, "Bibe." I see inside —she knows who I am.

MISSING my mother has heightened because of her inability to converse. I felt sad. Though, I expected this to be so. During our past online convos, I did most of the talking and now most times, our special "chit-chat," involve others. With a new caregiver hired, the care staff was shuffled around. Aleck is still heading Ma's care with a new hire as her back-up assistant.

It has been over a year since I last visited Ma. My longing intensified and became worrisome when I discovered Aleck has taken an emergency personal time off.

The internet connection has been sporadic through the month of September. I have been praying. God, please remove my wrestling concern.

Adding the bad news of a brown-out where my mother lives was troubling. Days before, I had an earlier conversation with the new caregiver and saw Ma looking distressed! I shared my deep concern and asked the caregiver to alert my niece, in charge of Ma's medical care. The new caregiver has contacted my niece and assured me—there is no reason for concern. A few days later, they rushed Ma to the emergency.

On September 11, 2014, early evening and through a four-inch mobile screen, I saw my mother struggling to breathe. Later, I saw my brother Rex by our mother's railed bed. The screen is transcribing life's passing scene. It won't be long after, I received a message that my beloved Ma has died.

Ushered by our Lord and Savior, Jesus, Mama Dolores stands with both feet on the heavenly grounds and meets her Creator, face-to-face.

I can only imagine! Ma is surrounded by God's glorious presence.

Encouragement:

∼

2nd Corinthians 5:6-8
So we are always confident, knowing that while
we are at home in the body we are absent from the Lord.
For we walk by faith, not by sight.
We are confident, yes well pleased rather to be absent from the body
and to be present with the Lord.

(NKJV)

∼

IN JESUS' name, I thank You, Oh my God, "hallelujah!"

How beautiful it is to imagine my mother standing by Jesus. She meets her Creator—I sing to You my God, "hallelujah." Dressed in an *angelic* bright red flowing gown, I see Ma, swiftly walking and gracefully dancing her heart away. Bright smiles for all who welcome her home in heaven. With red lipstick and stiletto-heel dancing shoes on—Mama Dolores "Loleng" graciously moves about her everlasting family!

See you later, Ma! Love, your Bibe.

THE TRUTH AND WHY (I) SAY, "YES"

God answers ALL prayers. Sometimes with: yes, no, or maybe later. Without a doubt, the "Yes" is the most favored answer. I too, love the *yes* answers that God gives me. Recipients of the *yes* answer experience relief and comfort at its best.

God's, "Maybe Later" and "No," answers have been the hardest to deal with for me—yet, these answers were when my faith grew mightily.

Patience is a virtue. Right? Impatience... Joseph, tells this to be the most accurate adjective in describing his wife (stressing on me here). But God knew this about me. So my transformation began with the noun, TRUTH. Remember?

"The truth shall set you free!"

In God's revelation of His absolute truth; I trusted—again.

Each time He said "No," was because He knew best. These answers given in all those years until now have been blessings pulled out by His own sovereign hands. Plain and simple right?

No, it ain't! My pride kicks in and I would feel unloved. *No, not true!* However, as the Bible tells me so, Jesus loves me. And, I trust Him.

Obedience unveiled the many truths surrounding my life. I did not always comply to God's Spirit's leading and sometimes... ok, OFTEN, I ignore His corrective words. And so my transformation took a longer route. Advance training took more time by my lack of trust and obedience to His calling for my day.

Since I didn't do my daily homework from God, my divine schooling took longer time than needed. Much later, in spending time with God, He equipped me with an improved trait—patience which developed through personal trials and sufferings—in perfect time, God would reveal His great response.

IN ALL THE TIMES, I answered "Yes" to God's invite, I was present in His divine presence—I faced His uncompromising truth. YES is the fitting *keyword* that unlocked God's treasures set for my life.

Unlike Noah, from the Old Testament, responding YES to God took me a long time to make. Albeit now, I am in God's Divine Transforming Program.

Though in some likeness during Noah's time, the similarities—uncanny to my *growing-up* setting. There were: *grieving* time for a lost father, *chaotic* lifestyle, *darkened* world, struck with *fear*, felt *isolated* and *lonely*. Ultimately, Noah's trust, obedience, and faith in God led his entire family into a new beginning in life. In leading, God kept His promise to Noah. The promise of a bright day showcasing a colorful rainbow—assurance of His presence—never leaving him alone. *God remains true to Himself offering endless hope to this hopeless world.*

~ WHY I SAY, "YES" ~
The Eight Pillars To Living Free

IN SEEKING THE TRUTH, I said, "Yes," to having my **HEART OPEN WIDE**. God is patient. He remained at the door of my broken heart waiting to unlock and open. He is my Security. Only after I tried everything that is humanly possible and failed—like a child, I looked up. God picked me up from deep futile attempts, and I responded, YES!

I **SURRENDERED**—EVERYTHING and EVERYONE in my life; placing all at His feet. *Submitting all of me to God*, called for my faith in the Lord Jesus, trust in His Word, and obedience to His calling. *Relinquishing all the standards I set*, meant letting go of my control over everyone and everything else. To this day, in goodness and in health—through trials and sufferings, the Lord stands by me. Having God's peace always guarding my heart, mind, and soul through Christ Jesus.

In asking God for healing, His calling to **FORGIVE** others as He has forgiven me—cut the bondage of sin that had tied me down for decades. As a result, He placed me, including the difficult and sinful others who inflicted pain in me, on the road to full recovery. Growing up, my mother exemplified utmost forgiveness by acknowledging my father's other children as legal heirs; and thus, gave them access to many valuable benefits. I admit, "forgiving others," was hard to do. Recalls of pain resurface vividly. The hardest is in forgiving myself for holding on to shame, which degenerated my life. I kept the painful past—dulled my present day—held for a dreary future. Thank God for His complete forgiveness, I am free to live life abundantly.

ACCEPT each one for who they are. Yes, everyone! This is not about those dissolute people. I speak of those others around, difficult to love. Just imagine, accepting others may push your altitude to new heights. Change may occur through you. Imagine that!

God's grace and mercy is undeserving—I am **THANKFUL** to the Holy One. Grateful for His loving presence; outweighs the burden of grief in losing loved ones. The blessing and liberty in ministering to many others is to experience His loving promise in my life. I walk in amazement and fully see His Grace surprising me in joyful blessings as His vessel for others to come on board life's heavenly "fun" cruise. God's commitment to His promise offers salvation through our faith in Jesus Christ.

I give God all the glory—my **DEDICATION** to share His great love to all mankind. As He continues to transform me in His likeness, praying God's story of love written on my heart—His promise fulfilled. Blessing you and others with an *open heart*.

God in His own image created mankind. He has a **PURPOSE** in my life and in each one of you in this, our temporary home on earth. God will finish the good work He started in me—in you. Trust and obey, there's no other way—pray and believe on the latter.

Below, I share a short list of the wishful ways that made me temporarily happy. Please sizzle here, on each unsettling method I tried:

- ~ ✓ Attention to Me, Myself, and I
- ~ ✓ Attraction to pleasure seekers
- ~ ✓ Casual sex, cohabitation, and pre-marital sex
- ~ ✓ Control everything and everyone
- ~ ✓ False happiness; alcohol and drugs
- ~ ✓ Idolizing
- ~ ✓ Loathing and wanting loads of money
- ~ ✓ Material possessions
- ~ ✓ Seek and have corporate power
- ~ ✓ Worship framed accolades, and
- ~ ✓ Busyness

I was so busy; my life was senseless!

There are many more to list. My point is:

None of the methods included above provided permanent happiness and completeness in my life.

I strived for my foolish plans rather than God's purpose in my life.

Only in walking with Jesus and living out God's purpose; interesting or mundane, big or small role—GIVES ME EVERLASTING JOY AND CONTENTMENT.

God gave me a "blueprint," though I did not recognize His gifts early on handed down through both my parents. **STEWARDSHIP**, directed by the Holy Spirit, examples displayed by my parents. Sharing my God-given gifts—skills, giving of time and service to others. Sharing His provisions to those in need. Each of which is an opportunity to grow in His likeness—experience joy forever. Teach if you love to teach. Share your talents with others by serving a person in need. Watch your contentment hit through the roof. Serving in the Special Needs Children's Ministry was gratifying. God's blessing our family with my son, Paul, is beyond our own interests. Serving in the community of distinctive needs, we represent God's agency in spirit and truth. I developed a health condition that kept me from serving further. Feeling confused I went to God for healing. In time, He did. Then placed me elsewhere; back at home!

Encouragement:

THE GREATEST COMMANDMENT
Deuteronomy 6:4-9
Hear oh Israel: The Lord our God, the Lord is One!
You shall Love the Lord your God with all your heart,
with all your soul, and with all your strength.
And these words in which I command you today
shall be in your heart.
You shall teach them diligently to your children,
and shall talk about them when you sit in your house,
when you walk by the way, when you lie down
and when you rise up.
You shall bind them as a sign on your hand,
and they shall be as frontlets between your eyes.
You shall write them on the doorposts
of your house and on your gates.

(NKJV)

In Jesus' name, I pray:

God answers our prayers in the most exciting and impeccable ways. During which, let's not take access to God for granted, His word neglected, and His calling, wasted. LISTEN UP, the Lord gives us much more than the world can ever give us. God provides us His tremendous peace, heightened joy, and everlasting love; keeping us, hopeful in life.

27

FREEDOM

*R*EFLECTION: Goodness, I stretched my writing all the way through several seasons. Yes, I am very excited to approach the finish line. We will part soon—still, hang on for a little while longer!

An upgraded high-tech life's "Roller Coaster Ride" picked me up! Assuredly, I say to you, "I didn't pay for this' ticket"—**God did**.

During the ride, there were many of God's revelations. More training, embellished with some pain and suffering. Topped with a few trials here and there but I had the Lord's Force in me—the Holy Spirit had us riding, "Whee" into my next journey! Yes, it was fun! I am learning. I am being transformed big time into the Lord's likeness.

Noting a statement given to an interviewer by the actor who played Jesus, Jim Caviezel, at the time he was filming "Passion of the Christ."

"We tend to want Resurrection without suffering. 'Yet, it was in suffering that I seek God.'"

I still hold on to His Word, daily. Two hours in the morning; another stretch of a time mid-day; worship and praise during dinner preparations. In between, confer with the Lord and have Him help solve any issues a day may bring. Though, I still get irritated, frustrated, tired, and sometimes cry—in joyful, sometimes—sad ways. Still and all, never ever lose sleep—that's the peace I have in my Lord. He is in control!

FREEDOM | 233

I FLEW TO MANILA, in tote—my love for Ma. Minus Ate Claudette, my brothers and I said farewell to our mother with showering kisses marked on her forehead. It is with mixed emotions that I leave; she is absent in the body, and now present with the Lord. AH, what a feeling!

After the funeral, we fellowship with few of the co-inhabitants from Villa Dolores. Most continued life in the nearby towns of Quezon City; all but one, have families and grandchildren. Only two of my co-inhabitants have migrated to the US.

Yet, a sweet blessing in seeing and chatting with my former playmates; infused, sweet loving memory of the past—a permanent joy in my heart. Each one changed; each one still connected. I see the permanent bond we have in their eyes—in their spirits. Connection, I still miss. Each one is in my prayers. I appreciate their unique part in my childhood years.

MY FAREWELL VISIT brought on one dreary day's thundering, sending off voluble proclamation, rain is coming.

In no time, memories of children's past:

I see fourteen youths scurrying, jumping, laughing, dancing, aspiring to cut through the warm drops of rain dousing the ground. Mud splatters on darkened-olive skin—adds to the joyful cheerful smiles that know zero bound. Splashing muddy droplets on skin and with glee, I reminisce sitting front row from this lovely scene.

As the muddy springing locale turns into puddles, a stream of pre-leaping age tadpoles by the hundreds, burst from nowhere land! Slimy creatures—wiggling—tickling and massaging in quadruple sets exiting in-between my fingers, diving back into moving water! I see with utmost curiosity, cumulative fresh water housed these tad-poles, splattering water—plead—begging to come closer to my face.

A personal invite I cannot resist. I cupped my hands together and formed a miniature swimming pond and scooped these energetic squirms. Fifty-something tiny, living, wild species resembling oversize papaya seeds with tails longer than its torsos, swim around and around. As the pond water seeps through my fingers, I move to investigate closer! Closer I did so. Warm and slimy seed-like living organisms are jumping. Blowing kisses on my cheeks; slimy lips all over mine. Tickles and twitches gave sudden visuals of baby frogs gasping for water—not blowing kisses but desperate to jump off my cupped hands and dive back into murky puddles.

I can't explain the phenomena. Strange as it sounds, playing with these little creatures was an action-packed entertainment... and oh so mucky! So much so, I yearned for the rainy season to come sooner than later, full-grown tads—ribbit frogs announcing their arrival! I was not alone in this super amusing fun play—my playmates join in cheerful laughter and jolt in joyous jumping. Several pairs of hands cupped, ladled in and out of the rainwater-formed tiny water pools. Not to forgo an opportune for fun, the boy's group members tease my longing for more kisses.

This imaginary moment brings sweet recollection of happy times; as fourteen young silhouettes faded into the days and nights—ending the scene. Still, years after, loving memories of our times past.

REFLECTION: Young silhouettes now come in the form of my children and grandchildren. There are no water meres nearby to take the children for a peek at these tadpoles. Nor, are there thunderstorms and heavy rain to orchestrate and introduce, hundreds of tiny water creatures. What I have is a story to tell. A story beyond telling. Wherein, my children and their children's children—in creative, imaginary ways— they too, would collect scripts from their own life. In due time their own gathered story clips will be on the pages for telling. Their storyline—the sweet sound of memory lane!

ELEVEN YEARS HAVE PASSED since that day I missed Sam's first day back to school. She has been dealing with much ambiguity. Obvious, my older daughter is suffering emotional imbalance. She has taken a fast pace and distanced herself from many—especially from me. In doing so, the world was more than ready to snatch her into *its* deceptive ways.

Sweet Sam! She has a big heart to please, entertain, and help. As a child her smiles come from a *heart open wide*. Contagious to all, each one reciprocated and loved on her. Admired for her wit in graceful styles. Soon and unsurprising, *mid-men* piled on.

Throughout elementary school and into the first year in high school, Sam received "A and A+" grades. She wanted to become a pediatrician. At age fourteen—a representative from Sam's high school pursued her to tutor college freshmen in two possible subjects. Tutor in either English or Mathematics subject, whichever one she prefers. Because she was dealing with critical things happening in her life, neither of us... her parents signed off the release form.

REFLECTION: It was during her first year in high school, she became a member of the popular Alhambra High School's Drill Team. She appeared to have found something to look forward to. Each morning, she takes her bike to school. After class, she goes straight to her team's practice. Despite that, in her junior year, she reverted to her old self... mind adrift. Life's brutality steering her further away, closer into the hands of the prince of darkness.

FOR A GOOD WHILE, I believed Sam could pull an easy "collegiate modus operandi," accomplish anything she sets her mind on. Yet, I sensed deep inside her spirit, though only she can impart, is a heart broken—unable to break through. Sam wore clear signs of a pained heart as far back as seven years old. She signaled strong emotional stress. The remaining last two years of Sam's high school, life became stale—life was unsure and hazy.

Identifiable. That was me.

I know exactly how that feels like—felt like!

Looking back to Sam's involvement into the arduous and lengthy process of her parents' divorce, I now recognize what had taken place.

Sam tried hard to wiggle out of continued heart-squashing games played before her presence. My heart remembers. The hurtful actions and scripts she witnessed and heard, over and again is a remake of an earlier version. An original scene made on the same harrowing stage my parents played.

Sam's heart crumbled. The neglect and feelings of abandonment by me, her mother. I didn't see then. Blinded, but now I see. Warning signs were loud and clear. We, her parents, placed Sam in dire predicaments. She needed to stay loyal to a parent. Embattled, she went along against her heart's desire. Sam, forced to misrepresent—betray the person she has placed on the pedestal... her own mother. Someone coerced her to tell untruths for the sake of selfish and unruly desires.

It was during this time Sam shares a growing resolution.

"Mom, I couldn't!"

"Couldn't what?" I asked.

My flesh and blood in weariness; I feel and see her troubled mind. She continued.

"I could not bear the imagery—the thought of your face—your heart!"

"My face!" I felt a sudden jolt in my heart.

"No, Lord." Please, no!

"Mom, I couldn't bear the thought of your face—if you're the one to find me DEAD!"

Bull's Eye! The arrow lodged in the center of my heart—shattering to pieces.

Oh, how it hurts! Seeing my precious and sweet Sam's torn heart—I see the familiar brokenheartedness. Though, unable to talk, I became defensive. Glad I didn't add hurtful words to her! "I didn't do that!" and thought more.

"I didn't say that!"

Truth being. I paid no attention! I was too busy with my own hurts. Now, admitting—there were no excuses rectifiable. Yes, I was in the dark; living in the pleasures of life.

"*Stop there, Annabelle.*"

God reminded me that Sam is His child. "*I created her with a great purpose, and I will reveal it in time.*" Surrender, *this,* Sam's burden, to her Creator—to our Creator. Pray for guidance. Be ready for action. As sure as a challenge—this one belongs to my Lord.

"*You know the drill, Annabelle... 'Follow Me, the Leader!'*"

With shattered heart, Sam followed the corresponding unruly path paralleling mine. On the outside appearance, her teen years were full of fun-loving times. Inside, her pain propagated and spirit mutated. Her behavior had become destructive—somewhat self-centered, self-absorbed into what she wanted. Thus, my daughter allowed no one in, especially me!

Unable to follow established house rules, Sam in her overt rebellious mode, moved out at age seventeen. Just the same, I cried. My tears for Sam, my child—an intense and painful feeling—knowing the path she is taking is not a yellow brick road; but a darkened and wicked, heaving evilness with only one hard sell in life—spiritual death.

Just the same, we kept the porch light on. She is always welcome to come back. It affected Joseph more than he showed. He tried—tried hard to have a healthy step-father role with both girls. Sam was too hardened. I know. I recognize her heart's condition.

After several weeks of playing with fire, an overbearing world humbled Sam, she returned home. She knows the rules. And will follow them, will try to. Yet, she is compromising. Sam continues to live life in doubt and untrusting of me.

SAM CAME home in time to celebrate her eighteenth birthday in the Spring and finished high school in June. Joseph and I were in high hopes encouraging Sam to at least graduate. We were much relieved; Sam graduated. To commemorate the victory, we celebrated with a trip to Cancun, Mexico.

Our TRIO trip, may seem odd to most graduates who prefer to celebrate their high school graduation in a *much* younger age group setting, than alone with their parents! Sam didn't appear disturbed by our presence. She chose this celebratory trip with us... rather, to be with her graduating class. Joseph and I were glad to be with her.

We laid and soaked up Cancun's hot and steamy air. Strolled on the warm, wet, powdery-feel sand, and even went horseback riding for a powerful "slo-mo" galloping on the cotton-smooth beachfront. Neither, we pulled back from Cancun's fun dining... no age limit on anything and everything. Super glad, Joseph and I were there with Sam, we watched as she giggled having fun with a group of mature strangers. Her laughter was music to my ears. We, ate and ate more.

I wanted to see and feel Sam's heart, up close and personal. She has been distant for a long time; we needed to reconnect. I felt hopeful. Emotionally, I see Sam, detached. Her mind seems far... a hemisphere distance. Half the time, she positions herself alone on the beach looking out towards the ocean's blue surface and into the deep horizon. I wonder what she was thinking!

After returning home from our celebratory vacation, Sam broke off from her "on-again, off-again" boyfriend. To be honest, I was praying for that final separation. Her new boyfriend, Len, has many similarities to Sam. Len seemed like a happy person, a "happy-go-lucky" kinda guy. Their relationship appeared serious. My prayers now include him.

Home seems to move in a joyful direction. De is very busy with high school and loves having her older sister back. She has always admired Sam in more ways than Sam could ever fathom. I hear De often boasting about her older sister's ability to receive the highest grade on any written test. Often, quipping, Sam needs only a small amount of time in studying versus her (De's) days of prepping for a test. Sam's wit, coupled with intelligence; fun ways and easy-going persona, creativity, and beauty; De wished she could be more like her sister. It gave me great joy to see the sisters' giggle and confide in each other.

THE WEATHER IS PREPARING to stage Springtime, a welcome season for me. Though I suffer a little with allergy, I welcome April showers; for they bring all the beautiful May flowers. I am in the best mood in these rainy and budding days.

One early evening, Sam walks in from a short school day's class at Pasadena City College. She sensed my happy mood and asked if she could talk to both Joseph and I after dinner. She must have good news about school; I am all ears and ready!

Kneeling in front of my bed where I sat with Joseph behind me.

"I have good news!" she started.

Okay, trying to get my mind away from all the newsflashes I could muster that Sam would have. From: "I am on the Dean's list," or maybe, she has pursued medical school after all. Oh, I could hardly hold it together! With Sam's biggest and sweetest smile ever, she said,

"I AM PREGNANT!"

I gasped. (Let me and you, my reader, sizzle here for a second.) Long silence. Eye's locked on each other. My thoughts, The news did not surprise me.

Yet, I have so much to share. The pain inside doesn't go away by any means. For most of my life as a mother... utterly, beautiful and a lovely time; but the chronic interruptions, surfaced from my pained soul. Un-attended hurts and pain quickly diluted focus on my children. In and out as it pleased.

I admit, I felt joy. Sam will have a loving focus in her life. My first grandchild is due near this coming Fall and not wanting to miss Sam's call when birthing comes, Joseph gave me a state—of-the-art, Nokia cellphone. My very own mobile phone. It would prove useful for a similar event in the next couple of years ahead.

REFLECTION: This may sound intense; in real-time and prayer-time, I have long conversations with the Lord about Sam. Often, I hear Him say, "I have not, because, I ask not." So I asked. God remained quiet. I prayed for His will for Sam. Then, God whispered "*Trust Me!*" into my rattled mind. Sam continued with her life's choices; she was moving and circling around in the lost world of deep hurt. In time, my prayer, though unfathomable; if at the least, God willing, He gives Sam a reason to live. In this my personal plea with an inscrutable prayer, God answered... "*Yes!*"

~ THE MOON APPEARED ~

WITHIN A FEW WEEKS Sam moved in with Len, the baby's father. I have been praying for health and wellness for both my daughter and her growing baby. Over and above, I prayed for the soon-to-be parents to seek God. Sam surprised me with an invitation to her birthing day. "Yes! I'll be there." I was ecstatic. In between the following weeks, Sam and I talked about labor pain and shared my personal experiences. She should not have asked—labor varies from a woman, to a woman. So, I replied and gave a lighter version—softer—down-playing labor intensity.

The time came, my mobile phone rang. Sam summoned me to the nearby Medical Hospital. When I arrived, Len was in the delivery room ready to coach. Sam was holding up well. She concentrated on her breathing technique. *Breath in, breath out*, focusing on what appeared to be a draping spider web off the ceiling. Okay, I am familiar with the "Lamaze" birthing method so I could aid in coaching.

After several hours of labor pain, Sam faced a ready birthing phase. Now dilated to the maximum, she pushed—and pushed. Seeing her pain and suffering, I bowed my head to say a prayer. My daughter looks at me, with obvious excruciating pain blaring out of her facial expressions. In a worrisome tone, she asked in a panic manner.

"What is wrong Mom?" her face shows a strained hold on the labor pain! (I wanted to tell her to exhale... but she appeared to hold some kind of explosion!)

"Why are you praying?" exasperated, my daughter waited for my answer.

Snapping out fast, I responded.

"Nothing is wrong. I am praying!"

My life flashed before me, but was saved by one of Sam's intensified labor pain grunt—spared my life. Phew! She pushed a few more times. "Push, another push," and her firstborn, my first grandson, was born.

J. Moon is perfect. He is healthy and created in perfect ways! I praised God for our new sweet blessing. The following day, I saw Sam covered with small red spots all over her face... she caught up to the first-time grandmother.

Please, call me, "Nay-Nay."

Sam with a slight sneer on her face.

"Not much pain, Ha?" her face piqued.

"And what was the bowing of your head about... MOM?"

Later, we both laughed referring to her graceful day.

REFLECTION: More graceful days came. Eleven years later, one more "bowing of my head" in prayers for Sam, took place in the hospital delivery room. "Z. Christian, say hello to Nay-Nay!" Once more in less than three years, after my genuine petition to God for a grand-daughter; I introduced myself to M. Pink,

"Hey there, precious one! Call me, Nay-Nay!" Graceful days indeed.

EVERY DAY SINCE MY RETIREMENT, God has kept my day filled with "*Bibe, God's calling!*" Wholly loving my retirement in Him! My background as an Executive Administrative Assistant, has placed my tech abilities in mid-point, between a novice and an expert. It was a natural continuum; keeping up with useful skills, technology-related everything. Though my birthright as a "Baby Boomer," there are days, I skip Generations Jones and X. Instead, on steady knees, I crawl towards my goal—to Generation Y.

Really, Annabelle!

Hard, as I try, admitting such a task is like looking for that extra fine needle in a haystack. Because, I don't always "have faith the size of a mustard seed"—God still moves the mountains for me!

Christian, aka CE, born in Nicaragua, was a scrawny fourteen-year-old, *mid-man* when he and I first met. He had been friends with De since high school. Adding to other activities in school and with friends, they shared interests in track and field. As fun partners, they went to dances together, and for sure—shared junk food together! In the four succeeding years, my family enjoyed a separate friendship with CE. His pleasant ways are refreshing—exuding contentment in life with and a positive outlook. He shared some heartfelt childhood experiences while in Nicaragua and his migration into the US. Raised by a single mother, CE has a relatable and moving life story. We connected. Akin to my co-inhabitants—his experiences similar to mine.

We saw CE fewer times after Joseph and I moved out of our townhome. De had also started college and took a residency at Cal Poly's apartment housing. We all parted ways.

SEVERAL MONTHS PASS and my family heard little from CE. Though I heard updates about CE from Sam, occasionally, through a mutual friend. Time is slowly passing during this period. De, is out living what every mother feared! Believing the lies of our mutual enemy; our adversary, the evil one—she went out seeking love from "his" (demonized) world.

REFLECTION: Our mutual enemy, does not sleep; he tirelessly works on hopelessness. Though the enemy, aka the Devil... knows what happens to a believer's prayer, he continues his pursuit to steal, kill, and destroy.

. . .

My time of worshipping God during lunchtime and praying during my walk, have me in hopeful days.

One evening, the doorbell rang while Sam and I sat in the family's nook, dining area. My daughter looks at me and asked,

"Expecting anyone?"

She got up and walked to the front and I heard Sam open the door. I heard her speak though I couldn't make out the man's deep sounding voice. The conversation was in high speaking notes—a welcome surprise situation.

"Hi!" followed by short talking but I can't understand what they are saying.

Followed by footsteps moving towards the nook area. The talking and stepping stopped. I sensed them behind me. I turned around. Yes, my eyes, mouth, and ears popped wide open after seeing who our surprise visitor was.

No more a *mid-man*, CE had grown to a towering six-foot two inches. An adult man and a whole foot taller than me.

Seated across from CE, I opened—talk about the recent past—with a sneak peek into a promising future. The pleasant visiting hours went by fast and we soon said our goodbyes.

"I look forward to your next visit Christian."

Waving his hand back, "I'll keep in touch, see you later, Annabelle."

Well, CE kept in touch. Subsequently, several months later, De came out of the world and reconnected back with her long-lost dear friend.

God nurtured my mustard seed faith into moving the mountain. He answered the many years of prayers for De to come back to "Jesus," her first love.

God didn't stop with moving the mountains for me—He unveiled His goodness. With baby EZ in her arms; CE, a new believer in Christ, asked De to be in her life; as De's husband and Dad to EZ. Making this "Gen Y," son of God, my son-in-law.

God is De's rock, fortress, and deliverer.

Officiated by my brother-in-law and Pastor, Carlos, my daughter married her best friend, CE, in front of a hundred plus guests. Ten months later... back in the delivery room, with my head bowed, I prayed silently. God blessed me in witnessing their family of three welcome the newest member—N. Christeanna.

IN THE EARLY days of April, Kuya BB's dear friend, Austin, alerted the Sabella siblings.

"Communication from our eldest brother regarding his health will be forthcoming."

There were news of a serious illness swirling around, though none of my other siblings have any details. His health and wellness concerns me, but I was not expecting any communication from my brother.

Kuya BB hasn't re-admitted me back in the infamous, "Fun Group" for decades. So, it did not surprise me when my brother, Ramon asked,

"Did you read Kuya BB's e-mail?"

His questioning concerned me about the matter and answered,

"No. What e-mail? I have receive nothing from him."

Upon hearing my response, Ramon went to his computer and opened his incoming folder, pulled up the subject electronic mail, and tapped on the forward button. In an instant, a sound came from my desktop, alerting me of a new e-mail. The subject showed: "Rick's state of health." Here, I noticed, he included my old invalid address in the earlier e-mail sent. Kuya BB did include me.

Apprehensive, I opened and read Kuya BB's e-mail dated on the last day of April! It blew my heart into pieces; I hurt for him. Not denying at first, in reading his e-mail, I sizzled on the medical terms used. I froze, and after re-composing, read the rest. I can hear his voice with these words: "Back pain. Ultrasound revealed a mass. Mass confirmed in the pancreas and liver. Admitted to the hospital. Nine doctors, to triple check the previous finding, ordered an 'MRI.' This revealed... ". I slumped further down my chair. He shared the gravity of his condition. "The results returned two days ago: Stage 4 Pancreatic cancer!" Albeit, they diagnosed him with Stage 4 cancer, his e-mail contained a sense of hope. Signing off with "God bless," and "keep the faith." In an earlier paragraph he typed: "Appreciate your loving prayers!" I cried for my brother! He has included me in this news and what news this is!

He started treatment without delay. Weeks later and with Ramon's encouragement, Kuya BB took his family home to the Philippines for a much-needed vacation. (Kuya BB introduced his immediate family members to Ma, three months before her passing.)

Upon BB's return to the US, wasting no time, he resumed his treatment. He endured intense pain but traveled back to Manila in September to pay his last respects to our mother. During the religious funeral mass, Kuya BB followed protocol—stood up, sat down—stood up, knelt down. This practice went off-and-on for an hour and my pained brother never missed a beat.

Believing my oldest brother had pardoning to complete—there was a heavy heart towards Ma—stemming from many things. What may be a greater possibility is Ma never knew the devastation that occurred during Pa's passing. I know. I witnessed what may have started—his spirit to break, and I shall not forget.

After my mother's memorial back in Quezon City, my siblings and I joined Kuya BB for breakfast before taking his flight back to the US. During our limited conversation, I offered to help care for him at anytime he wants or needed me to. He nodded and sidelined my offer; he suggested we try the restaurant's delicious pancakes. In quietness, without moving my lips, I asked Jehovah-Rapha—the God Who Heals, to please cure my brother. Asking God, further, to give me the opportunity to serve my Kuya BB. Remembering those times, he took care of me; allow me the privilege to serve my brother in return.

~V~
LORD, SOMETIMES I STILL WRESTLE WITH PEACE.
HELP ME TO REMEMBER, YOU ARE THE TRANQUILITY IN
MY LIFE; THE SOOTHING MELODY OF YOUR PRESENCE
HOLDING ME STILL AND KNOW THAT YOU ARE GOD.

KUYA BB'S FAMILY: his wife, Breana and sons have invited me to help care for their loved one. In due time, my brother—still with reservations said, "Yes," to my help. Many times before, Kuya Rolando, presented the idea, and BB always said, "No, not yet." We started chatting by phone. In several occassions, I would end our usual short talk and say, "I'm ready to come whenever you are." Kuya BB would bid goodbye with assertion.

"Don't worry, will call you when *that* time comes I need your help."

His assurance proved, "that" time came and his sons flew me to Texas. I thanked his family for entrusting me to help with their loved one, my brother. Meeting his wife and the rest of the family for the first time was moving. Seeing their genuine loving care in person is heartfelt.

Upon my arrival, I saw my brother looking at me from where he sat. Kuya's face shows an obvious battle within. I walked over, gave him a hug, and he patted my arm. (Hmm, good enough! Let's do this Lord—lead the way.)

I didn't need to acclimate, Texas is only a few hours' air travel from Los Angeles. Besides, I wanted to ride along and accompany Kuya BB to his doctors' appointments. His Oncologist had arranged for the family's presence on *this* scheduled treatment. The family kept me posted in earlier days of the pending appointment. What is to take place and all. Yet, between travel plans and updates on my brother's health, I joined in with mixed feelings of what was to take place.

What took place... his Oncologist's displayed with deep empathy —her approval—to stop further treatments. His doctor went on further and pressed his attention to the *quality of life*... for however longer that would be!

Outside the doctor's office, Kuya BB and I have a few minutes of private and personal talk. We sat side by side. Words assuring:

"I am here for you, Kuya." I felt my brother's deep emotions.

"Please Kuya... please let me serve you as you have me. I want nothing else but to help you."

His tears rolled down as I hugged my brother. Then, he answered in a softened voice.

"Yes, okay!"

Lord, did you hear? He said, "Yes." My tears joined in with my brother's and as dire the situation, we started to re-connect.

With his doctor and wife's approval, I stayed with him for this last day of treatment—noting, a lesser time he had spent in previous appointments.

Vewing Kuya's unwavering fight with this horrific illness is captivating. With every ounce of energy, he fights against the flesh consuming effects of pain-relieving drugs. In lucid moments, he struggles in great opposition to this indiscriminating disease. I watched a younger BB inside *this* tired, frail body, battles like he once did in that inherited, "father-role."

ACCOMMODATING his every desires mentioned since, Kuya BB was rather contentious with me. I sense the former "Leader of the Fun Group" at Villa Dolores is back poking at his favorite target. I say,

"Ok, game on!"

He was beyond thrilled and felt obliged to critique my personal style of prepping and cooking meals. The "Master Food Reviewer," Kuya BB, had only a few words; either is "not good enough," or better yet, "not as tasty as Ma's or Ramon's." My old self could have matched this—his, irking ways. I wanted to look up and roll my eyes, instead my heart's longing to help, softened and I understood. Serving him! Is what I wanted.

In between managing his physical pain, he would deal with other complications. We have called for emergency personnel in two incidents. In which, the time I turned loopy; asked everyone in the room to *You-tube*,

"How to give an injection?"

OMG! Really, Annabelle! Soon, another urgent situation came for the much-needed shot.

"Kuya, I'm sorry if this hurts."

Hand shaking, I jabbed the needle into his tummy. After a few minutes, his vitals came back to normal.

"Did the injection hurt?" I asked. He responded,

"Yes, a little!"

Kuya BB's condition has taken a fast dive. When I see my brother sound asleep, induced by a plethora of pain medicine, I thank God for some relief. Wishing sometimes—if it is all possible—to give him complete rest, I'd take on his pain.

Pain management with side effects... sleep, missing precious sibling time with my brother! Or, see him with relief? My personal desires—the medicine, allay his pain.

In the meantime, he took my administrative experience to work.

"It is time!" he started. Appearing assured.

"Annabelle, would you help me, please?"

"Yes. Let's do this!" I responded with no reservations.

He wanted his *home in order*. He fights with the lack of lucidness; sharing and wishing for more time for many unfinished items. He poured his heart out and in his asking, I poured mine to him. With time on his hands lessening each passing day, Kuya BB settled with what he had legally prepared in earlier years.

 LIKE, RESPECT, AND TRUST

THANKSGIVING IS fast approaching and Kuya BB is on a non-stop talking about one of the family's most celebrated day. Salivating, while in the midst of describing Austin's special turkey. I've met the renowned cook during the Sabella's earlier years from out west, through Rex, is Kuya BB's very dear friend.

Austin is in the building and construction business and has played a supportive role to BB. He was my brother's close ally at work. Today, his visit is twofold.

Two days earlier, Kuya BB, dealing with complications of his disease, struggled with physical balance. Though, Breana was on his left side, she strived to keep at bay. I was standing on the other side of the doorway... seeing his weight swaying backwards, I don't know what came over me but in a flash, I found myself standing right behind parallel against his back. I don't know how this happened. Like a Roman guarding a soldier's back, I was ready to catch BB's dead weight body! It was a reaction I instinctively followed, though realized later, was unsafe for the both of us.

Austin wasted no time, he installed the needed safety bars for his ill friend. My brother's loyal ally remembers me and we chatted, recalling our times in California. Soon after, I found myself engaged in a "matter of fact" conversation. Kuya BB stood sandwiched in between. Our chatting progressed to a serious discussion about businesses. I shared the three criteria I follow in doing business with someone.

"Criterion, I give credit to a wonderful Christian business woman, Mina, who exemplifies these principles."

"I have to like, respect, and trust the individual."

Expecting to hear something from my brother, the experienced businessman, I looked at him. Kuya BB did not react—said nothing. Yet, he appeared to be listening intently. So, I continued.

"Beforehand, my knowing the person is a critical component. Next, likability is a must to even develop respect. Finally, with respect, trusting comes easier." I paused here.

There are no comments, only nodding heads from both gentlemen. They briefly discussed Thanksgiving. Austin completed his work. My brother left me surprised. He said nothing. There were no words... usual comments from the experienced businessman, who stood in between his guest and I. Hmm, *who is this guy?* Speak, not a word regarding my shared business criterion.

The disease is not letting up. Inspire of the fact that Kuya BB fights the effects of his pain meds, lucidity lessens each passing day. With morning hours more tolerable, our sibling conversations continue to take place. His cognitive abilities are in play. Lucid moments, he takes advantage of.

Amid our discussing, organizing, and filing of many documents... from out of the blue, Kuya BB asked an odd question.

"Do you like me?" I was the only one around so that question is for me. I replied,

"Yes, I like you." Without missing a beat, he followed with the second question.

"Do you respect me?" looking down, appearing to search for something through folders of paperwork.

"Yes, I respect you," I said. Then, his third inquiry blurted with clarity as he looked up.

"Do you trust me?"

THE LIGHT BULB LIT UP! I answered,

"Well..." looking at those familiar bulging eyes directed at me, sight repositions—ready in a defensive stance.

"Well, I'm not sure if I trust you... too!" his defense—immediate.

As soon as he finished saying "you," I finished my answer.

"Yes, I trust you, Kuya!"

It was not clear at the time why he asked those odd questions until he reminded me of his business offer—presented a few days earlier. I turned him down then. Reason being, my presence alongside him is not business or money-related. Persistence has not left my brother for sure, he asked me the second time. Sticking to my words in our private talk at his last treatment, I am flattered, but said,

"No, thank you."

To help appease his mind, I suggested we focus on first things first.

"Let's take care of your personal business—your priorities."

Negating my earlier response, he rebutted back.

"I am taking care of business and you fit the position, Annabelle!"

(We both left the scene and replayed at a later time.)

PREPARING foods to taste like my brother Ramon's and our mother's cooking, was just never going to happen for Kuya BB. So, I rolled up my sleeves and prepared a dish from my personal recipe box.

At last, I see my brother smile as he continued to eat. He looked at me; took a bite again, chewed, and smiled again. My brother in a satiated state of mind was silent, but visually complimenting beyond my expectations.

"Raw foods, and I like it!" was BB's final remark.

Yes, I'll take those *complimenting* words. Our "brother-sister," bonding time seemed to have softened Kuya BB's demeanor towards me in the kitchen—to everyone and in other areas. His heart is opening. Catching up on our families' life events of the past decades was making him more comfortable. Sharing our experiences in life's choices, I felt his appreciation for what I have become... transforming. Hearing his defense of my choices and scrutiny of mistakes made, reminded me of the "father-role" persona and apparently, still holds. Empathy grew for each other. I love our personal bonding time. I felt his respect developing; trusting more in me.

More health-related incidents with my brother justified the reason to move my flight to Los Angeles, back a few days. Thanksgiving is fast approaching, and I promised to celebrate with my family. In each of the next five days, Kuya BB would inquire of my departure. In each passing day, I responded,

"Not yet, Kuya."

Travel day arrived. My nephews arrived about an hour early to take me to Houston Airport. My brother knew my day to fly has arrived. Noticing, this time that he is silent. His wife took pictures of Kuya BB and I, along with his sons. In a subtlety move; my brother quietly rolls his wheelchair towards his bedroom. I don't recall a time BB watched TV by himself. Neither have I seen him watch TV in his bedroom, let alone in later morning hours. Hmm! With my luggage packed, my nephews waited by the front door near their father's bedroom, where my brother appears to be "watching" a TV program.

There's... His nudging again. He's powerful. And with that, I realized one important item—stuck in my carry-on bag. God said,

"What are you waiting for, Annabelle? Go!"

ONE HOUR and a half before departure, I pulled a large envelope from my carry-on. With my sight directed at my nephews and my sister-in-law, I turned about-face to walk towards Kuya's bedroom. Turned around and in a steady voice, I said,

"I need to go back in to see Kuya, he wanted to sign a letter he had prepared earlier, for a later use! With a directive from himself, 'To distribute after he is gone.'" Breana gave me the nod.

In quick steps, I went straight into their bedroom. I shut the door behind me. My brother "appeared" engaged in a TV program. I interrupted. He looked at me. I reminded him of his personal letter he wanted to sign. Kuya BB signed the one-page, hand-written paper and handed it back.

Then he went right back to his TV show. I bent down to kiss him on his forehead.

"I love you, Kuya!" I turned around, and stepped away in fear of crying. When...

"I love you too!"

Caught off-guard, I stood still. Did I hear my Kuya BB say, "I love you too?" The answer is, "YES," and for the FIRST time—he voiced his sibling love for his little sister, Bibe! I did a quick U-turn, stepped forward, knelt down on the cold hardwood floor and leaned on his wheelchair. The Lord's Spirit nudging is now clear in my mind.

"*Ask him!*"

"Kuya, do you want to be free from bondage?" He looks me at eye level and asked.

"Bondage?"

"Free!"

"Free from bondage? Yes!" he answered in repeated head-nodding with his eyes fixed on mine. At this time, I feel his spirit lightened.

OH GOD, YOU HEARD HIM—HE SAID, "YES!"

"Please know God loves you so much; He can forgive you of all your sins—big and small!"

He looks and nods. His eyes bulging and in awe! Like he has never heard of God's total forgiveness. Then I asked,

"Kuya, do you want to ask God to forgive you of your sins?"

"Yes! I do!" he answered.

"Please repeat after me." Word for word, Kuya BB repeated:

"Father God, please forgive me. I repent of all my sins. Thank You for your grace and mercy. Jesus, I believe You are the Son of the Living God. Thank You for cleansing me with your sacrificial blood. Please, purify my conscience and give me a new mind and a new heart. Make me a new man. Jot my name in the Book of Life, forever, in Jesus' name, I pray!"

With our hands touching, together we said,

"Amen!"

Seated in front of me is God's child who has come back home to Him. I witnessed my Kuya BB experience relief—forgiven and redeemed—Spirit-filled and light-hearted. The heavy burden of sin; I witnessed *that* young and broken soul from long ago, come to life a new man in Christ.

I felt millions of Angels rejoicing.

"Hallelujah!"

I cannot drum up words to describe the feelings of this joyful moment—for Kuya BB and for me! The much-needed relief. The intensity. Why was I chosen? Indescribable! To lead my brother and beloved father-figure to the loving hands of our Lord!

God's goodness overwhelms my heart.

"Hallelujah," to the good, good Father in heaven! "God so loved the world, He gave His Only Begotten Son, (the only Way) that whoever believes in Him shall not perish" (John 3:16).

> Ultimate hatred and ultimate love
> met on those crosspieces of wood.
> Suffering and love
> were brought into harmony.
>
> — ELISABETH ELLIOT

GLORY BE TO GOD

A WEARIED HEART. Meanwhile, chaos was awaiting at home. Pressing on my joy is here to stay.

Did Satan ask for my name?

Whether God complied, I trust in our sovereign God. Many things are in disarray. Situations at home have taken sharper turns. My husband's life issues have become more intense, and I feel the pressure on me to help resolve them. My daughter, De, has expressed discontent in my missing her birthday celebration for the *third* time in thirty-something years! I felt seated in the middle cart of a heavy-loaded roller coaster ride.

Unsurprised, temptations are funneling through my head. It's Thanksgiving. I thank God for everything. Including the most recent blessing—my brother, Kuya BB's, salvation.

Our mutual enemy is at it again—using my loved ones to tempt me. Having what scientists refer to, "clock-gene," in his inhumane genetic spirit, he never sleeps. He doesn't mute. Knows he is in a time constraint. Not his last-ditch… with all his might, lays down his evil works to anyone who will listen and believe his lies! He is back to his favorite target and is using every power, thinks he has on me.

God is the power. God is in control. My Lord, my hope, my fortress and salvation. His Grace and Mercy—sufficient. I press on.

~V~
OH LORD,
MY SHELTER IS IN YOUR LOVING PRESENCE.
MY HOPE IS IN YOUR PERFECTION.
MY PEACE IS IN YOUR GOODNESS.
AND HERE I AM—NEEDING YOU.

〜

GIVE ME REST, Oh Father! I need Your peaceful presence in my life. Jesus, please remind me of Kuya BB. My hope is in you. And the promise of seeing my brother again is definitive. I hear my God say,

"I am with you, Annabelle."

"And we know that all things work together for good to them that love God, to them who are the called according to his purpose" (Romans 8:28 KJV).

Encouragement:

〜

Psalm 28:6-7
Blessed be the Lord because He has heard
the voice of my supplications!
The Lord is my strength and my shield;
my heart trusted in Him and I am helped.
Therefore, my heart greatly rejoices and with my song,
I will praise Him.

(NKJV)

〜

IN JESUS' name, I pray:

Lord, Only Your Spirit's great yearning allows me to pray for others. Give me the sensitivity to those who need Your saving grace. Seeing their brokenheartedness—needing Your gracious and merciful love.

. . .

Ramon made a last-minute travel plan to visit our oldest brother. He arrived in time to celebrate Thanksgiving with Kuya BB and his family. The entire Sabella and Juaner Families know about our brother's diminishing condition. Love and prayers from relatives and friends are pouring in.

Standing by Ramon's side, I see my ailing brother wearing a familiar smile. Kuya BB displays an array of smiling expressions; a replica of our mother's, as well depicts various feelings. From feeling happy, sad, irritated, frustrated, angry, mad, mysterious, in pain, and often wears that... "strategizing" smile. Features, I have been able to identify. On display, he wears a happy and relieved beam.

Though his pain is visible, my computer screen also reflects spiritual calmness and inner peace! I can see it. I can feel it. The Holy Spirit is with us both! For sure, his generous smiles show gladness in seeing Ramon. Kuya BB appeared a bit anxious. He leaned over Ramon's shoulder—looks towards Ramon's iPad screen and seeing me on the screen, leaned closer.

His words spoken in slow motion—asked me about his business proposition. He added,

"But first, discuss my proposal with your husband, Joseph, and get back—soon, please!"

Did he mention my husband's name? When was the last time he used Joseph's name? When was the first time? His persistence won me over.

REFLECTION: I felt God's perfect timing. Together, my older brother and I, freely walked away from that ruthless day—we lost our father. Hurtful words intending to destroy young souls, no longer have its *stronghold* on us.

We are "free from bondage."

I responded.

"Yes, I will!"

I see, the answer, "Yes" pleased my brother. I want nothing more than to make life easier for my Kuya BB.

"Let's talk about the details, Kuya, when I get back to Texas." I see relief. Smiles flashing as both my brothers said,

"Bye for now."

After we disconnected, I felt restless. I have been dealing with the slow healing process from bronchitis. My doctor advised against my impending travel plans... instead, he advised I stay at home and rest. Concerned with the high probability of infecting my ailing brother, I postponed my travel back to Texas.

Rex and Carmen S. arrived in Texas days early to celebrate Kuya BB's birthday. His health has turned for the worst and was back in the hospital. On his birthday, led by the celebrant himself, the family joined in the "Happy Birthday," chorus-singing. Ending the last stanza with his finger up in a maestro-like motion, Kuya BB, the musical conductor, sang,

"Happy birthday to me!"

In the meantime, waiting for Ramon in Manila is a backlog of urgent business-related matters. As well, the management amid busy preparation for the Sabella Fashion Annual Christmas Celebration. Though he agonized over leaving Kuya BB at a critical time, Ramon flew back to Manila. He left with hopes to come back first thing in the new year.

Kuya Rolando flew in. He joined Rex and Carmen S., who have been by Kuya BB's hospital bedside. Seeing our older sibling still fighting, and appearing to lose his battle with the cancer—nothing could describe their helplessness with the severe pain they are witnessing! Explaining! Describing the disease's atrocity to our brother's body. There is no need for more description. I've seen and heard this impartial disease apply its mastery of agony and suffering to our Kuya BB. I don't want to imagine... I won't.

Rolando aches. I hear it in his voice. Having the same birthdays, these two brothers have celebrated with each other's company most of the past years. A rarity this year, they celebrated on their own in separate occasions.

∼

Kuya BB and Kuya Rolando are like two peas in a pod. I say... much deeper in brotherhood and friendship. Even though each one has close friends; these two are by far, way beyond blood brothers, who share the same birth month and day. Each one thinks of the other, always with one key element—the older still carries the cultural headship. Thus, Kuya BB leads.

They share pretty much everything in life. They talk—well as can be. One talks more; the other nods. Together, they traveled the *ups and downs* journeys of life. Holding on to each other, riding in and out of life's bumpy roller-coaster carts. These two peas held together in their pod! Two hearts beating as one, per se. They have not allowed the rest of the siblings, membership in their exclusive relationship. From birth, they were inseparable. It is of no wonder my brother, Kuya Rolando, finds himself deeply tormented. Disheartened with the painful reality of losing his longtime and personal life partner.

Although I couldn't be with my Kuya BB, it comforts me to know members of his immediate family, including our siblings—our personal playmates for life, surrounded him even for just a few days. For personal reasons my siblings and Carmen S. flew back to California.

Meanwhile, I rested and nurtured myself back to health. Healthy enough to travel back to Texas. Receiving a clean bill of health days later, my physician gave me the thumbs up to travel. Financial help given by my nephews, enabled me to schedule travel on the earliest flight for the later morning in mid-December.

I kept in touched with Austin all the while and had asked him to relay my flight schedule to BB. My brother, in weakness, whispered his response...

"Annabelle... I am no longer! I am no longer!" and faded off.

Dealing with the chaos, poor health and travel plans, I felt physically exhausted. After rushing through L.A. Airport's security, I have just enough time to get a cup of coffee and jump-start my body.

I was in much anticipation. I have been in constant longing to be back to my ailing brother. *He did mention my name to Austin—he is waiting for me.* My spirit in high hopes. *How has Kuya BB changed? How is he dealing with the pain? How will our reunion be now that he is also a "Brother in Christ?"* A sweet sound to my ears.

I walked around the boarding gate to find an empty corner seat for my hour wait. Flopping into the seat, relief soon came in from my quiet talk with the Lord. Moments later, my cell phone pinged. I received a text at past 10 a.m. from my younger nephew.

"My father passed away, just a little over fifteen minutes ago."

I looked down and... cried.

My head emptied. Saddened, my heart ached. Though my shoes felt like a ton, I walked towards the gate where my plane awaits outside. Several more steps towards the window, I stopped. There, I stood looking out through this soundproof window and up into the clear blue sky. My head drooped... in remembering Paul the Apostle's credence; I looked back up, my eyes reaching towards the heavens, picturing my brother.

"We are confident, yes, well pleased rather to be absent from the body and to be present with the Lord" (2nd Corinthians 5:8).

I envisioned the Lord Jesus' arms around Kuya BB's shoulder. Our Lord, escorting my brother—presenting him pure—to our Heavenly Father, Who awaits at His throne.

"Welcome home My child; welcome home!"

I realized my smile *is* an *ear to ear* as tears dropped to give me a salty taste.

"Oh, God!"

I boarded the plane. Slumping into the plane's isle seat, my head now spinning overwhelmed with flashes of our last time together with the "I love you's" exchange. With my eyes closed and in the sudden moment, I asked.

"Why God?" then cried more.

In stillness, after the realized pause that God is in control; I praised God. My grief stricken soul relieved in deep gratitude for God's gift of salvation. Kuya BB is no longer suffering. Pain free! Joyfully remembering his face when he accepted the Lord Jesus Christ just three short weeks ago is an assurance—we will see each other again.

My tears of sadness are now tears of joy. Same liquid, same salty taste; now, with pure joy. Knowing my brother and I will continue our bonding in heaven. We can talk about *that* business deal then!

REFLECTION: Answering yes to the business proposal is a reflection on my saying, "Yes," to God. Kuya BB experienced the chain of bondage break off when he too said, "Yes," to God's gift of salvation.

"Hallelujah!"

~V~
GLORY BE TO GOD

~

MY HEART IS over-flowing with God's love everlasting. His grace and mercy is sufficient. I am back in His Humble Spirit, ready to receive His sweet goodness for the day. There is no need to worry about another life's roller coaster ride coming down steady and ready to take me for a ride.

God seated in the front engine is the train's Conductor-in-Chief. His arms and hands raised high, Jesus sits beside me as the Holy Spirit pushes the weighty caboose through to my next journey.

"Hold tight on Me, Bibe."

Holding tight—I will never let You go, Oh Lord!

Whee!

Jesus Christ sits at the right hand of God the Father; interceding every day for me. Through the power of His Holy Spirit, I feel His faithful representation and secure love—safeguarding me always and forever—Grace in me.

REFLECTION: Where does a wearied heart go? Who can take our place? To pay the price for our sins. Who will?

Jesus Christ is the answer.

There is nothing like His Love. Our salvation is in Jesus Christ; our Lord, Who has already paid the price and finished the work for ALL to receive this gift. Therefore, why would one continue in the bondage of sin? Open your heart to God. He is waiting patiently to have fellowship with you.

~

Encouragement: All Things Made New.

∼

Revelation 21:3-4
And, I heard a loud voice from heaven saying, "Behold the tabernacle of God is with men, and He will dwell with them,
and they shall be His people.
God Himself will be with them and be their God.
And God will wipe away every tear
from their eyes; there shall be no more death, nor sorrow, nor crying.
There shall be no more pain, for the former things have passed away."

(NKJV)

∼

Revelation 21:6
And He said to me,
"It is done!
I am the Alpha and the Omega,
The Beginning and the End."

(NKJV)

∼

∼

∼

∼

∼

∼

∼

∼

GLORY BE TO GOD | 261

THE CHARACTERS AND MORE

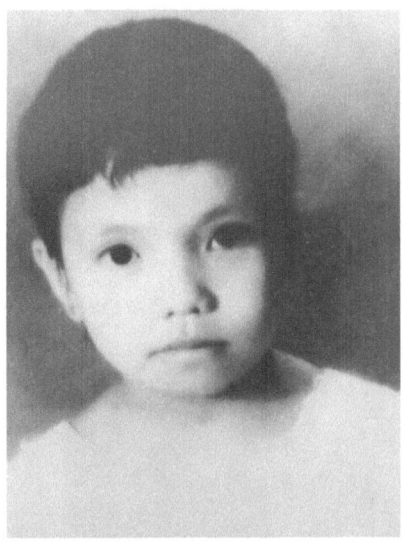

Me, "Bibe," at 5 years old.

From the left: Ate C, carrying a doll; Me, sporting my new hairdo (You guessed right, I wasn't too thrilled about wearing a dress.) Ma with Rex; Pa standing in the back; Kuya Ricardo, Jr. (Kuya BB)—carrying a big stuffed monkey; Kuya Rolando seated in front. Note: a neighbor is the first family photo bomber, 1957.

Standing in our front yard at Villa Dolores, Tatalon, facing the bungalow, 1958. From the left: my beautiful sister, Ate C; my gorgeous Ma with Ramon; Me—holding one of the two dolls I owned (I had a big smile here since I didn't have to wear a dress, no top—LOL); and Kuya BB. Notice the barbed-wire fencing behind where I pulled my ankle through. Ouch (Aray)!

Photoshoot, top left: Kuya BB and Kuya Rolando. Bottom left: Rex and Me, Circa 1956-57. I know what you're thinking… so, let's hear it!

Me, Kuya Rolando leaning on Kuya BB, and my beloved Pa seated on the stairs by the driveway at our former home situated at the Welcome Rotonda on Espana Boulevard, Quezon City, Philippines, 1954.

My beautiful sister, Ate Claudette (aka Ate C).

With Ma at the Sabella Fashion Group's 25th Anniversary celebration. Praying for all the guests, including the group's employees was a privilege and an honor. Thank you, Ramon!

Me, Joseph, De-was crowned: Alhambra H.S. Homecoming Court Princess, with Sam in 1998.

I'm such the nerdy Fiance' here... still feeling my new engagement ring, December 1992.

Joseph, giving me the second, or was it the third kiss (?) on my cheek at our Wedding Day Photoshoot, May 22 1993.

GLORY BE TO GOD | 265

At Calvary Chapel, Pasadena, Ca. Upper left: Walking down the isle with Rex. Upper right: Deanna (De), Sabella (Sam), Me, and Paul. Bottom left: Ma, Me, and Joseph. Bottom right: Paul, Auntie Peling, Rex, Ma, Kuya Rolando, Me, Joseph, Sam, Ramon, and De, May 22 1993.

The Reza family and Me, the new member, May 1993. From the left: Brother Luis, Kathie, Dad Rudy, Me, Joseph, Mom Annie, Susie, and Yvonne.

De, Paul, and Sam, posed in the back of my pick-up truck. I had to get rid of the Nissan because it only seated three in the front.

Paul, De, Me, and Sam at Ma's 87th birthday celebration held at the Almansor Court.

Me, Paul, and our beloved, Granny. Yosemite National Park, 1974.

At Knott's Berry Farm. Marley (M. Pink), Navi (N. Christeanna), Zen (Z. Christian), and their NayNay (Me) 2015.

I'm simply drawn wading in water. Here, I was crossing more waterways. There were fishes, but no tadpoles! Grasshopper Point Swimming/Picnic, Sedona, Arizona.

Left picture: Our wedding party included the groom's sisters—Yvonne, Joseph, Susie, and Kathie, is the modern-day photo bomber. Top center: Joseph, Jonathan (J. Moon), and Paul, Easter celebration. Top right: Carlos, J. Moon, Joseph, Kathie (seated) and Susie—celebrating J. Moon's high school graduation, June 2015. Bottom center: J. Moon and his "Tata" (Joseph) fishing at the Sedona's Trout Farm, in Arizona, Summer 2003. Bottom right: Me and my BFF and bridesmaid, Carmen.

Celebrating De's 40th birthday. Standing from the left: Violet (CE's mom), CE, EZ, Joseph, and Me. Front: N. Christeanna with the Celebrant, De. Temecula, November 2019.

GLORY BE TO GOD | 269

Rex, Carmen S., Me, Kuya Rolando, and Kuya BB. There are two photos combined here. I took Kuya BB's picture as he was leaving. BB's last visit to his ranch home, Texas, November 2014.

Rex, Me, Ate C, Kuya Rolando, and Ramon seated in front of an oil painting by Wendell Cristobal, with the inclusion of Pa (Note: from an original photograph setting without Pa).

My beautiful Ma, in a Filipiniana Red Dress, celebrating her 87th birthday.

Pa, wearing his doctoral regalia (robe).

I captured this loving moment between Auntie Peling and Ma—as they separate for the night with a graceful kiss! Taken at my Auntie's 80th birthday celebration, 2002.

J. Moon and Sam, M. Pink, and Z. Christian at J. Moon's High School Graduation from Alhambra H. S., 2015.

N. Christeanna, CE, De, and EZ. Taken at the Calvary Chapel Bible Fellowship courtyard in Temecula, 2018.

272 | A KISS WITHOUT ANY SHAME

In Sedona, Arizona, June 2019—I look up and see You, Father God. Thank you for my life. I sit here midway on Bell Rock and catch sight of life surrounded by Your beautiful creations. Father in Heaven, the existence made by Your mighty hands; I feel the wonders of Your loving presence. Jasper-colored Buttes, shrubs, trees, cacti on hematite grounds each were formed in wonderful ways. Likewise, in creations with Your divine manner, You made me unlike any other. Created in Your image—every fiber of my being in caring ways, made for the greatest role on earth is to follow my Lord, Jesus Christ, on the road to heaven.

LOVE IS FUN

Cycling on Bell Rock with Joseph in Sedona, Arizona.

Joseph and I, taken on our wedding anniversary, 2018. To my readers, I hope that you find the love of God, open the door to your heart, and invite Him in. Experience a life filled with fun, excitement, and freedom in knowing the Lord is in control and has the best plan for you. Then brace yourself... hold on for more thrilling rides of a lifetime, whee!

GOD HAS THE POWER. GOD IS IN CONTROL. OUR LORD—OUR HOPE, FORTRESS, AND SALVATION. HIS GRACE AND MERCY—SUFFICIENT. WE PRESS ON FOR GOD IS LOVE.

WORDS OF LOVE: FOR YOU

ear Reader,

THANK you for accompanying me through the re-calling parts of my life's journey. All the way through, praying that my story would encourage you to know, just as God was with me all along, He is also with you. As I've been journaling and pondering writing this memoir, thoughts of you have taken me to levels higher than one could ever imagine. You have provided the bright lighting in completing my story.

If you, or someone you know, relates to any of the heartfelt experiences I have shared here—I pray that God comes to your aid. May He stretch His presence; and, give you grace and mercy. Remove all feelings of hurts and pain—guilt and shame from within your mind and soul.

God loves you. "God so loved the world that He gave His only begotten Son, that whoever believes in Him, should not perish but have everlasting life" (John 3:16). And Jesus says, "I am the way the truth and the life, no one comes to the Father but through me" (John 14:5). Then Jesus solidifies and gave His promise, "I will never leave thee nor forsake thee" (Hebrews 13:5).

Hope is never far away for the expecting person. Hang on to His mighty Word. Reach out to a trusted person and pray that God gives you the strength and confidence to share your feelings.

Is your "heart open wide?" Do you want the Truth to set you free from the bondage of sin? Are you ready to accept Jesus as your Lord and Savior?

Did you say, YES?

If you did, ask,

"Father God, please forgive me of all my sins. Thank You for Your grace and mercy. Jesus, I believe You are the Son of the Living God and thank You for Your unconditional love—cleanse me with Your sacrificial blood. Please, purify my conscience and give me a new mind and a new heart. And, write my name in the Book of Life, forever—in Jesus' name, I pray. Amen."

If you implored for God's forgiveness and accepted Jesus as your Lord and Savior—WELCOME TO KINGDOM COME! God's sweet gift of salvation in His Son will empower you with His Holy Spirit and fill you with His everlasting love, joy and hope in Christ Jesus.

Celebrate your full freedom. Experience newness in life with God! Bask in His glory and enjoy the gift of salvation. Experience love unlike anything you have had before. Read the Word of God and be in His Holy Spirit—providing you wisdom, courage, strength, and laughter.

And enjoy life. Especially, those new tears of joy!

God bless,

ANNABELLE "BIBE"

P.S. Jesus loves you!

WORDS OF LOVE: FOR A BROKEN FELLOWSHIP WITH THE LORD

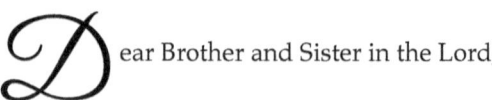ear Brother and Sister in the Lord,

I HAVE BEEN PRAYING for you, as God presented these pages of my story in your hands, please know, God's Word stands firm.

Sometimes in life we walk away from the soft-caring hands of our Father, the Almighty. We evolve into self-regarding individuals, depreciating God's abundant blessings. We take the first fast train to never, never land; where we get drowned by the overflowing sounds of the world's irresistible, plethora servings of pleasures for us mankind. Or fall into the conducting hands of self-gratifying activities, siphoning our reliance for God. Only to find emptiness and loneliness once again.

Are you feeling discouraged in life? Dismayed? Disappointed with yourself? In others, who may have broken their promises to you... who left and have not returned? The betrayal of others, causing you to lose faith in God. And, that fire you had for the Lord, has it sizzled down to a lukewarm level because of reasons that have no matter to Him? Have these, or something and someone else, caused your fellowship with God to break?

"And the LORD, He is the One that goes before you. He will be with you... do not fear nor be dismayed" (Deuteronomy 31:8).

Don't lose heart! God is the Healer of hurts. God is the Mender of brokenheartedness. He is the Lifter of souls.

There are words composed to spell out many reasons, and or, many excuses written out but will have no effect on God wanting to see you return to Him. God wants you back; and, just as before, just as you are.

"And the son said to him, Father, I have sinned against heaven, and in your sight, and am no more worthy to be called your son. But the father said to his servants, bring forth the best robe, and put it on him; and put a ring on his hand, and shoes on his feet" (Luke 15:21-22).

Much to the story of the "prodigal son" in the Bible, God is ahead, looking for you... near or far, where ever you are; and, is readying for your coming home celebration.

Shamed by your own choices; feeling unworthy? Like Peter the Disciple when he denied Jesus?

As Jesus thought and uttered Peter's name at His resurrection, "But go, tell His disciples—and Peter—that He is going before you" (Mark 16:7); He thinks of you—always. And the Lord is waiting for you to come home. Nothing has happened that will keep you from the love waiting for your return.

Are you ready to come back home to Jesus?

If you answered "Yes" please say:

Father God, I don't know how I got here, but You do. I don't how You could wait by my side every time I need, interventions—and You're there. My Savior, my God, and my Redeemer—forgive me. I am lost without Your Spirit of love and understanding. Guiding, protecting, lighting my path to see that I am not alone. Always, and forever, I can count on You, my Lord Jesus.

I can hear Him saying:

"Welcome back home, My child. Come, sit, let's sup and fellowship," as He greets you,

"With a kiss of love" (1st Peter 5:14).

Hallelujah! Welcome back home.

YOUR SISTER IN CHRIST,
    Annabelle "Bibe"

WORDS OF LOVE: KISSES FOR OUR HEAVENLY FATHER

Dear Father God Who art in Heaven,

YOU ALONE KNOW our heart's desires and what becomes of each one. And this I know that You are our good Father in heaven.

As I share Your mighty Word—not from the pulpit—remind me, my identity is in Your Beloved Son, my Lord and Savior Jesus Christ. May Your Holy Spirit continue to nudge and use me as a vessel for your children. Equip me with Your divine power and may I endure the race set before me. Bless Your love story written on my heart, revealed in this book. Touch the reader looking for the truth; and, open his or her heart wide to You.

Words of love, revealing who I am in You my Father in heaven—God's child—beautiful, and victorious. I am lavished by Your love, every moment of the day. The richness of Your glory gives steadfast confidence to my soul with strength to carry on.

As Your star—the brilliance shining brightly for others, I aim to glorify You and give You all the honor for what You have done in my life; are doing now, and will do, while doting on me Kisses Without Any Shame!

. . .

Love and kisses from Your daughter,
   Annabelle "Bibe"

UNMOVED, CIRCA 1958

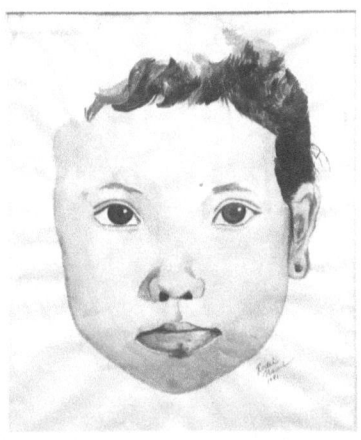

"Unmoved." Bibe's personal collection. Drawn by: Rodel Naval, 1981.

ACKNOWLEDGMENTS

WITH LOVE AND GRATITUDE

Twenty-five years in the making—the story written on my heart for you is finished. I do not take the lead role in shaping each chapter—God, the Executive Creator of life itself, directed the accounts of my true story revealed in these pages. In the same manner, the chosen cast was in perfect harmony with His divine message. Citing sweet moments when each one touched my life sensing God's loving presence.

Each contributor's part has been an inspiration fueling my desire to finish writing. I am grateful to the many gifted and willing individuals in my life. I thank you:

To Maria Becerra and Mina Ruiz—Beta Readers. Maria—for squeezing my project into your very busy life. Your steadfast prayer dealing with my "last-minute" treaty is beyond what I had hoped for. My thanks to your husband, Ricardo, for his prayers (I know he did, LOL!) and for allowing me to "borrow" some of his family time. Mina —I appreciate your prayers. You have been an encourager in my life. Always, the positive persona and a lifter of others.

To Violet Tapec—my Co-Inhabitant and first "Employer," for every time I needed to talk to you about our childhood memories. To the rest of my Co-Inhabitants—Cousins: Rodolfo Banzon, Corazon Felix, Alice Matatquin, Rolando Ancheta, Rose Olaer, Arnold Cuevas, and Evelyn Cuevas. For being a part of the greatest group of playmates ever. To my "Juaner" Aunties: Basilia, Felisa, Virginia, Remedios, Leonora, and

Dominga—for all your loving help "Filipino-Mestiza" style and steadfast loyalty to Ma. I have missed you all.

To my In-laws, the Reza's: Dad Rudy—for all your help in rougher times. Mom Annie—for your persistence and comments, often, made me laugh. To Yvonne Flores, Luis Reza II, Susie Maldonado, Kathie and Carlos Mendoza—for the many fun and happy times together. For opening your hearts extending loving care to my children.

To the Sabella Sisters-in-law: Esperanza, Carmen, and Bonita—God bless you for having lasting love for your husbands. Nieces and nephews—I pray for each one of you and your families by name!

To my Pastor, Pancho Juarez—for showing up week-in and week-out. Your commitment to the Word of God has helped keep me grounded for the past twenty-six years. My gratitude to your beautiful wife, Millie—for praying for my daughters. Her genuine example of faithfulness and unwavering love for the Lord is an inspiration to me.

To Carmen Rosenblum—my BFF and Prayer Warrior. Your support never ends, always believing in me. Your continued comments to my manuscript kept me on my computer typing away to completion. I love you my dear.

To our dear "Lady Di," Shooshanig Diana Agajanian—for your generosity, the love and genuine interest you show my entire family and countless others, never seize to amaze me. Love you, lots.

To Michael Lirag—I am blown away with your artistic abilities. Thank you for the perfect cover design. I love it!

To the Prayer Warriors: Suzanne Aroz, Millie Juarez, Karin Vogt, and Kristine Sabella for your steadfast prayers for our families. To all the prayer warrior princes and princesses—please keep praying. Your prayers and supplications for others are in a *queue*, giving peace and comfort to many.

To my siblings and co-inhabitants: Claudette Weaks—for stepping up; helping Ma, and your siblings. To Rolando Sabella—I appreciate your generous heart. Continue dancing and entertaining. To Rex Sabella—my sibling "Confidant," thanks for being there with listening ears and encouraging words. To Ramon Sabella—you never seize to surprise me. Thanks for your generosity. We have good times together and wonderful memories to rehash. My dear Siblings, we might be seniors but the best is yet to come. Hold on to your britches... here comes life's roller coaster ride! Whee!

To my "Sabella" Siblings: Raul Madarang, Linda Sabella Chommanard, Esmeralda Shirley Sabella, Rosario Sabella, Helen Sabella, and Ricardo "Boning" Sabella—thank you for the love. Though we grew up separated by distance; we are always connected in Christ.

To my children: Paul Moore—for showing and living humility. Love at its best when God chose me to bring you, one of His special creations into this world. God trusted you to show me His ways. I am still learning, son. To Sabella Moore—thank you for your uniqueness. May God continue to give you His love and confidence to bust out and show the world His supreme creative formation in you. To Deanna Espinal—thanks for opening your heart wide to God. Enjoy the transformation. Always stay receptive to God's Word and see your diligence achieve many more successes. To my son-in-law, Christian Espinal—for answering my daughter's and my prayers for a delightful, responsible, generous, and dedicated husband. David Walker—your amazing creativity even shows in the kitchen! And the fastest cook I know.

To my five grandchildren: Jesus loves you!

Jonathan—for all the wonderful memories Tata and I have with you; we will forever cherish them and for your helping hands with the rest of the little "monkeys." To Ezekiel—for your contagious laughter and whopping energy. Slow down and enjoy many greater and fun times in your journey that the Lord Jesus has in stored for you. To Zen—for your overflowing sweetness and sensitivity; yes, Jesus has His sight on you. Keep smiling. To Marley—for being a girl, an answered prayer. Your quiet demeanor displays God's calmness for all to see. Your awesome artistic abilities are obvious to many; someday for all to see. To Navi—and, "Yes," for being a girl too! Your energy is catchy and makes me happy. Our joyful times are memorable and I pray for many more to come.

To my husband Joseph Reza—my "Knight in Shining Armor," my lifetime coach and partner, my truest friend. Your patience in the editing process is greatly appreciated. Thank you, my love for all the sweet times we have together. Your amazing support keeps me afloat. Loving and providing for all of us is a blessing, I thank God every day. You are the greatest step-dad and the BEST "Tata" ever!

To my former In-Laws: Nettie Mae Moore—I miss your genuine love and uncompromising faith in God. For your Godly ways and patience, dealing with my hardened heart. Do I ever... understand the struggle you went through with me. I can't wait to see you again. Faye Moore—for your welcoming and understanding heart. I have missed our times together just walking and talking. To Ruth Williams—for mirroring your mother, Granny's unconditional love. I cherish the years we had together. To Angie Reece—for your commitment to the family. To Calvin Moore—for being there when I felt alone—giving soothing words that consoled my soul.

To my beloved older brother and father-figure, Ricardo Sabella—for caring and sacrificial love. God allowed your unquestionable love in my youth to remind me of God's great love. I am eternally grateful for the memories of our unmatched childhood fun together. Until then, dance with Ma in our Almighty God's presence. I will see you later!

To my beloved parents: Ma, Dolores Juaner Sabella—I miss your smile. (Salamat po!) Thank you for passing your forgiving and generous DNA. Though hard to match, without your teachings, I would still be floating looking for love in all the wrong places. I strive to mimic your loving ways, enduring commitment, and loyalty to Pa. To my beloved Pa, "Doktor" Ricardo H. Sabella—I have missed you for so long! The kisses and love you have imparted are forever imprinted on my heart. Thank you for your economic (frugal) trait, I practice regularly. Wish you were both here to read the love story God has written on your little girl, Bibe's heart.

To the difficult people in my life—I continue to pray for each one of you. God uses all things for good.

And finally, Lord, thank You that as the Master Artisan of life—with love, You pick up the loose and dull fibers of broken hearts, mending them with Your healing hands. As Your stars—the brilliance shining brightly for others. I give You all the glory and the honor for what You have done in my life—are doing now, and will do, while doting on me Kisses Without Any Shame!

With love,
    Annabelle "Bibe"

ABOUT THE AUTHOR

Annabelle Sabella-Reza is a passionate "tell-all," spokeswoman who thrives on helping others. She reads and writes, on most days; and daily practices a healthy lifestyle. A former corporate employee and factory worker—she had farmed on a ten-acre land and performed on a live stage audience. She loves humming praise music for inspiration and would flip to disco dancing in a heartbeat! She is married with three children, five grandchildren, and lives in the San Gabriel Valley, California.

To connect with Annabelle or to request for a speaking engagement, visit her on Facebook and Instagram.

facebook.com/a.bibesabellareza
instagram.com/asabellareza

www.ingramcontent.com/pod-product-compliance
Lightning Source LLC
Chambersburg PA
CBHW020358080526
44584CB00014B/1066